Deliberative Democracy and Human Rights

Deliberative Democracy and Human Rights

Edited by Harold Hongju Koh and Ronald C. Slye

Yale University Press

New Haven and London

Published with assistance from the foundation established in memory of Philip Hamilton McMillan of the class of 1894, Yale College.

Set in Adobe Garamond type by The Composing Room of Michigan, Inc.
Printed in the United States of America by BookCrafters, Inc., Chelsea, Michigan.

Library of Congress Cataloging-in-Publication Data

Deliberative democracy and human rights / edited by Harold Hongju Koh and Ronald C. Slye.
p.   cm.
Includes bibliographical references and index.
ISBN 0-300-07583-9 (cl. : alk. paper). — ISBN 0-300-08167-7 (pbk. : alk. paper)
1. Democracy.   2. Democracy—United States.   3. Human rights.   4. Human rights—United States.   5. Representative government and representation.   I. Koh, Harold Hongju, 1954–   . II. Slye, Ronald.
JC423.D3894   1999
323—dc21   99–27517

A catalogue record for this book is available from the British Library.

The paper in this book meets the guidelines for permanence and durability of the Committee on Production Guidelines for Book Longevity of the Council on Library Resources.

10 9 8 7 6 5 4 3 2 1

Contents

Part One **Introduction**

Deliberative Democracy and Human Rights: An Introduction

Harold Hongju Koh

Ronald C. Slye

Half a century after its birth, the modern human rights revolution stands at a crossroads. At this writing, the first international criminal trials since Nuremberg have commenced in The Hague and Arusha; a treaty to create a permanent international criminal court has been ratified by dozens of countries; numerous countries are prosecuting war criminals and other human rights abusers; United States federal courts have awarded millions of dollars in damages against individuals who have violated well-established norms of international human rights law; and governments from Latin America to Eastern Europe to Africa are struggling to make the transition from regimes of repression to ones committed to human rights and the rule of law. Human rights nongovernmental organizations have reached newly sophisticated levels of development; the United Nations has finally created a high commissioner with an express mandate to promote and protect human rights; and plans are finally under way to establish a permanent international criminal court. Yet at the same time, the world has been watching silently as plans for what may be a new genocide unfold in Burundi and Kosovo; civilians have become explicit targets in armed conflicts from

Chechnya to Bosnia to the Middle East to Liberia; and women, children, homosexuals, and ethnic and religious minorities continue to be targets of brutal violence and discrimination throughout the world.

Which of these paths will predominate at the turn of the century remains obscure. As the Cold War recedes into the past, it becomes apparent how little we understand causes of human rights abuses, the legitimacy and content of universal human rights norms, and the most effective strategies for addressing gross violations of human rights. A yawning gap looms between our understanding of the moral and philosophical justification of human rights and our prescriptions for addressing the gross violations that confront us daily.[1]

This volume brings together academics and advocates, philosophers and lawyers, theorists and policy analysts to address some of the most pressing issues facing the contemporary human rights movement. The contributors to this volume gathered in September 1994 at Yale Law School in a conference organized by the Orville H. Schell, Jr., Center for International Human Rights, an organization dedicated to promoting more sophisticated understanding of the theoretical, philosophical, and moral issues raised by our commitment to international human rights. The participants assembled in memory of Carlos Santiago Nino (1943–1993), a remarkable Argentinean lawyer who had uniquely bridged the gap between human rights theory and practice. As professor of law at the Universidad de Buenos Aires, academic director of the Centro de Estudios Institucionales, and visiting professor at Yale Law School, Carlos Nino wrote prolifically on a wide range of theoretical issues in the fields of human rights, political theory, and moral philosophy. In addition, fate led Nino to become a major political actor in one of the most important human rights events in the twentieth century. In the early 1980s, Nino became a legal adviser to President Raúl Alfonsín, entrusted with overseeing the transition from the military junta that had orchestrated Argentina's "dirty war" of 1976–1983, a brutal tragedy that had witnessed the death or disappearance of approximately nine thousand persons. As adviser to Argentina's president and coordinator of the Commission for the Consolidation of Democracy, Nino became the key architect of the government's decision to place members of the military junta on trial for the atrocities perpetrated under their rule. All the defendants were eventually pardoned by Alfonsín's successor, Carlos Menem, an experience that profoundly influenced Nino's understanding of the theoretical justifications for criminal punishment and the practical demands of moving toward a democratic rule of law.[2]

Shortly after Nino's untimely death, a group of philosophers, lawyers, judges, and activists who had known and admired him gathered at Yale to consider four areas of inquiry. First, what is the moral justification for the concept and content of universal human rights?[3] Second, what is the relationship among nation-building, constitutionalism, and democracy? What are the political implications for a conception of universal human rights? Third, what is the relationship between moral principles and political practice? Fourth, how should a society confront what Kant called "radical evil"? What moral principles and practical realities must a successor regime address in seeking to hold a prior regime accountable for gross violations of human rights?

Nino's death invited reexamination of these four fundamental questions, for his life had posed challenging answers to each. His book *The Ethics of Human Rights* (1991) had sought to answer the first question—the theoretical justification for the concept of universal human rights—by deriving a moral justification for human rights from Kantian moral theory. Under Nino's constructivist account, human rights ultimately derive from three basic moral principles on which there is a high degree of societal consensus: autonomy, inviolability, and dignity. Nino posited a normative notion of personhood, in which persons must be treated as autonomous beings, capable of fully engaging in moral discourse and freely accepting or rejecting moral positions.

Nino's posthumously published book *The Constitution of Deliberative Democracy* (1996) addressed the second and third questions. Assessing democracy's relationship to constitutionalism, Nino argued that democracy was a normative conception—not just an end in itself, but a vehicle for the creation of a more just society. Nino sought to develop an epistemic theory of deliberative democracy, through which he asserted that majority decision-making preceded by a process of deliberation constitutes a more effective method of ascertaining the moral good than any one person's individual reflection. Finally, Nino's last manuscript, *Radical Evil on Trial,* an ambitious attempt to reconcile criminal punishment, deliberative democracy, and moral philosophy, explored the theories underlying the political question he had tackled as a presidential adviser: how successor regimes should deal with their predecessors.[4]

The essays collected in this volume deliberate and build upon these leitmotivs that consumed Nino's intellectual and political life. The authors of the works assembled here viewed Nino's passing less as an occasion for festschrift than as a collective opportunity to test his theses and to extend the debates in which he had so vibrantly participated. Although Nino held the monopoly on wisdom in none of these debates, his energy and range rendered him an engaged participant in all of them. Nino's efforts as a moral philosopher, lawyer, political theorist, policy-maker, and human rights advocate exemplified both the nobility and the difficulty of striving to unite the theory and practice of human rights within a single lifetime. Nino's struggle is vividly described in chapter 1, by Nino's friend and colleague Owen Fiss, an essay that captures the energy that surrounded Nino and touched all who came into contact with him.

The essays in the first section address two broad issues: the relationship of philosophy to "real-life" politics and advocacy; and the substantive content of those fundamental human rights norms that enjoy sufficient legitimacy to be called "universal." The latter issue in turn raises two related questions: What makes a right universal? And what standards should we use to judge whether a particular norm rises to the level of a fundamental right? These essays take as their starting point *The Ethics of Human Rights* and *The Constitution of Deliberative Democracy,* which chart Nino's own efforts to translate his philosophical ideas into political reality.

How do we determine what rights are fundamental? In an age when cultural relativism threatens to replace sovereignty as the leading barrier to both the idea of universal human rights and the practice of preventing abuses, the question of what rights are fundamental and universal has grown dramatically in importance. The section's opening essay, by Tom Nagel, treats the rights to be free from torture and to rent pornographic videos under the same moral heading of human rights. Yet Nagel focuses not on the former, for he finds that "the flagrant violation of the most basic human rights"—in particular, rights of bodily integrity—"devoid of philosophical interest." He turns instead to the latter, one of many contested issues that are the subject of heated discussion both within the international human rights community and within the civil liberties community in the United States: the rights of gays and lesbians, the regulation of hate speech and pornography, sexual freedom, and sexual harassment. Key to Nagel's discussion is an adherence to the traditional distinction between the public realm and a private realm into which no invasion is allowed. Nagel posits that each of us is "a separate and irreducible node of freedom and value, not to be dissolved into the general welfare." The most distinctive value expressed by a morality of human rights, he claims, is "a form of moral equality that accords to each person a limited sovereignty over the core of his personal and expressive life." That sovereignty, he argues, is under attack, by the "radical communitarian view that nothing in personal life is beyond the legitimate control of the community if its dominant values are at stake." But what are the limits of that private realm? Where do personal rights end and so-called public space and the legitimate demands of societal order begin? Nagel leaves the task of definitive answer to others, suggesting only that some areas that some communitarians have sought to regulate—sexual fantasies, means of sexual gratification, and noncoercive expressions of sexual interest or sexual proposals—belong properly in the private domain. No matter how grotesque observers may find some of these activities, Nagel argues, they should not be subject to external disapproval that is "converted into a claim of personal assault which can be used as a basis for public control."

Bernard Williams shifts focus to the question of how we legitimate those fundamental rights that we assume are universal. Unlike Nino, who would anchor the legitimation of fundamental rights to a normative conception of the individual, rooted in such values as individual autonomy, inviolability, and dignity, Williams invokes instead what he calls "the deed," a phrase that he borrows from Goethe via Wittgenstein. In Williams's view, theory or philosophy alone cannot provide a satisfactory justification for what we consider universal rights, because what we consider legitimate is in part informed by historical context. To be considered universal, he suggests, a right should come close to being self-evident, through a process of dynamic interaction among philosophy, politics, and real life that creates the conditions of legitimacy for various practices. In his view, attempts (like Nino's) through foundationalism or constructivism to equate liberal values with universal rights ignore the self-evident truth that liberalism (like all political theories) is itself the product of a particular political and historical situation.[5]

This reasoning leads Williams to reject the cultural relativist argument, now often asserted by opponents of universal human rights, that what is right or good in one society may not be right or good in another. There is, he argues, a universal paradigm of injustice—the coercive use of power to force one set of people to do something against their will that benefits another set of people. The problem is to identify in which situations this paradigm is operating. Williams sets aside the polar cases that Nagel addresses, instead identifying as the hardest cases those in which "a style of legitimation that was accepted at one time is still accepted in some places but not others," for example, theocratic conceptions of government and patriarchal ideas of the rights of women. The difficult question in such cases is "how far [can] the acceptance of these ideas . . . itself be plausibly understood as an expression of the power-relations that are in question?"

Williams suggests, "to the extent that the belief system can be reasonably interpreted as . . . a device for sustaining the domination of the more powerful group, . . . the whole enterprise might be seen as a violation of human rights."

Yet again, what is critical is the context. No political theory, he concludes, can determine its own application. "The conditions in which the theory or any given interpretation of it makes sense to intelligent people are determined by an opaque aggregation of many actions and forces," some of which are political. Thus for Williams, real-life events in the world of political action must inform our understanding of what fundamental rights are legitimately considered to be universal, of what issues are considered philosophically interesting or challenging, and of what actions—including philosophical inquiry—are most needed to legitimate fundamental human rights.

Martin Farrell takes up Nino's defense and uses the essays by Nagel and Williams, as well as their earlier writings, to locate Nino's moral philosophy of human rights along the spectrum of other moral philosophers. Farrell asks why individuals prefer actions that benefit society at large—whether defined by utilitarianism or otherwise—over actions that benefit themselves. Farrell describes this as the distinction between "agent-relative" justifications for action, which focus on the subjective desires of the actor, and "agent-neutral" justifications, which focus on an impartial view of the good of society. In Farrell's view, Nagel's agent-relative approach emphasizes individual desires, and thus carves out a realm of individual autonomy or sovereignty into which no invasion is legitimate. He defends this realm of autonomy not only because of its utilitarian effects, but also because of its deontological value. Farrell shows us how Nino's theory of moral action cannot be easily characterized as utilitarian, deontological, or consequentialist, and thus provides the seeds of a theory of moral action that reconciles utilitarianism with both the agent-relative and deontological justifications that Nagel adopts.

Elaine Scarry finds both Nagel and Williams unduly skeptical about the relevance of philosophy to the question of what constitutes fundamental human rights. Nagel asserts that philosophy has nothing interesting to say about flagrant violations of these rights, while Williams falls back upon a notion of "self-evidence" in identifying fundamental rights. Against their common position, Scarry argues that philosophical inquiry *does* have relevance to the discussion of fundamental rights, through what she calls "the lapse of practice." Unlike Nagel, Scarry turns her attention to those flagrant violations of rights that Nagel found so devoid of philosophical interest. She argues that it is the very lack of consensus on the rights that Nagel discusses—that is, the fact that these rights are in danger of being lost because they are not adhered to in practice—that provides them with their philosophic interest. "Only during periods when rights are fully enshrined do they seem self-evident," she argues; "the moment their practice is interrupted, their self-evident quality also seems to be interrupted."

Taken together, the first section's essays suggest the evolutionary nature of fundamental rights. Nagel's essay pushes the concept of fundamental rights to include issues of freedom of expression in the context of hate speech and sexuality. Williams argues that rights evolve through the historical process; that practices are recognized as illegitimate not just through the development of better moral theories of rights, but owing to changing perceptions of the validity of those arguments brought about through other historical forces. Farrell, like Nino, argues that theories of rights must be coupled with theories of personhood, based on agent-relative reasons of autonomy that constrain society's utilitarian calculus. Finally, Scarry focuses on the proleptic role of rights—as recognized in Williams's assertion that rights can move forward either by extraordinary theory or by extraordinary actions that go beyond current understanding, and as illustrated by Nagel's act of advocating for a particular set of rights that have not yet become self-evident. Scarry asserts that the question of what constitutes a fundamental right, like the question of what constitutes beauty, requires us to fall back on the ancient notion of "claritas"—a form of self-evidence that resides in the right itself. Paradoxically, she argues, we must continue to use philosophical inquiry to seek out and strengthen even those rights that are self-evident—that exhibit the quality of claritas—or they will lapse and lose their self-evident quality. Although ideally rights are "things whose rightness or justness would arrive in our perceptual field without our ever having to seek them out," in a less-than-ideal world, "for some time to come, they will no doubt require us to seek them out."

The second group of essays, on nation-building, constitutionalism, and democracy, ask how constitutions can preserve human rights in a manner compatible with both democracy and a stable social order. While the essays in the first section concerned justifications for the concept of fundamental, universal human rights, this section's focus on constitutional principles resembles John Rawls's inquiry concerning moral and political deliberation and the "middle game" explored by James Nickel.[6] How does one create a social order strong enough to prevent anarchy, yet constrained enough to prevent tyranny, while providing maximum protection to the human rights of its members? Understandably, the international human rights movement has long focused upon the tyranny of the state and its unique ability to marshal its monopoly of legitimate coercive power to oppress its own citizens. Yet human rights scholars and advocates have increasingly turned their attention toward the positive role of the state—through constitutionalism and democratic institutions—to preserve and protect fundamental human rights. Human rights crises in a host of "failed states," exemplified by Somalia, Haiti, Yugoslavia, Rwanda, and Liberia, have fostered increasing interest among human rights advocates in the positive role that democracy and constitutionalism can play in creating and sustaining a society friendly to human rights. In *The Constitution of Deliberative Democracy*, Carlos Nino grappled with the question whether a commitment to human rights requires a particular form of democracy or constitutionalism. In particular, Nino asked whether the value of democracy was instrumental or intrinsic, procedural or substantive. Does democracy's value lie in its ability to avoid tyranny, or in its ability to promote a stable environment for the enjoyment of individual preferences?

The first two essays in this section, by Ronald Dworkin and Stephen Holmes, sharpen and deepen Nino's inquiry. How one talks about a constitution's role in a democratic order that respects human rights depends first on whether one is looking at an established constitutional order or at newly emerging constitutional regimes. The contribution by Ronald Dworkin focuses on established constitutional orders, most particularly that of the United States, while Stephen Holmes focuses on the newly emerging constitutional orders in the postcommunist societies of Russia and Eastern Europe. While both are concerned with creating a society that encourages deliberation and protects a core set of individual rights, Dworkin emphasizes the legitimacy of a mode of constitutional interpretation that allows judges to incorporate explicitly moral principles (what he calls the "moral reading" of a political constitution). Holmes, by contrast, focuses on the creation of a stable political and economic order as a necessary precondition for the preservation of individual rights.

Constitutional orders must walk a tightrope between establishing sufficient order so that individual rights are not violated in an environment of anarchy, and establishing sufficient limits on government power to prevent official tyranny. Dworkin's focus on constitutionalism is driven by fear of tyranny, by either the majority or the state. Holmes, drawing on the lessons learned at the end of the Cold War in postcommunist societies, addresses the role of constitutions in preventing anarchy. Thus, while Dworkin's focus is on the autonomy of the individual, and the preservation of individual rights, Holmes focuses instead on what he calls "positive constitutionalism," the proactive role of constitutionalism in nation-building.

Dworkin's essay begins by addressing the "majoritarian difficulty." This familiar criticism contends that allowing individual judges to decide important fundamental issues of society without the input of the democratic majority is inherently undemocratic. Dworkin argues that, in fact, the majoritarian premise of democratic theory is not at all incompatible with judicial constitutional interpretation that adopts his theory of moral reading. Instead, Dworkin defends what he calls "the constitutional conception of democracy": an account that rejects the majoritarian premise and "denies that it is a defining goal of democracy that collective decisions always or normally be those that a majority or plurality of citizens would favor if fully informed and rational." Instead, Dworkin argues, the defining aim of democracy is that "collective decisions be made by political institutions whose structure, composition, and practices treat all members of the community, as individuals, with equal concern and respect." Although this alternative goal leads to much the same structure of government as does the majoritarian goal, it does so "out of a concern for the equal status of citizens, and not out of any commitment to the goals of majority rule." Majoritarianism, in Dworkin's view, is thus merely a means, not an end: "when majoritarian institutions provide and respect the democratic conditions [of equal respect for all citizens], then the verdicts of these institutions should be accepted by everyone for that reason. But when they do not, or when their provision or respect is defective, there can be no objection, in the name of democracy, to other procedures that protect and respect them better." Nor can there be "any moral cost," he argues, to a court invoking its moral reading to strike down the defective procedures as unconstitutional.

Dworkin focuses on the role of constitutional interpretation in preserving freedom and equality within established democracies. Holmes asks instead what role constitutionalism and democracy play in preventing state decay. In contrast to Dworkin's jurisprudential argument, Holmes offers a contextual, historicist, and functional thesis, which draws lessons for constitutional legitimacy from the real-life experiences of the postcommunist societies of Russia and Eastern Europe. Like the contributors to this volume's first section, Holmes believes that philosophical inquiry and moral legitimacy must be driven by what is happening on the ground: "In 1989," he wryly notes, "most of us thought that good had conquered evil (that we had achieved a liberal revolution)"; "what we've got instead is Chicago in the 1920s." The experience of statelessness in postcommunist societies leads Holmes to adopt an instrumentalist view of constitutions as only one part of state-building. Constitutions should be judged, he argues, on how well they order society, not on their procedural origins or some philosophical notion of right and wrong. Holmes emphasizes this societal-ordering function of constitutionalism as the key prerequisite for the creation of liberal democracy: "the Hobbesian problem has to be solved," he submits, "before the Lockean solution looks attractive." Recent events in postcommunist societies also lead Holmes to embrace an "interest-based analysis" of constitutionalism and nation-building. This reasoning posits that states are created not from some sense of collective need, but from bargaining among interest groups who buy into particular governmental structures only when they receive tangible benefits in return. The minimum requirement of this first stage of constitutional democracy, as Holmes describes it, is not as an idyllic constitutional moment, but a cynical, rough-and-tumble "moderated kleptocracy."

Alberto Calsamiglia uses a Marxian analysis to take issue with Holmes, noting that the prevention of anarchy may be necessary, but not sufficient, to justify constitutional democracy. Yet like Holmes, Calsamiglia evaluates a state not by its form of government but by the substantive norms it protects. Calsamiglia asserts that a state is legitimate not because of its compliance with certain norms of representation, but because of its fulfillment of certain substantive individual rights. Calsamiglia rejects the argument that those universal rights are to be found through natural law, which does not allow for the evolution of our conception of rights.

The first three essays in this section broadly agree on the functions of constitutions, but engage one another strongly on the role of *constitutional courts*. Dworkin and Calsamiglia see constitutional courts as imposing important constraints on majoritarian impulses. But Holmes sees danger in constitutional courts "refus[ing] to identify with the goals of the political branches—to solve society's problems [through energetic action]—and see[ing] themselves as a breed apart, custodians of higher values which executive and legislatures fail to appreciate or understand." Underlying their division is a deeper, unresolved debate regarding the extent to which courts energetically defending rights will undercut or encourage republican deliberation, political stability, and constitutional legitimacy. Dworkin, for one, suggests—but only tentatively—that active judicial review of constitutional questions may in fact provide a superior kind of republican deliberation, by provoking widespread public discussion on important questions of political morality.

To this discussion, Ian Shapiro adds a new question: how should democracy fit, not just with judicial review and societal ordering, but with the identities and aspirations of groups within society? Shapiro urges that "democracy's place is as a subordinate, or conditioning, good." Democracy seeks to shape the terms of common interactions and the pursuit of goals that implicate power relations, without decreeing the end result of those interactions and pursuits. He takes as examples various antidemocratic group-based claims raised by Palestinians seeking self-determination in Israel and political groups in South Africa during their transition to democracy between 1990 and 1994. The challenge for nations seeking to build constitutional democracy, he argues, is not simply to suppress such group-based claims. Rather, the task is to devise electoral mechanisms that will avoid exacerbating intergroup antipathies and make it more, not less, likely that group-based claims can be expressed in ways that are compatible with conditions of inclusive participation and nondomination.

The complex relationship among democracy, voting, deliberation, and human rights also emerges as the focal point of the third set of essays. In *The Constitution of Deliberative Democracy,* Carlos Nino sought to reconcile democracy and human rights through a theory of deliberative democracy. For Nino, democracy was a normative, not a descriptive, concept. The practice of deliberative democracy, he argued, would create a citizenry educated and engaged in the politics of governance, and would thus lead to a stronger and more stable society that would better protect human rights. Establishment of deliberative democracy was thus not just an aspirational goal, but an immediate necessity to begin the creation of a more just and democratic society.

Two essays in this section seek to test Nino's broad thesis in concrete factual settings. Societies in political transition pose a particular dilemma to scholars and policy-makers, who regularly disagree on the extent to which stages of economic development, political structures, cultural beliefs, and national history affect a society's ability to embrace simultaneously the ideals of democracy and human rights.

Irwin Stotzky, a legal adviser to the newly democratic Haitian government and longtime advocate of human rights in Haiti, first tests Nino's thesis, using the troubled history of Haiti as a case study. Stotzky's essay assesses the development of democracy and human rights in Haiti through a detailed application of Nino's theory of deliberative democracy to current realities. His conclusion— that the development of deliberative democracy requires a level of material and political development not yet achieved in Haiti, as well as a coherent justificatory theoretical base—raises challenging questions about Nino's ambition immediately to apply principles of deliberative democracy within ravaged and economically underdeveloped countries.

Jaime Malamud Goti, who worked closely with Nino in Alfonsín's Argentina as a presidential adviser and later Solicitor General, supplements Stotzky's contribution by examining the feasibility of applying a theory of deliberative democracy to Argentina during the military dictatorship from 1976 to 1983. Malamud Goti's essay provides a valuable counterpoint to Stotzky's by illustrating that different obstacles arise to applying a theory of deliberative democracy within an economically developed society that is also a highly developed totalitarian state dominated by state-sponsored terrorism.

Stotzky and Malamud Goti both assume that deliberative democracy is a goal worth pursuing, even if not immediately attainable. But the test cases they explore force us to reexamine whether the very concept of deliberative democracy is sufficiently complete and coherent. Although the four remaining essays in this section do not disprove Nino's hypothesis, they do challenge it from a variety of theoretical angles.

Jeremy Waldron first tests the completeness of the idea of deliberative democracy by asking how we reconcile the value of deliberation with the reality of voting. One of Nino's core claims is that policy decisions that result from a process of deliberation are more likely to further the good of society than decisions achieved without such deliberation. For Nino, deliberation solves the puzzle of how to justify majoritarian decision-making in a society composed of individuals with differing conceptions of the good. Nino sees deliberative, as opposed to merely pluralist, democracy as having the power to transform people's individual preferences to more closely reflect an impartial view of the good of society, through the process of collective deliberation that results in majority voting. Nino goes even further, asserting that collective deliberation results not only in impartial solutions, but also in solutions more consistent with those prescribed by valid moral principles.

Waldron responds by pointing out that even individuals who collectively deliberate often reasonably disagree about what constitutes a just result. Deliberation may not lead to a greater consensus on what constitutes the good, instead only crystallizing bases for disagreement. Voting provides a political answer to the problem of how to deal with deliberative disagreement. At some point, a decision must be made, and most political deliberative bodies have embraced majoritarian voting as the means for reaching that decision. Using the U.S. Supreme Court as his example, Waldron argues that a key overlooked factor in deliberation is "the circumstance of politics": "the felt need among the members of a certain group for a common policy or decision or course of action on some matter even in the face of disagreement about what that policy, decision or action should be." It is precisely because the Supreme Court faces circumstances of politics that it resorts to a vote as a way for resolving disagreements. Waldron does not seek to provide us with a general theory of deliberative democracy, nor does he claim that there is any Archimedean point from which the justice, morality, or constitutionality of a given decision can be assessed. He does, however, argue that a theory of deliberative democracy is radically incomplete unless it dovetails its account of deliberation with an account of what procedures the participants invoke to resolve disputes when deliberation fails. Again using the Supreme Court as an example, Waldron claims that voting is the natural upshot of deliberative democratic decision-making, not something that indicates the inadequacy or unsatisfactoriness of the deliberation that takes place. Waldron concludes by suggesting that the transformative work that Nino attributes to deliberation may really trace to deliberation *in the shadow* of voting, in circumstances of "final equality of decisional authority" among those who deliberate and decide.

The Supreme Court is only one institution that faces the relationship between deliberation and voting. Moreover, the Court's approach provides only one acceptable solution to the problem of how to reach an ultimate decision. Amy Gutmann urges us to focus less on Waldron's issue—the need for a justification of voting—and more on the need to redress the "deliberative deficit" and make our democratic institutions more deliberative. Gutmann takes strong issue with Waldron's (and other majoritarian democrats') attention to majority rule, arguing that democracy, "understood as a moral ideal, is far more than majority rule." To prove this point, Gutmann focuses not on the Supreme Court but on criminal juries. The fact that criminal jury verdicts require unanimity, not majority vote, does not lead us to think of criminal juries as undemocratic, so long as individual equality is respected and deliberative decision-making procedures closely followed. Like Dworkin, Gutmann argues that "majority rule typically comes into its own, morally speaking, only when it turns out to be the best way of either expressing the equal political status of citizens or securing at least provisionally justifiable outcomes or both." Like Nino, Gutmann suggests that deliberation "with justifiable agreement as its primary aim," not voting, is the critical element in our efforts to achieve a democratic society.

Waldron's debate with Gutmann highlights the need for additional work on justificatory theories of democratic institutions—a theme addressed by Carlos Rosenkrantz and Paul Kahn. Both Rosenkrantz and Kahn challenge Nino's acceptance of an "epistemic" justification of democratic institutions: the claim that there is a principled connection between majority rule and moral reason, because a properly structured democracy has a greater tendency to impartial solutions than any other method of reaching group decisions. Rosenkrantz finds Nino's epistemic theory of democracy lacking in its ability to justify the constitution as a legitimate democratic institution. Despite Nino's far-reaching claims, Rosenkrantz argues, the epistemic justification of democracy in fact needs to be supplemented with other theories that explain why and when a restriction of the democratic system is justified. Kahn takes a different tack, using the essays by Stotzky and Waldron to remind us of how truly revolutionary Nino's project was. If asked "can a moral philosopher be a democrat?" Nino would answer yes, because his justification of the state's authority makes of the state a deliberative community that satisfies the conditions of moral inquiry. Yet Kahn argues that this is possible "only if the state is completely restructured to meet the conditions of philosophical inquiry," reworking every aspect of the modern nation-state into the form of "the Socratic model of a dialogical community." Kahn calls Nino's epistemic theory "essentially an anti-political proposal," for it flattens politics and eliminates the role of history in constructing a citizen's identity. The Haitian case study, he argues, disproves Nino's theory of deliberative democracy, for it reminds us that communities are formed by their history long before the politics of an impartial, discursive morality begin. Politics begins, he says, only "after the needs of the body have been met." Waldron, by contrast, abandons Nino's epistemic defense of democracy by abandoning Nino's goal: to mount a philosophical argument for supporting democratic institutions that are linked to truth, not discord. In politics, Kahn argues, the moral philosopher's mission is not to justify the institutions and procedures we have, but rather to rebuild those institutions by insisting that moral truth be the judge of power.

All the essays in this section call for a coherent theory that both justifies deliberative democracy and has relevance for the diverse range of societies who today seek to move toward more "human rights-friendly" regimes. They highlight the unfilled requirements of Nino's conception of deliberative democracy—both the need for radical changes in societal structures that Stotzky and Malamud Goti outline before the conditions for deliberative democracy may attach, and the need for further thinking about our theoretical justifications of democratic institutions (raised by Waldron, Gutmann, Kahn, and Rosenkrantz) before any particular theory of deliberative democracy can be embraced.

The final set of essays addresses one of the most vexing issues facing human rights advocates today: how should a successor regime respond to human rights abuses that have been perpetrated by a prior regime? Examples of societies confronting past abuses abound in such diverse countries as South Africa, El Salvador, Argentina, Bosnia, Rwanda, Albania, and South Korea.[7] How does a successor regime balance the creation of a stable democratic order (discussed in the essays in the second and third sections) with accountability for past abuses? Nino grappled with these issues in both his writing and activism until his death, in his posthumously published manuscript for *Radical Evil on Trial.* Moreover, our response to these questions has a profound impact on whether we consider legitimate the Nuremberg trials and the war crimes trials begun in the 1990s in The Hague and Arusha, in light of past failures to punish similar transgressions, such as the genocidal reign of Cambodia's Khmer Rouge.

What do we seek to achieve by holding individuals criminally responsible for their past misdeeds? Varied justifications have been offered, including retribution, rehabilitation, deterrence, reconciliation, and compensation. The justification for criminal punishment and the limits of successor justice were issues that daily confronted Nino as counselor to President Alfonsín during the Argentinean trials, and that haunted him after that experiment ended in presidential pardons for the accused.[8]

Nino rejected retribution as a legitimate goal of punishment, in part because he thought that such a justification would require punishing all who were guilty of an offense, an option his Argentinean experience had taught him was unrealistic. Tim Scanlon also rejects retribution as a justification, distinguishing the retributive rationale from deterrence, affirmation, and fairness as moral values that can be served by a system of punishment. Citizens cannot reasonably demand retribution from their criminal justice system, he argues, only that it effectively deter; that it affirm the victim's sense of being wronged; that it be fair; and that it be safe, for law-abiding citizens and law-breakers alike. The fourth requirement—that the system be safe—Scanlon sees as providing a limiting principle for the application of criminal justice.[9] A criminal justice system is safe if it offers a defensible justification for punishing some people and not others. Criminal trials undertaken by one regime against the members of a previous regime are particularly vulnerable to criticism, especially to a claim of illegitimate retroactive justice. This was the dilemma that faced the Allied powers at Nuremberg, as well as the U.N. Security Council when creating the international criminal tribunals for the former Yugoslavia and Rwanda.[10]

In *Radical Evil on Trial* and earlier writings,[11] Nino offered *consent to punishment* as a solution to this problem. In committing gross atrocities and voluntarily violating the law, he argued, human rights abusers implicitly consent to being held accountable for the normative consequences of their actions. Scanlon critically analyzes the consent solution, questioning in particular its strong requirement of knowledge of the legal normative consequences of one's actions. Scanlon distinguishes two roles for the "mental element" in the definition of a crime: as a condition of the appropriateness of condemnation and as a condition for the permissibility of inflicting losses. Retributivist theories of punishment, he argues, improperly lump these roles together, while nonretributivist theories of punishment, like Nino's, concentrate unduly on the latter condition over the former.

While Scanlon addresses the justifications and limits for application of criminal sanctions, Ruti Teitel looks at how recent successor regimes have in practice addressed the punishment-pardon dilemma. Surveying examples throughout Latin America, she deconstructs the purposes of a criminal justice system into the functions of storytelling versus punishment, truth or justice. Drawing on these distinctions, Teitel looks at transitions in Chile, Argentina, and Eastern Europe in the 1990s to develop three conceptions of successor justice: limited sanctions, historical justice, and "poetic justice." Limited sanction, she claims, is made possible by the modern separation of the punishment and prosecution components of criminal sanction, with prosecution manifesting itself in modern transitions in the form of a truth commission. Teitel sets forth the purposes and effects of truth commissions and concludes that, even while they lack the trappings of traditional punishment, these narratives create a poetic transition from retrospective desires for accountability to the prospective need to create a new society.

Ernesto Garzón Valdés draws upon his experience with successor justice in Argentina to justify criminal punishment based on its deterrence value. If deterrence is our justification for criminal sanctions, he reasons, the official truth-telling and the limited sanction discussed by Teitel do not go far enough. For Garzón Valdés, the lessons of Argentina are that knowing the truth may not be sufficient to avoid future catastrophes, and that stopping short of full criminal punishment may not provide sufficient foundation for the creation of a just and stable society.

Finally, John Shattuck, the first Assistant Secretary of State for Democracy, Human Rights, and Labor in the Clinton Administration, concludes this section with an essay on accountability written from the perspective of a high-level government official charged with daily formulation of human rights policy. With respect to several key policy questions facing the United States, Shattuck emphasizes the practical importance of accountability for past abuses in facilitating reconciliation in transitional societies, and in emphasizing justice as a means to stability and redevelopment.

The essays collected here were inspired by the work of an extraordinary philosopher, statesman, and patriot, Carlos Nino. But they were equally influenced by the troubled times in which they were written: a moment when efforts to ensure accountability in the Balkans, to entrench democracy with justice in Latin America, and to create political and economic stability in Haiti stood at the forefront of global concern.

What holds these essays together is a common intellectual project: the development of a political philosophy of human rights. That project requires—and will continue to require—exploration of four fundamental relationships: the relationship between ethics and human rights; between constitutionalism and democracy; between democracy and deliberation; and between morality and punishment. Understanding these relationships, and the links among them, is a task that overlaps theory and practice, and that centrally challenges the future of the international human rights movement.

Exploring these relationships was both Carlos Nino's life work and his unfinished journey. His life testifies to the truth that just as human rights theory without practice is lifeless, human rights practice without theory is thoughtless. This volume attests that, even if the markers Nino laid are not always followed, they still chart courses for future action and inquiry that we cannot ignore.

NOTES

1. While there have been many efforts to address the philosophical underpinnings of human rights, few have focused on the link between such theories and the practice of human rights advocacy. Most attempts to make such a connection were published prior to the end of the Cold War and thus stood in the shadow of a global political conflict that often manipulated the concept of human rights. See, e.g., James W. Nickel, *Making Sense of Human Rights: Philosophical Reflections on the Universal Declaration of Human Rights* (Berkeley: University of California Press, 1987); Morton E. Winston, ed., *The Philosophy of Human Rights* (Belmont, Calif.: Wadsworth, 1989). For an interesting post–Cold War treatment of some of these issues, see Stephen Shute and Susan Hurley, eds., *On Human Rights* (New York: Basic Books, 1993).

2. Nino recounts the story of retroactive justice in Argentina and shares his last thoughts on this issue in his posthumously published book *Radical Evil on Trial* (New Haven: Yale University Press, 1996), 41–104.

3. This question has dominated most recent philosophical inquiries concerning international human rights. See, e.g., Nickel, *Making Sense of Human Rights*, and Winston, *The Philosophy of Human Rights*.

4. Nino, *Radical Evil on Trial*.

5. By Williams's lights, Nagel's inquiry into the limits of freedom of expression in the context of sexuality and hate speech is in fact driven in part by "a culturally injected overdose" of the peculiar political culture of the First Amendment to the United States Con-

stitution. For an attempt to move beyond a purely liberal conception of human rights, which accepts the possibility of illiberal human rights-friendly regimes, see John Rawls's well-known essay "The Law of Peoples," in Shute and Hurley, *On Human Rights.*

6. For Rawls's inquiry concerning moral and political deliberation, see his *A Theory of Justice.* Nickel, for one, seeks to apply Rawls's inquiry to the concept of universal human rights. See Nickel, *Making Sense of Human Rights.*

7. For an excellent and thorough compilation of some of the most current writings on the theory and practice of justice in such transitions, see Neil J. Kritz, ed., *Transitional Justice* (Washington, D.C.: U.S. Institute of Peace Press, 1995) (three volumes).

8. It now appears that the presidential pardons have failed to shield completely some of the Argentine perpetrators from accountability. At this writing, prosecutors in Spain and Italy are attempting to hold certain Argentineans criminally accountable for the death or disappearance of their citizens during the "dirty war" in Argentina.

9. The need for such a limit becomes evident when one looks at the use of the criminal justice system by the Argentinean military junta, for example, as described in Malamud Goti's contribution to this volume.

10. For a recent defense of retroactive justice and criminal trials, see Mark Osiel, *Mass Atrocity, Collective Memory, and the Law* (New Brunswick, N.J.: Transaction Publishers, 1997).

11. Carlos Santiago Nino, "A Consensual Theory of Punishment," 12 *Philosophy and Public Affairs* 289 (1983).

Chapter 1 The Death
of a Public Intellectual

Owen Fiss

In 1976 the military seized power in Argentina and, in the name of maintaining order and combating left-wing terrorism, established a heartless and brutal dictatorship that was without parallel in Argentine history. The reign of terror included kidnapping, torture, rape, and murder, and led to the death or disappearance of some nine thousand persons suspected or accused of being subversive. In the early 1980s, the generals sought to counter a decline in their support by trying to retake the Malvinas Islands from the British by force, but they failed in that endeavor and were soon defeated at the hands of Margaret Thatcher. Embarrassed by this turn of events and burdened by a deteriorating economy, the generals then decided to relinquish power and call for national elections, always assuming that the presidency would be won by the candidate—a Peronist—who promised to leave them alone.

The election was held in October 1983, and to the surprise of many, certainly the generals, the Radical Party candidate, Raúl Alfonsín, won. He had campaigned on a platform that promised to bring to justice those responsible for the human rights abuses of the previous seven years, and he was true to his word. In the spring of 1985, the leaders of the junta were put on trial before a civilian tribunal in downtown Buenos Aires. The spectacle that then ensued absorbed all the energy of the nation; it was an extraordinary event in the history of Argentina and, for that matter, the world. It was not the first time that a successor government put the leaders of a previous regime on trial for human rights abuses, but it was one of the very few times that such a feat was attempted without the assistance of a conquering army.

In the midst of that trial, I, along with a small group of lawyers and philosophers from the United States and England (Ronald Dworkin, Thomas Nagel, Thomas Scanlon, and Bernard Williams), was invited by the government to come to Argentina. I immediately accepted and began to prepare for the trip with a certain measure of eagerness, although, to be perfectly frank, I did not have the least idea what lay in store for me. I did not know the language, I hadn't a clue about the legal system, and my impressions of Argentine history were based entirely on a quick read of Joseph Page's then recent book on Perón. Among close friends, I was at a loss to explain the purpose of the trip. I also found it difficult to form a concrete picture of our host and the person who had conceived of this odd academic junket—Carlos Nino. When I innocently inquired of Thomas Nagel and Samuel Isaacharoff—the two I always assumed were most responsible for this extraordinary turn in my life—they simply described Carlos as an adviser to the president.

My own image of a presidential adviser was shaped during the Watergate era. At that time I was working for the Committee on the Judiciary for the House of Representatives, which was trying to determine whether there were grounds to impeach President Nixon. I spent a great deal of my time during the summer of 1974 inquiring into the activities of two of the most notorious presidential advisers in American history, John Ehrlichman and H. R. Haldeman—dour, cynical political opportunists who were intensely faithful to Richard Nixon the man, but not to the nation nor even to the office they served. Some ten years later, on that first plane ride to Buenos Aires, interrupted by a short stop on the beach in Rio, I kept wondering who this adviser to President Alfonsín might be. How far would he fall from the American standard? Little, little did I know.

At our first meeting, Carlos Nino bubbled with conversation. There was a warmth and openness that immediately drew me to him. He was curious about his visitors, attentive to their every need, and always in the best of humor. He loved to tease and joke. He seemed to be the embodiment of life itself. These personal qualities immediately distinguished Carlos from his American counterparts (I'll put to one side the chaos and confusion that seemed to emerge spontaneously from his desk). Even more significant was Carlos's love of philosophy. I found in Carlos Nino a presidential adviser who loved ideas—big ideas, abstract ideas, deep ideas, sometimes even strange ideas, but always ideas—and who, by his devotion to speculative thought, distanced himself from everything American, not just the Ehrlichmans and Haldemans of the world, but even our most honorable officials.

Carlos believed in moral truth. He believed that there were certain principles that were right, and others wrong, and that these principles could be used by an individual or a nation for choosing the proper course of conduct. These principles were set forth in *The Ethics of Human Rights,* first published in Spanish in 1984, revised and published in English in 1991. This belief of Carlos's in the objectivity of ethical judgments was entirely admirable, and also much to my liking, but at times difficult to reconcile with the two other ideas that were foundational for him—a belief in deliberative democracy and the rule of law. What value can democratic politics have if there is an objective moral truth? A similar doubt might be raised about law.

Carlos was not the first philosopher who made his career by embracing a number of contradictory propositions, but like the very best, he openly confronted the contradictions and tried to reconcile them. He was always so honest. The result was his epistemic theory of democracy, which assigned a value to democratic politics because it enlarged the range of interests that would be taken into account in the formulation of public policy. He spoke movingly of "the difficulty each of us has in representing vividly the situations and interests of people very different from ourselves" and saw the democratic process as a means of transcending those limits and achieving a measure of impartiality. For Carlos, democracy was a surrogate of the informal practice of moral discussion, and in a fallible world, democracy was the best means available for discovering moral truth. Similarly, he embraced law as an indication of moral truth and gave it a value only insofar as it was the product of democratic deliberation.

Theories like this are grist for classroom discussion and academic journals. Indeed, Carlos explored these ideas for over a decade in countless articles in academic journals and in one of his final books, *The Constitution of Deliberative Democracy.* Remarkably, Carlos did not confine these inquiries to the academy. He also pursued them when he served the president. Carlos conducted his meetings within government as though they were graduate school seminars, analytically tough, but also speculative and broadly inquisitive. He assumed that every participant—even the president—had just put down Kant or Kelsen.

During that initial visit to Argentina, Carlos made certain that the visitors from abroad met the president, and I was struck by the affection and mutual respect that held them together; the president treated Carlos as a beloved son. But even more striking was the scope of discussion between the two, which ranged broad and far, and eventually settled on the work of Joseph Schumpeter, the great political economist who made his career during the first half of this century. In the presence of a few interlopers, Nino and Alfonsín sat around a conference table at the Casa Rosada at this dramatic moment in Argentine history, speculating about the inadequacies of Schumpeter's theory of democracy. Perhaps such discussions occurred in the councils of power during the days of Madison and Jefferson. I tried to imagine that kind of conversation occurring within the Oval Office in the early 1970s, in the 1960s, or even today, but found myself simply unable to do so.

In this devotion to philosophy, Carlos distinguished himself from the typical American public servant, but his engagement with practical politics distinguished him from most philosophers of his stature in the academic world. It was not just that he was prepared to address public affairs, which might now be commonplace in the American academy, but he was also prepared to act on his theories. Philosophy was an integral part of his effort to make the world just.

When the military seized power in 1976, Carlos was not politically active. He lived wholly in the kingdom of ideas. This did not insulate him from the reach of the dictators, who were prepared to kill those who did no more than espouse unorthodox ideas. As a result, Carlos spent some of the time during the dictatorship living abroad, in England, Venezuela, Mexico, the United States, and Germany. He feared that one day the military would force him to abandon Argentina permanently, and that he would have to adopt one of his temporary refuges as "home." By June 1982, however, the generals began to stumble: They lost the Malvinas War with Great Britain, and, as news about the generals' humiliating defeat came to light, public unhappiness with the regime grew. Carlos saw a faint opening and entered the realm of action, determined to restore democracy to his country.

In July 1982, still a year before the junta relinquished power and decided to call for elections, Carlos began meeting informally with a group of lawyers and philosophers who shared his commitments. This group included some of the most distinguished figures in Argentine intellectual life. Among its members were Genaro Carrió, who later became chief justice of Argentina; Eugenio Bulygin, later the dean of the Universidad de Buenos Aires and a judge of the federal court of appeals; Eduardo Rabossi, a professor of philosophy and the undersecretary for human rights during the Alfonsín administration; Martín Farrell, a noted legal philosopher and judge; and Jaime Malamud Goti, who later served Alfonsín as an adviser and then became solicitor general of Argentina. Like Carlos, these individuals were committed to restoring democracy to the country and were willing to run all the risks that entailed. Even more remarkable from the perspective of the cloistered American academy, they were also prepared to participate in partisan politics to achieve their purposes.

The first meeting of this group had its difficulties—Carlos lost the address and he, along with Eduardo Rabossi, raced up and down Avenida Pueyrredón frantically trying to find the apartment where they were to meet. From the start the group turned to the Radical Party, for it had been the traditional bearer of liberal values in Argentina, but they wanted to meet with various contenders for the leadership of the party for the purpose of deciding which one might best serve the democratic cause. They made one false start, but felt they had struck solid gold when they were introduced to Raúl Alfonsín. The feeling was reciprocated. President Alfonsín made this group part of his inner circle, and affectionately referred to them as "the philosophers." Carlos began his political life as a member of "the philosophers," advising Alfonsín in his quest for the leadership of the Radical Party and in his campaign for the presidency. Later Carlos served as the president's adviser on human rights, then as the director of a commission devoted to constitutional reform.

For the philosopher king, the field of action is merely a means to actualize his ideas. For the public intellectual, as Carlos was, the causality flows in both directions. His ideas were shaped by actions just as his actions were shaped by his ideas. Carlos's intellectual agenda reflected the needs and crises of Argentina and all the other countries that summoned him; he constantly reformulated and refined his theoretical views in light of lived experience. He spoke to the world, but also was part of it.

In opening oneself to the world in this way, the public intellectual always stands in danger of being corrupted. He can easily put to one side the entrapments of petty politics, or the desire for personal advancement—never a temptation for Carlos. The real danger is that the public intellectual may forget the duality of his commitments—that he is committed to the world of thought as well as to the world of action. He may compromise his devotion to the truth in all its fullness, because he is anxious to get on with the project which he has become part. This was Carlos's burden. We talked about it on countless occasions and it weighed heavily upon his soul.

The great, great public event of his life was indeed the trial of the leaders of the junta that occurred in downtown Buenos Aires in the spring of 1985, the occasion of my initial visit, and his involvement in that event left its mark on *Radical Evil on Trial,* a book that Carlos wrote with great gusto and passion in the months immediately before his death. One cannot read a page of it without sensing that Carlos was moved in his writing by his profound belief in the justness of the administration's cause and the need he felt to explain the basis of that belief.

The original strategy of the administration was to focus on the leaders of the junta. Judgment was entered against fifteen of the highest-ranking officers in December 1985, but in time the swath of the prosecutors, not fully in the control of the executive, broadened. In the first few months of 1987, there was a sudden upsurge in the number of indictments, partly in response to a new law passed by Congress that closed off the time for new indictments. By the spring of 1987, more than four hundred officers, including many from the lower and middle echelons, stood indicted. Dissension within the ranks grew and in April 1987, just before Good Friday, a number of garrisons openly rebelled, requiring the personal intercession of Alfonsín to restore order on Easter Sunday. No one knows exactly what transpired in the negotiations between Alfonsín and the leaders of the rebellious forces on that day, but in May 1987, President Alfonsín proposed to Congress a law that would insulate the middle- and lower-level officers from prosecution for many human rights abuses, including torture. The intent was to create an irrebuttable presumption that those officers acted in accordance with higher orders and thus, according to Argentine law, did not have to answer for their misdeeds.

Carlos was upset by this turn of events and was unable to hide his sense of disappointment from the president. Carlos's exuberance knew no limits, and my hunch is that Carlos responded to the Alfonsín's initiative with one of his favorite expressions, "Incredible." The president asked Carlos if his opposition to this new law was based on moral grounds. Carlos answered in the negative, and then, very much the teacher, reminded the president that he, Carlos, was not a retributivist. No, Carlos said, his opposition to this new law was based not on retributivist theories of punishment, which he felt were untenable because they would require every single wrongdoer to be punished, but rather on a fear that the new concession would only escalate into an endless series of demands by the military. In that case, Alfonsín replied, the decision was a matter of political smell, and whose sense of smell, he affectionately inquired of Carlos, should I follow, yours or mine? Carlos, being true to his beliefs but at the same time trying to define the limits of his involvement with the administration, answered, "Yours, of course. After all, the people elected your nose, not mine."

During the waning years of the Alfonsín administration, Carlos was exhausted by the day-to-day involvement with the business of government. He hungered for the freedom that rightly belonged to him as a professor at the Universidad de Buenos Aires and as a regular visiting professor at Yale. Yet his commitment to the world of action did not lessen. Outside of government, he helped build the Centro de Estudios Institucionales, an independent research institution in Buenos Aires that was to provide a home and base for a new generation of Argentine intellectuals. He also continued to worry about constitutional reform in Argentina and elsewhere.

Carlos died on August 29, 1993, at the age of forty-nine. He was on his way to Bolivia for the second reading of the constitution that he had helped to draft for the country, when, arriving at La Paz airport, so high in the mountains, he suffered a fatal heart attack. On earlier occasions the altitude greatly had affected him, and he approached this trip with a certain measure of trepidation. On the day after he died, I received this much-delayed message from cyberspace, forcing me to relive his death once again: "Tomorrow I am going for three days to Bolivia. The new deputies need to know what is inside the Constitution because they must decide whether to give to it the necessary second reading. I hope that the highness does not affect much my explanations."

Why, why, Ernesto Garzón Valdés once asked me, trying to make sense of this enormous tragedy, did Carlos ever go to Bolivia? When Ernesto first posed that question to me in his home in Bonn I sat in silence. Nothing I could say could adequately respond to the grief we were both feeling. But there can be no doubt about the answer. Carlos was impelled to go to Bolivia, and to Germany, Czechoslovakia, Colombia, and countless other countries, by the same sense of civic obligation that drove him in Argentina, and now embraced all the world.

In August 1994, a year after his death, I was in Buenos Aires once again. Carlos was nowhere and yet he seemed to be everywhere. I could see him in the smiles of his sons, Mariano and Ezequiel. I could see him in the eyes of his wife, Susana, and remembered how deeply he loved his family and how much he enjoyed their times together—in their apartment in the mornings before he walked to his office, in their country house, or on their vacations in Córdoba, Brazil, or even Hamden. I could also see him in the public debates of the day.

Politics is the lifeblood of Buenos Aires. Public debate does not await some precipitating event. Yet in July 1994, weeks before my visit, a bomb had exploded in front of a Jewish organization, not far from where the Centro was located, killing a hundred people. The country was once again taking stock of itself. Like myself, Carlos was a Sephardic Jew, and soon after we first met in June 1985 we became enmeshed in broad-ranging discussions about the role of anti-Semitism in Argentine society. Those early conversations were prompted by Jacobo Timerman's book, *Prisoner Without a Name, Cell Without a Number,* which described in painful detail Timerman's imprisonment by the junta and the anti-Semitism that seemed to inflame his jailers. Always the believer in the essential goodness of people, and so in love with Argentina, Carlos tended to minimize the presence of anti-Semitism. I wondered how he would respond in the face of the new calamity.

Anti-Semitism was not the only issue on the public agenda in August 1994. As the country tried to recover from the bombing and to make sense of that tragedy, a convention opened in Santa Fé for the purpose of amending the Argentine constitution. During his presidency, Alfonsín pushed for constitutional reform, but was blocked in his efforts by the Peronists. Alfonsín's term came to an end in 1989 and the elections of that year brought to power a Peronist, Carlos Menem, who soon found himself uncomfortable with the provisions of the Argentine constitution regarding the presidency. The constitution provided for a six-year term but with no opportunity for immediate reelection. In November 1993, President Menem, anxious for a second term, pushed for a convention and the Radical Party, still headed by Alfonsín, saw this as an opportunity to achieve some of the reforms they had sought earlier. The result was the Santa Fé convention of August 1994.

Carlos had worked for constitutional reform, both in the Alfonsín administration and afterward. It was therefore difficult for his family and friends to accept the fact that the convention he had labored so long to bring into being was now being held—in his absence. Yet, in truth, his ideas were present, and for those who cared to look, Carlos could be seen in the persons of Jorge Barraguirre, Gabriel Bouzat, Roberto DeMichele, Marcela Rodriguez, Carlos Rosenkrantz, or Agustín Zbar, a number of the young people he had trained and inspired at the Universidad de Buenos Aires and the Centro—*los jóvenes.* They had become the advisers to Alfonsín, who led the Radical Party delegation in Santa Fé. Now and then, facing some fork in the road, Alfonsín would turn to one of *los jóvenes* and ask wistfully, "I wonder what Carlos would say."

All the political battles of the Santa Fé convention were hard fought, and there is no easy way to assess the outcome. The good was often mixed with the bad. Not all would have been to Carlos's liking, but in the end, there seemed to be a lot of the good, and I think it fair to say that those provisions enhancing the protection of human rights, limiting the executive power, and establishing a mechanism to coordinate the work of the executive and legislative branches seemed to vindicate Carlos's vision and to memorialize all that he had worked for.

Soon after the close of the convention, I received a letter from President Alfonsín. In it, he reminisced about his earlier visits to Yale, while Carlos was teaching there, and praised Carlos for laying the groundwork for the human rights policy of his administration, which he described as one of his "proudest accomplishments." Then the letter ended with this paragraph:

> If the Argentine Constitution of 1994 has an intellectual author it is Carlos Nino, who during my government, as coordinator of the multipartisan Commission for the Consolidation of Democracy, laid the groundwork which permitted those of us who labored in the Constitutional Assembly to come up with most of the ideas and proposals that are enshrined in that document. Carlos was a maker of ideas that worked; his life was too short, but it was also bright, full and good; he is missed.

On the last afternoon of my trip to Buenos Aires in August 1994, I had lunch at El Café de Paso, a restaurant in Parte Once, the Jewish Quarter in Buenos Aires, just a few blocks from the site of the bombing and the former offices of the Centro. The café was Carlos's favorite luncheon spot. I had made one of my usual trips to Argentina in August 1993, and in the course of that trip Carlos made certain that we had lunch there before the time came for us to say goodbye. The café is a Sephardic restaurant, and we spent hours and hours eating *bohios* and reminiscing about the kitchens of our mothers, and, of course, talking about justice. Two days later, I left for Chile and Carlos prepared to leave for Bolivia. The next August, when I returned to El Café de Paso, Carlos was not with me. His absence was painful, and here I am referring not just to the personal pain, which was greater than words could describe—I came to love Carlos like the brother I never had—but a public pain. I knew that there was so much work to do, not just in Argentina but in all the world.

Although Carlos was not with me, I was not alone. I had brought *los jóvenes* to Carlos's luncheon spot, not just the Argentine *jóvenes,* this time Martín Böhmer and Roberto Saba, but also a number of Americans who were there as part of an exchange program Carlos helped establish between Yale and the Centro—Victoria Graff, Julian Kleindorfer, Janet Koven Levit, Ken Levit, and Linda Rottenberg. Having *los jóvenes* with me helped, it helped a lot. Glancing around the table, I realized that Carlos had introduced them to books and ideas that they had never heard of, nor even dreamed of, and that he had broadened their vision in just the way a teacher should. I knew Carlos would live on through his teaching and the institutions he built and shaped. Even more, I realized that Carlos had created for himself a unique form of life and that by his example he had showed *los jóvenes*—no, showed all of us—how we might make our way in this world and perhaps, if the gods are kind, achieve the endearing nobility that so belonged to him.

Part Two **Ethical Bases of International Human Rights**

Chapter 2 Personal
Rights and Public Space

Thomas Nagel

I was once at an international seminar devoted substantially to the discussion of individual rights, their moral basis, their boundaries, and their relation to other values, moral and political—the aim being to present recent developments in American political theory to interested parties from elsewhere. The Americans in the group were much concerned over such issues as freedom of expression for racists, access to pornography, affirmative action for women and minorities, and restrictions on abortion. After listening for a while to the admirably subtle discussion of these issues, some of the other participants began to grumble. They pointed out that in the countries they came from there were no free elections, no free press, no protections against imprisonment or execution without trial or against torture by the police, no freedom of religion—or that their countries were threatened by radical religious movements that would quickly abolish such freedoms if they came to power. Why were we not talking about those things rather than these ridiculous issues of detail which were of no concern to them?

One could understand their point of view, but unfortunately the flagrant violation of the most basic human rights is devoid of philosophical interest. The maintenance of power by the torture and execution of political dissidents or religious minorities, denial of civil rights to women, total censorship, and so forth demand denunciation and practical opposition, not theoretical discussion. One could be pardoned for thinking that the philosophical interest of an issue of human rights is inversely proportional to its real-life importance. One might even be tempted to go further: perhaps the subtle refinements that worry the inhabitants of liberal democracies, in which the most basic protections of the individual are taken for granted, do not even belong to the same subject matter. Is there any meaningful sense in which freedom from torture and freedom to rent pornographic videos both raise an issue of human rights? Is there really one subject or one moral concept here, at all?

I would like to make a case for the view that, once one recognizes the most basic human rights, the ones whose violation fills the reports of Amnesty International and the various Human Rights Watch committees, and makes your flesh crawl, one is committed to taking seriously the sort of highly refined and subtle issues that can easily seem unreal to those who do not enjoy the luxury of being able to take the most basic rights for granted, in virtue of a fortunate political and legal system. This means that there is a connection between being opposed to torture, political imprisonment, censorship, and dictatorship in China, or the political and civil exclusion of women in Saudi Arabia, and being concerned about pornography and the regulation of racist speech in the United States. The fact that in the United States, having secured the canonical blessings of liberty to ourselves and our posterity, we have the luxury of arguing about fine distinctions in the definition and demarcation of individual rights does not mean that we are talking about a completely different subject.

Carlos Nino understood that all these issues were connected. He dedicated much of his inexhaustible energy to the battle for recognition, understanding, and protection of human rights of every kind. In Argentina he was forced to confront the unbearable atrocities committed by a lawless military regime, and to try to respond to them under the rule of law when democracy was restored. But he also understood that human rights must form part of a comprehensive system of moral and political values, and he aimed at a theoretical understanding that would connect the many different issues that fall under that heading. In *The Ethics of Human Rights* he investigated the special features of rights of all kinds that will particularly concern me: their distinction from aggregative goods and the priority they have over other values. He also understood rights as the expression of a distinctive ideal of moral equality.[1]

My focus will be the type of rights usually called negative—forms of freedom or discretion for each individual with which others, including the state, may not forcibly interfere. I believe that if we start with the basics, the fundamental human rights that over the past fifty years have begun to make such a large international impact, however much they may be resisted by the cynical appeals to cultural relativism with which authoritarian regimes defend the cruelties they use to stay in power, then we will find that a fully developed understanding of these rights makes unavoidable the kinds of questions and disagreements that occupy American liberals today. Contrary to the suggestion of the Declaration of Independence, rights are not self-evident: they require precise argument, definition, and adjustment, which will always give rise to controversy, and there is room for very considerable disagreement and development in the details of their design.

One can be against the worst abuses—torture, summary execution or imprisonment, religious or racial persecution, censorship of political criticism—for various reasons: their wrongness is morally overdetermined. But what does it mean to object to these common horrors as violations of universal human rights? I believe it has two implications. First, it means that these are forms of treatment to which no one should be subjected—that any person, anywhere, is wronged if maltreated in these ways. Second, that the wrongness is not a function of the balance of costs and benefits in this case—that while in some cases a right may justifiably be overridden by a sufficiently high threshold of costs, below that threshold its status as a right is insensitive to differences in the cost-benefit balance of respecting it in each particular case. Rights are universal protections of every individual against being justifiably used or sacrificed in certain ways for purposes worthy or unworthy.

I believe it is most accurate to think of rights as aspects of *status*—part of what is involved in being a member of the moral community. The idea of rights expresses a particular conception of the kind of place that should be occupied by individuals in a moral system—how their lives, actions, and interests should be recognized by the system of justification and authorization which constitutes a morality. Moral status, as conferred by moral rights, is formally analogous to legal status, as conferred by legal rights. It is a normative condition, consisting of what is permitted to be done to persons, what persons are permitted to do, what sorts of justifications are required for preventing them from doing what they want, and so forth. Because this normative status is possessed by all persons or none, it is nonaggregative: It is not the kind of good that can be redistributed or increased in quantity.[2] The difference between moral and legal rights is that the existence of moral rights does not depend on their political enactment or enforcement, but rather on whether there is a decisive justification for including these forms of inviolability in the status of every member of the moral community. The reality of moral rights is purely normative rather than institutional—though of course institutions may be designed to enforce them. That people have rights of certain kinds that ought to be respected is a moral claim that can be established only by moral argument.

When appeal is made to human rights in the international context, the aim is to rest one's case on features of moral status so basic that they can be invoked without having to consider in detail the broader circumstances of the situation. If someone has been tortured, or shot for demonstrating peacefully, or imprisoned for criticizing the government, we don't have to investigate the economic performance or popularity of the regime that has done it to decide that this was an impermissible violation of the person's rights. The particulars of the treatment are enough. The appeal to human rights is supposed to be an appeal to values more fundamental than those issues of social policy and political organization over which people can disagree so vehemently.

Of course we often believe that it would be better if the regime that is using these methods to stay in power were displaced by those who are being suppressed. But that need not be the case. The real test of a belief in human rights is whether we are prepared to insist that they be respected even in the service of worthy causes—prepared to condemn their violation not only in the suppression of the democracy movement in China but also in the Peruvian campaign against the Shining Path and the Algerian campaign against the Islamic Salvation Front. The recognition of rights, even if they make more difficult the achievement of a good or the prevention of an evil, expresses that aspect of morality that sees persons not only as objects of benefit and protection but also as inviolable and independent subjects, whose status as members of the moral community is not exhausted by taking their interests into account as part of the general good. Each of us is also a separate and irreducible node of freedom and value, not to be dissolved into the general welfare. Rights form an essential part of any morality in which equality of moral status cannot be exhaustively identified with counting everyone's interests the same as a contribution to an aggregate collective good whose advancement provides the standard of moral justification.

But what is to be included in this core of inviolability? That is the question which links the fundamentals of international human rights policy with the refinements of American civil liberties debates. The farther we get from the fundamentals, the more difficult it is to answer, and the more plausible it seems that the answer can legitimately vary from culture to culture.

Within limits, I am prepared to be a relativist about the ways in which equality of moral status is expressed, not only by the legal systems of different societies, but in the moral systems of different cultures. That is, I believe that individuals can be accorded an adequate form of inviolability by various alternative allocations of individual discretion, privacy, and freedom from interference, provided certain basics are included in the package. Circumstances may have a big effect on the kind of space for personal autonomy and discretion that ought to be left protected by individual rights—circumstances ranging from economic development to population crowding to racial, religious, and ethnic conflict. But when determining the scope of individual rights in the light of the circumstances, the issue is always the same: what kind of force may be used against people, and for what reasons? The limits always represent a balance between collective goods and individual independence, but I believe that every morality should accord some substantial space to personal independence, immune from coercion by the will of others.

One can make a rough division between two domains in which the issue arises, the public and the private. Of course any issue of individual rights depends on there being, at least in the offing, a contention that something or other is the public's business and subject to public control; but the contested conduct itself may be more or less evidently part of public life. In this sense, the public segment of the issue of rights concerns the form of independence from external control that people must be allowed to retain when they enter explicitly into relations or transactions with others that give rise to competition and conflict, notably political and economic relations. Freedom of expression and association in political matters is the core right in this domain, but I would also include some form of economic freedom.

The private domain includes the realm of choices of personal pleasures, sexual fantasy, nonpolitical self-expression, and the search for cosmic or religious meaning. But of course the privacy of these matters is precisely what is at issue: it is only because some individuals' personal choices can seem to others to encroach or impinge on the public space that we have the issues of individual rights in these areas that we do. The idea of rights exempts a core of individual discretion from the authority of others—removes it from the category of conduct that *might* be regulated if good public reasons so indicated.

Those who hold political power are usually inclined to use it to push people around. This can take more or less outrageous forms. Shooting demonstrators in Tiananmen Square is not in the same category as outlawing marijuana or making it illegal to deny that the Holocaust took place. Still, these exercises of force by the state all destroy individual freedom under the authority of some misguided idea of legitimacy. That is why it is so important to decide what limitations on control over the individual should be built into the conditions of political legitimacy—the legitimate use of political authority. We shouldn't be asked to trade in our autonomy completely in exchange for the benefits of political society: contrary to what Hobbes thought, it is not necessary.

Yet the maintenance of such limitations is a constant struggle. They come under pressure from various directions, even in societies with strong democratic traditions. I believe that the repressive impulse has a common source in all these cases, in spite of the great differences in the brutality of its expression. I find myself outraged by all its manifestations, and one of the things that prompts this discussion is a wish to account for the reaction, particularly to exercises of state power that do not have terribly harmful effects. My sense of the illegitimacy of the censorship of pornography or Holocaust denial is quite out of proportion to the actual harm done by such prohibitions. It's like the reaction when someone cheats you out of a sum which, in itself, you can easily afford to lose. A sense of wrong disproportionate to the resulting loss is a good sign that a sentiment of justice, fairness, or right has been aroused. I am aware that life without pornography is perfectly livable, and that the prosecution in Europe of negationists or sellers of Nazi memorabilia is overwhelmingly merely ridiculous. But the idea that state power may be legitimately used in such ways seems to me grossly wrong, and its instances of use to be serious injustices, however modest their actual costs. What I want to understand is the basis of these judgments—of the sentiment that we have absolutely no right to control other people in those ways.

There is a very important instrumental justification of individual rights that I shall leave aside. First formulated by Hume, and developed by Mill and the tradition of rule-utilitarianism, it accounts for much of the value of certain rights—particularly those of property and contract—in terms of the large contribution to the common good that a secure system of such rights provides for a society because of all that it makes possible. I believe that this advantage attaches also to other rights of personal liberty and in particular to the rights of free speech and freedom of the press—whose effects benefit a society vastly beyond the sum of their direct advantages to those whom they enable freely to express themselves. Freedom of expression is a protection of everyone against abuses of power and public outrage and neglect of all kinds. In instrumental value it is comparable in importance to democracy and the rule of law, and its personal value to writers and intellectuals, as Joseph Raz has observed, is slight by comparison.[3]

I believe that the justification of rights in terms of their effects is not the whole story, however, and I want to concentrate on the other major value they have—that of the form of inviolability they confer on everyone, not as an effect but by virtue of their mere existence—their normative essence, so to speak. This is certainly part of what we find important about free speech, in spite of its great instrumental value. That the expression of what one thinks and feels should be overwhelmingly one's own business, subject to restriction only when clearly necessary to prevent serious harms distinct from the expression itself, is a condition of being an independent thinking being. It is a form of moral recognition that you have a mind of your own: even if you never *want* to say anything to which others would object, the idea that they *could* stop you if they did object is in itself a violation of your integrity.

The worst, of course, is the suppression of dissenting opinion because of the danger that it may persuade people, thus depriving the reigning orthodoxy of support and threatening the stability of the regime based on it. Apart from its epistemological stupidity, this is the ultimate insult not only to the dissenters but to the rest of us, their potential audience, who are not trusted to make up our own minds (a point emphasized by Scanlon in this volume). There is no way one could be justified in conceding to the holders of political power this kind of control over the ideas and arguments we will be exposed to, for we would deprive ourselves thereby of any grounds for confidence in their judgment.

Although this kind of thought control is an element in the repressive impulses to be found in modern liberal societies, it is not the main one. Most civilized threats to individual autonomy are motivated by the desire to prevent offense, insult, or social discomfort, or to ensure a moral environment of one kind or another. The greater the ambitions of those who hold power to supply a certain kind of harmonious social environment, the greater will be the pressures on individuality and against variations in divisive individual expression: sexual, racial, religious—or narcotic. The common factor in disputes over the control of such conduct is the question of what should be assigned to the core of a person's life and how he lives it, and therefore regarded as really his own affair, where others should not meddle even if they don't like what he does, and where the authority of the state does not extend. It is this formal character that refined disputes about civil liberties share with the much cruder and more basic issues of religious persecution, crushing of political opposition, and physical cruelty. To be exempt from different kinds of *invasion* is the common denominator of human rights, and the definition of specific rights depends on an argument about where these boundaries fall.

At the present moment in modern democratic societies, an important source of questionable restrictions on individual liberty is the desire to protect people from offense or insult by those whose public expressions or private fantasies assault the sensibilities of others, making them feel they are living in a hostile or threatening environment. I want to discuss the two most prominent versions of this kind of control: attempts to regulate expressions of racial, religious, or sexual hatred or contempt, and attempts to regulate sexual behavior.[4]

Because of the Constitution, regulations of the first kind have been generally limited to the private, nonlegal sphere in the United States, but even this can be a substantial form of restriction. Moreover, in Europe, Britain, and Canada, government is under no such inhibitions, and laws against the expression of racial or religious bigotry are common. Now it would be easy to criticize such laws on the ground that they lend themselves much too readily to abuse, catching the wrong people. For example, the eminent scholar Bernard Lewis was recently taken to court in France for having expressed doubt in an interview with *Le Monde* that the mass slaughter of Armenians during World War I qualified as an example of genocide—the doubt being about the motives of their Turkish killers.[5]

But I don't want to make the case on those grounds, for I think it is already sufficiently outrageous that anyone should be jailed or fined for denying that the Holocaust took place, or selling books which deny it, or for conducting a mail-order business in Nazi medallions, small busts of Hitler, and so forth. Like others whose family photograph albums contain snapshots of people who subsequently died in concentration camps, I suppose I am one of those whose sensibilities are supposed to be protected by such restrictions, but I find them deeply offensive in themselves, and believe they are damaging to the situation of Jews in those societies which enforce them. Such restrictions carry the message that the reality of the Holocaust and the evil of Nazism are propositions that cannot stand up on their own—that they are so vulnerable to denial they need to be given the status of dogma, protected against criticism and held as articles of faith rather than reason. To claim the need for such protection of one's beliefs invites only contempt. Willingness to permit the expression of bigotry and stupidity, and to denounce or ignore it without censoring it, is the only appropriate expression of the enlightened conviction that the proper ground of belief is reason and evidence rather than dogmatic acceptance.

I find it a personal affront to be protected from the expression of such claims by others—thinking as a person with a mind of my own. But I also find it an affront that the state should have the power to silence anyone—and therefore to silence me, if I were to start spouting equally contemptible nonsense. The censorship of a fanatical bigot is an offense to us all.

The same can be said about the pressures to control racially offensive and sexist expression in the United States. And here again I am not just talking about the more ridiculous excesses of political correctness, but about the prohibition of hard-core, intentional expressions of hostility. The situation where those who hold such opinions or attitudes are prevented from expressing them publicly seems to me extremely unhealthy, with its suggestion that the opposite, right-thinking view is a dogma that cannot survive challenge, and cannot be justified on ordinary rational and evidential grounds. The status of blacks and women can only be damaged by this kind of protection.

I don't deny that direct personal insult, if it is offensive enough and not a part of public political commentary and debate, can legitimately be considered a form of assault liable to legal action. But this should be true whatever the content of the insult, and not only when it has to do with membership in a politically sensitive group. It is bad to be nasty and wounding, and while the law is not a very effective instrument for the imposition of civilized standards of discourse, perhaps it can be used in extreme cases—provided, again, this does not serve as an excuse to stifle political polemic or the criticism of public actors. Limits on verbal aggression are a reasonable regulation of the public space in which free individuals must interact—and it makes sense to try to enforce them socially, and sometimes even legally.

Let me now move to Topic A. Our political culture is in a condition of generalized adolescent panic with regard to sex, brought on by a sudden overthrow of puritanism without a concomitant development of worldliness. This is manifest in the absurd intrusions of sexual prurience into electoral politics. When the *Miami Herald* staked out Gary Hart, and the rest of the press and television promptly joined in hooting him off the political stage, I could hardly believe it. If every American citizen who had ever committed adultery had sent him a dollar, he would have been the best financed politician in the country. Since then things have only gotten worse, and we are subjected to a chronic orgy of journalistic hypocrisy that shows no sign of slowing down.

My concern, however, is with the broader problem of the conflict between individual sexual expression and the sexual character of the common culture. What about the range of cases where sexual expression offends or does harm, from unorthodox sexual practices to private consumption of pornography to the display of nude photos in the workplace to sexual harassment? Here my views are determined by a very strong conviction of the personal importance and great variety of sexual feeling and sexual fantasy, and of their expression. Sex is the source of the most intense pleasure of which humans are capable, and one of the few sources of human ecstasy. It is also the realm of adult life in which the defining and inhibiting structures of civilization are permitted to dissolve and our deepest presocial, animal, and infantile natures can be fully released and expressed, offering a form of physical and emotional completion that is not available elsewhere. The case for toleration and an area of protected privacy in this domain is exceptionally strong.

Relations between the sexes form an important aspect of the public space in which we all live, but their roots in individual sexuality are so deep that the protection of individual freedom within the public sexual space is an overwhelmingly important aspect of the design of a system of individual rights. Having made great progress in the past few decades, we are now threatened with a reactionary movement that is probably inevitable, given the size of the recent changes. The effort to recapture some of the domain of sexuality recently lost to public control is not limited to abortion, but extends to the impingement of private sexual fantasy and impulse on public awareness. The reduction of censorship and the decriminalization of all kinds of nonmarital sex has made unavoidable a spreading consciousness of things that some people find disturbing and an affront to their own sexual feelings. Yet in this respect, as with differences of religion, it is essential that we learn to live together without trying to stifle one another's deepest feelings.

A common public understanding of sexual life is very difficult to achieve, because each of us has such a limited supply of information. The sexual republic is a huge population of individuals with different, often incompatible fantasies and imaginations, and each of them has full-scale sexual relations with a very small proportion of his or her fellow citizens. We are all dependent on our own sexual experience, and the sexual experience of our sexual partners and perhaps their sexual partners, for whatever we really know about the subject. Even this source is problematic, since intimate sexual relations do not automatically overcome the barrier of imaginatively noncongruent sexual feelings and fantasies. People who sleep together don't know everything that's going on, and often they know very little. In any case, the selection of partners is hardly a random sample of the electorate.

The literary and cinematic culture doesn't do much to foster a less private understanding of sexual reality. Sex is one of the most difficult subjects to treat artistically, and what appears in the public domain is largely dominated by conventions that change over time but are not very reliable guides to the truth. Sex tends to be treated for the most part from a safe distance, however explicitly. Occasionally a brilliant writer like Henry Miller will get closer, but it does not happen often.

The result is that when a political or legal issue forces us to argue with one another on the basis of our sexual feelings, we find that what comes to the surface to be expressed in the public arena are profound and sometimes alarming differences in the way people see the world and one another. We do not inhabit a common sexual world in the sense—limited, to be sure—in which we inhabit a common natural, or economic, or medical, or military, or educational, or even artistic world. When we try to discuss sex publicly for policy reasons, what usually results is a great clash of expression of private sexual feelings and fantasies, generalized without warrant into conflicting conceptions of universal sexual reality. All this is stoked with the heat that always infuses the subject, and the result is a type of political argument like no other. The beginning of wisdom is to recognize this fact, and not to confound sexual fantasies with objective reality.

The area in which we have seen the most important progress, I believe, is the treatment of homosexuality. There has recently developed in our culture a fairly widespread (though still far from dominant) attitude of toleration which is remarkable because it is not based on general sympathy or understanding. (Of course that's why *toleration* is the word for it.) My guess is that many of the heterosexuals who have come in recent years to oppose laws against homosexual conduct or discrimination against homosexuals are still, viscerally, homophobic. The imagination of homosexual feelings and relations alarms or disturbs them; they hope their children won't be homosexual; their own sexuality shrinks from the full appreciation of this alternative form and finds it threatening. We can see from the arguments over admission of homosexuals to the military that one of the most threatening prospects for the heterosexual man in the street is having to imagine that he is an object of the homosexual fantasies and desires of others with whom he is in personal contact. (This is not an element in male heterosexual attitudes toward lesbianism—an important fact, since it has made the persecution of lesbians less virulent than that of male homosexuals, which in turn has helped the campaign for a general lifting of restrictions.)

But even without imaginative sympathy, there has gradually developed a widening acknowledgment of the obvious fact that the role of sexual relations is as central and fundamental in the lives of homosexuals as in those of heterosexuals, and that it therefore demands the kind of protection that can only be provided by rights of personal discretion, choice, and privacy. This is simply a consequence of the removal of homosexuals from their former official role as monstrous fictional characters at the boundaries of the sexual fantasies of heterosexuals and their reconstitution as people with lives and sexual imaginations of their own and claims to be treated as members of the public moral community. It has resulted, very importantly, from the courageous refusal of homosexuals to keep quiet any longer.

All this has required the end of control over the public sexual space by forces, particularly religious forces, which would prefer that people whose primary desires are homosexual should feel guilty and abnormal, and should try to deny themselves sexual expression and gratification or, failing that, pursue their pleasures in secret. There is no doubt that many people would be more comfortable in such a world. But if we take the idea of moral equality that is at the root of human rights seriously at all, this seems like an exceptionally clear case for exempting a central area of individual choice from public control in the interest of communitarian values. Acknowledgment of the failure of understanding and of the dangers of projective illusion is the primary insight in this area. People are finally beginning to realize that they cannot understand one another's inner lives by consulting their own emotional reactions to what other people do.

If this seems obvious, I emphasize it because I believe it bears directly on another set of vexed contemporary issues, the relation of sexual life to the moral equality of men and women. Here too there are conflicts between individual autonomy and features of the public space that many would find desirable, so the issue of the scope of individual rights inevitably arises. Here also the clash of private sexual fantasies, illegitimately generalized and spilling out into the open, tends to generate obstacles to a fair accommodation.

The status of women in any society—all women, not only those engaged in a heterosexual life—is strongly affected by the public norms of heterosexual relations, because these resonate throughout the social structure and are also intimately connected with the family and the division of labor within it, which is the dominant influence on general expectations and opportunities for women. There is a great deal to be said about how the resulting economic and social inequalities between men and women might be attacked directly, but that is not my subject here. I want rather to discuss the perceived and actual conflicts between equality of status for women and the form of sexual life itself.

The most important advance in this area has been the extension to many, perhaps most, American women of a degree of sexual freedom close to that of men—the abolition of the ancient double standard, with the help of easily available contraception, and finally abortion. While the old dichotomy between sluts and virgins is not really dead, it has certainly weakened its hold on the public imagination, as we can observe both in popular culture and in real life. This is an immense liberation for both sexes, and the more it is confirmed and extended to all social classes the better it will be.

But something else is now happening, also in the name of equality, which seems to me unhealthy, both politically and sexually—an attempt from some quarters to take greater control of the sexual atmosphere and environment by restricting the expression of forms of sexuality that feel threatening, at least to many women, and whose unrestricted indulgence is perceived as creating a generalized status harm to women who have to live in a society that permits it.

Now I am quite aware that plenty of heterosexual men hate and fear women and regard them at an instinctive level as less than fully human, and that these attitudes are often woven into their sexual desires and sexual fantasies. I'm talking now not only about rapists and wife-beaters, but about large numbers of ordinary slobs who aren't about to attack anyone. And there is something else, which is in its way even worse: the insidious and nearly subliminal idea that it is in itself *better to be a man* than a woman. I believe that it is a very deep and essentially inevitable result of the longstanding inferior social and economic and interpersonal status of women in our culture, as in every other, that simply being a woman is instinctively felt to be worse than being a man—a kind of misfortune that afflicts half of the human race, a less valuable form of existence, and one whose interests matter less. This is the most profound form of status injury, caused by the psychologically natural association, at a level beneath thought, of good or bad fortune with a corresponding valuation of any other defining property consistently and pervasively associated with it. And the victims are as susceptible to this miserable evaluative reflex as those on top. It accompanies all status hierarchies—of aristocracy, of class, of race, of sex—and helps to perpetuate them.

So I don't think that the situation of women, even in modern secular liberal cultures, is just fine. But I believe that the wish to improve it by the device of in-terfering with the sexual fantasy life and sexual expression of heterosexual men, as long as they do not directly harm specific women, is unwise and morally ob-tuse. I even think that the level of society's tolerance for offense in this domain should be quite high, nearly as high as it should be for political and religious expression.

My reason is that the impulse to control some people's sexuality on the ground that it makes others feel threatened comes from a misguided desire to treat the riot of overlapping and radically incompatible sexual fantasies among which we live as if it were part of the public environment, and to subject it to the kind of control and accommodation that is suitable for the public space. But this is com-pletely ridiculous. We all have to live surrounded by sexual fantasies, of which we are sometimes the object, and which are often potentially extremely disturbing or alarming in virtue of their relations of incompatibility or resonance with our own sexual imaginations. No one is sufficiently polymorphously perverse to be able to enter with imaginative sympathy into the sexuality of all his fellow citi-zens. Any attempt to treat this psychic jungle of private worlds like a public space is much too likely to be an expression of one's own sexual fantasies, rather than being an accurate appreciation of the meaning of the sexuality of others.

Reactions to pornography vary enormously. Many women like heterosexual pornography and are aroused by it. But it is clear that some women find it ex-tremely disturbing and think it reveals a world around them which is over-whelmingly hostile and dangerous to a paralyzing degree. I believe that this it-self has to be seen as a reaction of the sexual imagination. The offending images arouse disturbingly violent sexual fantasies or fantasies of threatening degrada-tion, which clash with the sexual feelings that the viewer can accept. The vio-lence is then projected onto those who derive sexual pleasure from this form of pornography. (In extreme cases I have the impression that a quite generally vi-olent sexual fantasy life is at work behind the projections—in the interpretation of all heterosexual relations as charged with aggression and rape, for example.) But the fact that a pornographic film evokes unacceptable feelings in someone who would not choose it as a source of sexual stimulation is no indication of what it means to someone who watches it for that purpose. The blind clash of sexual fantasies in this case is directly analogous to what happens when a homophobic heterosexual projects his own horror of homosexual feelings onto the actual sexual relations between men, so that they are seen as unnatural and revolting in themselves.

I would say the same about sadistic and masochistic fantasies, about which I do not know much, but which can be extremely disturbing to those who do not share them. To take these things at face value, as equivalent to real threats, seems to me laughably naive about the way the sexual imagination works. I do not want to see films depicting torture and mutilation, but I take it as obvious that they do something completely different for those who are sexually gratified by them; it is not that they are delighted by *the same thing* that revolts me; it is something else that I do not understand, because it does not fit into the particular configuration of my sexual imagination—something having to do with the sense of one's body and the bodies of others, release of shame, disinhibition of physical control, transgression, surrender—but I'm guessing.

Life is hard enough without trying to impose a sexual grid of the normal and civilized on the wildly various sexual inner lives that result from the complex and imperfect individual histories that have formed each of us. We live in a world of separate erotic subjects and we are all surrounded by sexual fantasies all the time. Who knows what unspeakable acts you are performing in the imagination of the mortgage officer as he explains to you the relative advantages of fixed and variable interest rates, or the policewoman who is giving you a traffic ticket, or the butcher who is wrapping your pork chops? If some men get their kicks by watching movies of women with big breasts engaged in fellatio, and if others get theirs by watching depictions of gang rape or flogging or mutilation, this really shouldn't give rise to a claim on anyone's part not to be surrounded by, or even included in, such fantasies. We have no right to be free of the fantasies of others, however much we may dislike them. If the division between the public and the private means anything, sexual fantasies and means of sexual gratification belong firmly in the private domain. An awareness that things go on there which might disturb, disgust, or frighten you, together with an unwillingness to regard this as providing any ground for interference whatsoever, should be a fundamental aspect of the kind of recognition of inviolability that makes up a commitment to human rights.

Here again what I am saying may seem obvious. But let me turn finally to the most difficult case in this area, the definition and control of sexual harassment. I believe that the charge of sexual harassment should be essentially confined to coercion, plus fairly extreme forms of offensiveness. By coercion I mean forced physical contact or the solicitation of sexual favors (explicitly or implicitly) in exchange for professional advancement, grades, and so on. By extreme offensiveness I mean lewd personal remarks that would embarrass any reasonable person. What I exclude from the category are noncoercive expressions of sexual interest or sexual proposals, even between people who are in a professional relation; and general remarks expressing what may be offensive attitudes about sex. People shouldn't be forced, as a condition of their employment or educational affiliation, to be subjected to gross sexual expression, just as they shouldn't be faced with it unavoidably in the street or on the display racks of newsstands. But they have no right to protection against being made aware of the sexual attitudes or feelings of others, even if those attitudes or feelings are distasteful to them. People can feel offended by anything if they disapprove of it strongly enough, and it is essential for the preservation of sexual as of other kinds of freedom that mere disapproval not be converted into a claim of personal assault that can be used as the basis for public control. Crude male sexuality is as deserving of protection against public repression as any other kind.

The radical communitarian view that nothing in personal life is beyond the legitimate control of the community if its dominant values are at stake is the main contemporary threat to human rights. Often, of course, it is invoked in bad faith by ruling minorities claiming to speak on behalf of the community. But sometimes the values and even the majorities are real, and then the only defense against them is an appeal to the form of moral equality that accords to each person a limited sovereignty over the core of his or her personal and expressive life. My contention has been that this sovereignty or inviolability is in itself, and not just for its consequences, the most distinctive value expressed by a morality of human rights.

NOTES

1. Carlos Nino's engagement in the prosecution of crimes against humanity, in constitutional reform, and in moral philosophy were all expressions of that confidence in the natural alliance of reason and decency, which was so prominent a part of his large-hearted attitude to life.

2. For fuller discussion see "La valeur de l'inviolabilité," *Revue de Métaphysique et de Morale* 2 (1994), 149–166.

3. See the essay "Rights and Individual Well-Being" in *Ethics in the Public Domain* (New York: Oxford University Press, 1994): "If I were to choose between living in a society which enjoys freedom of expression, but not having the right myself, or enjoying the right in a society which does not have it, I would have no hesitation in judging that my own personal interest is better served by the first option. I think that the same is true for most people" (39).

4. I shall leave aside the issue of drugs, because although it has much in common with these other two areas of control, it also includes a strong component of paternalism that makes it different.

5. This was a criminal charge, but it was brought by a private party—an Armenian organization in France.

Chapter 3 In the Beginning Was the Deed

Bernard Williams

Carlos Nino was a brave man and an admirable philosopher who gave his country notable service and stood against a tyrannical and corrupt regime on the basis of a robust belief in liberal political values and universal human rights. In his own mind and in his life, his philosophy and his political values were intimately linked. His philosophy not only expressed his political values, but firmly claimed a certain type of foundation for them. He was deeply opposed not only to those who rejected liberal values but to those, such as Richard Rorty and myself, whom he saw as trying to detach those values from their proper and necessary philosophical base. Even John Rawls was thought to have fallen away in his more recent work from the correct objective of putting human rights on a solid base, one that would have universal application.

As Nino himself recognized, I do not share his faith in that style of legitimation of liberal values.[1] Although I disagree with Nino about the *basis* of his values, I hope here to offer an even more direct link than his own account offers of the connection between such values and a political life.

The human rights that I shall discuss are the most basic ones: those that, at Thomas Nagel puts it in his essay in this volume, stand against such things as "the maintenance of power by the torture and execution of political dissidents or religious minorities, denial of civil rights to women, total censorship." Nagel says of these that they "demand denunciation and practical opposition, not theoretical discussion." He also says, a little more surprisingly, that "the flagrant violation of the most basic human rights is devoid of philosophical interest." I do not think that means that there is no philosophical interest in discussing the basis or status of these most fundamental rights. Moreover, reference to their flagrant violation is not a bad way of recalling what these rights are. Nagel does not disagree, and his point indeed fits in with this: he wants to say that no very elaborate and refined philosophical discussion is needed to establish what these right are. In this they differ from the issues he addresses, of freedom for hate speech and for pornography and a high level of sexual toleration.

We differ because I agree with the critics he mentions at the beginning of his essay in wondering whether these are matters of fundamental human rights at all. The fact that elaborate philosophical distinctions are required to define and establish these rights supports my uncertainty. Fundamental human rights, it seems to me, had better get slightly nearer to being what their traditional defenders always took them to be, that is, self-evident, and self-evidence should register more than the convictions of their advocates if the claims to human rights are to escape the familiar criticism that they express only the preferences of a liberal culture. This point seems to me all the more telling if they express the preferences of only some liberals. It is simply a fact that many European liberals, fully respectable (I hope) in their liberal convictions, find it a quaint local obsession of Americans that they insist on defending on principle the right to offer any form of odious racist insult or provocation so long as by some argument it can be represented as a form of speech. I should have thought that these were obviously matters of political judgment, above all in telling the difference between the point at which the enemies of liberalism have been given only enough rope to hang themselves, and the point at which they have enough rope to hang someone else. The fact that many trustworthy people elsewhere see it in that light should itself, I think, encourage American liberals to ask whether the powerful personal conviction that Nagel very clearly describes, to the effect that this is not a policy question but a matter of ultimate right, may not be partly the product of a culturally injected overdose of the First Amendment.

On the other matter Nagel discusses, sexuality, I very much agree with him, both with his psychological views and with his policy recommendations in our actual situation. But here also I wonder how much of this can really rest in the territory of fundamental human rights. Just because of the basic truths he invokes, about the power of sexuality, it is unsurprising that many and various conventions obtain in the world, and it must be a matter of judgment, I suppose, and one that to some extent will turn on local cultural significance, to decide where and when an accepted tradition becomes a matter of an unambiguous case of abusive power, which is what I take to be the subject matter of fundamental human rights. No one supposes that the drawing of boundaries is easy in such matters, and for reasons well known in semantics, it is no easier to draw an unambiguous boundary around just the unambiguous cases. I shall say a little more about this at the end. I would like to concentrate, however, on those only too clear and familiar cases of fundamental human rights: torture, assault, and arbitrary power.

Nino's own account of human rights is based on Kantian moral theory. Human rights are derived from moral principles, which could secure agreement and reduce conflict under certain postulated conditions of discussion, conditions which set constraints on what the moral principles can be like.[2] This constructivist enterprise implies a certain conception of the person as someone capable of enjoying these rights; this conception confers a very high value on autonomy. Autonomy, understood as the capacity and opportunity to choose one's own values and way of life without coercion or undue persuasion, is taken as the basis of other values as well, not just in the sense that it is, through the construction, presupposed in the articulation of other values, but because it confers the value on other valuable items ("the source of almost all social value").[3] Nino was prepared to say that the reason why it is wrong to abuse others is that it is an assault on their autonomy: "an individual who is killed, raped, cheated, etc., has less opportunity for choosing and realizing moral standards."[4]

This last idea presents a problem, which comes from the basic disposition of Kantian theories (in direct contrast, here, to utilitarianism) to make the beneficiaries of morality co-extensive with its agents. If the wrong of killing or abusing someone rests in its being an assault on his or her moral autonomy, an inability to be a moral agent will undercut one's protection against being killed or abused. One would hope that the theory could avoid this result without losing its general shape and motivation. However, there is a larger difficulty near at hand: what is involved in being a person in the sense relevant to morality. Nino was very emphatic that he did not want his theory to be seen as a dogmatic derivation of moral principles from some factually given account of what persons are. He thought that this might offend against the is/ought principle, and would in any case expose the theory, with its claim that persons in the relevant sense are equal, to empirical attack. He accordingly stressed the idea that the notion of a person that the theory required was *normative*.[5]

This, in turn, means that persons must be *treated as* autonomous, as capable of freely accepting or rejecting moral positions, and the justification of accepting this normative idea must be, Nino said, that it is implicit in the business of moral reasoning: it is "necessarily assumed when we participate in the practice of moral discourse."[6] Nino directly contrasted this strong approach with Rawls's more recent view that such conceptions are implicit only in certain political practices, those (roughly) of the modern democratic state. Nino's view is stronger perhaps even than Rawls's earlier position, and comes nearer to the outlook of Habermas, though Nino himself does not offer any elaborate presuppositional or communication-theoretical argument for it.

There is a problem with the internal economy of this argument. It looks as though the normative conception of the person enjoins us to treat others as possessing equally the powers relevant to autonomy, but one consideration that motivated the normative conception in the first place was precisely the fact that people do not empirically possess such powers equally. This is, once again, a recurrence of a type of difficulty that Kant encountered, in his dealings with God, for instance, where he seems to be involved in a kind of doublethink; he offers as a regulative idea a conception that seems indistinguishable from a constitutive idea which is false but which we are enjoined to treat as though it were true.

However, I do not want to pursue this line of criticism. I want to ask, rather, where this interlocking set of aspirations is supposed to touch reality. Are the items in the circle rights-principles-moral discourse-person-autonomy-rights merely identified in terms of each other? It will not matter in itself that there is a definitional circle here, if the circle is long and interesting enough, but we do need to identify a place in the world, a practice, that will give the set of concepts a grounding in reality. This is what Rawls does when he identifies something like this as the discourse of modern democratic states. But Nino rejected this approach as relativist, and it is clear that he wanted to get beyond any such idea to something universal. Where did he think he had found it?

I think that the item in this set that he supposed could in principle apply to everyone, and so lead everyone to recognize the force of the other notions, was moral discourse, with its associated ideas of reducing conflict and bringing about agreement.[7] The "social practice of moral discourse"[8] is one that will, properly understood, mobilize these other notions, including the normative conception of the person, in terms of which we can understand human rights.

But then, as so often, the gap between reality and aspiration appears in a new place. Where, among which human beings, under what conditions, do we actually find the social practice of moral discourse? Certainly not universally: some human beings do not even want agreement and the elimination of conflict, or at least its universal elimination, as Nino perfectly well knew and pointed out when condemning "tribalism, nationalism, and religious sectarianism."[9] Many who want agreement and co-existence, and indeed enjoy them, do not share the aspirations of autonomy. It is not true that every human group, or every human group enjoying a measure of peace, engages in the "social practice of moral discourse," as that notion is defined in the circle of concepts that delivers the normative conception of the autonomous person and, along with it, human rights.

Of course, any human group living in a moderately stable order under peace shares some set of ethical understandings, some rules and concepts that govern their relations. If these were all tantamount to what Nino called the social practice of morality, everyone would already have implicitly accepted liberalism, at least as an ideal, and one would merely have to spell it out. But this is manifestly not so, and the mere fact that there is so far for the liberal to go, and the fact that societies of the past, as well as recalcitrant societies of the present, have had relatively stable ethical systems that were not based on these presuppositions, make it clear that the practice of morality, in this distinctive sense, is not the only possible basis of peaceful social existence.

Liberals sometimes give the impression that the practice of morality, understood in liberal terms, is the only alternative to an overtly coercive or deceitful regime. When Nino wrote, for instance, "When we resort to the exacting task of discussing the moral merits of a solution instead of availing ourselves of propagandistic, seductive, or coercive means to promote its adoption,"[10] he exploited the idea that morality, and by implication the liberal ideals of autonomy, stand as the only alternative to means which are described in terms that will elicit disapproval from almost anyone except the most ruthless Realpolitiker or nihilist. At another point, the practice of morality in the liberal sense is seemingly equated, as it was by Kant, with the practice of reason itself: "we must accept that there may be some people or societies which do not follow the same practice of moral discourse; that is, that they follow a practice of moral reasoning and discourse which differs in relevant respects from ours. This usually provokes the question, 'What can we do to convince those people?' My answer is 'Nothing.' If there are people who refuse to listen to reasons—depending on what we understand by the word 'reasons'—it is as if they covered their ears. We can induce them or compel them but we cannot convince them."[11] The phrase "depending on what we understand by the word 'reasons'" hangs a little awkwardly in that sentence, no doubt because it registers a discomfort. Can we really suppose, as Kant supposed, that reason itself is liberal reason, and that an ethical practice which is other than the morality of autonomy involves the refusal to listen to reasons at all, the equivalent of covering one's ears? Surely not.

There are indeed universal paradigms of injustice and unreason. They consist of people using power to coerce other people against their will to secure what the first people want simply because they want it, and refusing to listen to what other people say if it goes against their doing so. This is a paradigm of injustice because institutions of justice, wherever and whatever they may be, are intended to stand precisely against this. "Might is not, in itself, right" is the first necessary truth, one of few, about the nature of right. Simply in this form, the universal paradigm excludes many bad things, but it is indeterminate about what it requires: it says not much more than that coercion requires legitimation and that the will of the stronger is not itself a legitimation. It is already clear, however, how long a journey the liberal would have to make to arrive at the conclusion that morality in his sense and its notion of autonomy provide the only real alternative to injustice and unreason. He would have to show that the only considerations that could count as a legitimation were those of liberal consent. In fact—and this is a point I shall come back to—he would have to show something stronger, that only his considerations could even decently be supposed to count as a legitimation. That seems, as it surely is, a wildly ambitious or even imperialistic claim.

It may be said that the liberal's legitimation is the only universal one, or at least the only universal one that is not simply dogmatic. One who believes in a revealed religion with universalistic pretensions has his view of a legitimation which can make coercion just and desirable, but he has the problem that not everyone accepts it, and the coercion will, obviously enough, not be legitimate to those who do not accept it. Only a constructivist solution, it has been thought, can get around this problem. But it does not ultimately get around it. For if it involves a top-down argument from a certain substantive conception of the person, for instance, it will (as Nino noted) have enough in common with dogmatic positions to run into a stand-off with them; liberalism sees persons as free autonomous choosers, and so forth, and religious fundamentalism sees them as something else. If, on the other hand, liberalism makes its conception of the person normative, as Nino wanted it to be, we are back to the point we have already discussed, that the circle of normative notions cannot be forced onto a recalcitrant world; in particular, it cannot be forced on to the world through a certain concept of moral discourse, one that turns out to be no more universal than any other element in the circle. Liberalism is no worse off in these respects than any other outlook, but it is not, at any absolutely general level of principle, better off. It may possibly, and for historical reasons, be rather better off now. But it will have a chance of being so only if it accepts that like any other outlook it cannot escape starting from what is at hand, from the kinds of life among which it finds itself. Like everyone else, it must accept the truth that in the beginning was the deed.

This famous line from Goethe's *Faust,* "Im Anfang war die Tat," is known best to philosophers, perhaps, from being quoted by Wittgenstein in *On Certainty,* where it steals into the text rather surreptitiously, in brackets. It follows a passage that says that there are statements about material objects that "form the foundation of all operating with thoughts (with language) . . . they do not serve as foundations in the same way as hypotheses which, if they turn out to be false, are replaced by others." Goethe's line can indeed help us to understand this Wittgensteinian theme, by reminding us in particular that the "primacy of practice" (in a familiar exegetical phrase) is not the primacy of descriptions of practice. It is not that when we represent to ourselves our practices, we can see in that representation a ground of our beliefs. The relation between a practice and a set of beliefs cannot be anything like that of premises and conclusion, or indeed any other relation of two sets of propositions. There could not be a description of our practices which adequately represented the way in which belief was grounded in practice, if only because the understanding of that relation itself would have to be grounded in practice. It follows from this that the powers of reflection on this relation are limited; indeed, that we must rethink what it is for reflection to get anywhere at all. (Those who attempt to recast the later Wittgenstein's philosophy as a theory, or, slightly more reasonably, to accommodate it to philosophy which consists of theory, have not fully grasped this point.)

It is even more important to bear these considerations in mind when we bring Goethe's saying back to politics. Moral and political philosophy supposedly influenced by Wittgensteinian ideas can easily slide into an uneasy communitarian relativism, under which we reflect on our (local) practices and take them as authenticating a way of life for us. This cannot be right. For one thing, no Wittgensteinian argument tells us who, in any given connection, is meant by *we*.[12] The particular passage in *On Certainty* is in fact one of those in which "we" seems to extend itself most generously to anyone who can share a language, that is, to more or less everyone, and the political analogue to this would be, if anything, a Kantian universal constituency of human beings (at least), rather than some community to be identified as consisting of some human beings as distinct from others. Moreover, even if *we* in the political interpretation meant a local *us*, the communitarian interpretation of this runs straight into the point often made by Ronald Dworkin and other liberals, that in any sense in which *we,* this local *we,* have identifiably local practices, one of them consists in criticizing local practices.

What the Wittgensteinian idea does mean for politics is that foundationalism, even constructivist foundationalism, can never achieve what it wants. Any such theory will seem to make sense, and will to some degree reorganize political thought and action, only by virtue of the historical situation in which it is presented, and its relation to that historical situation cannot fully be theorized or captured in reflection. Those theories and reflections will themselves always be subject to the condition that, to someone who is intelligently and informedly in that situation (and those are not empty conditions), it does or does not seem a sensible way to go on.

This important negative conclusion is, in my view, basically as far as the Wittgensteinian idea in itself will take us. Given simply this much, it might seem possible that the liberal project could in our circumstances make sense, even in a strongly foundationalist or constructivist form. (The *we* now appropriate to political practices is approaching the Kantian limit.) But this is not really so. For by virtue merely of the Wittgensteinian idea, the foundationalist project cannot in the end do what it really wants to do, and since that is both true and (granted these sorts of considerations) now evident, the liberal project, *in this particular form,* does not in fact any longer make sense. Moreover, Goethe's saying, not now as recruited by Wittgenstein but in its own right, reminds us how far such a project falls short of making sense. For political projects are essentially conditioned, not just in their background intellectual conditions but as a matter of empirical realism, by their historical circumstances. Utopian thought is not necessarily frivolous, but the nearer political thought gets to action, as in the concrete affirmation of human rights, the more likely it is to be frivolous if it is utopian. Those circumstances almost always are created not by our thought but by other people's actions. It follows, in fact, that whether our thoughts even make political sense depends to an indefinite degree on other people's actions.

Some of those actions are bad ones. The circumstances in which liberal thought is possible have been created in part by actions that violate liberal ideals and human rights, as was recognized by Hegel and Marx, and, in a less encouraging spirit, by Nietzsche. Equally, some are good actions that have gone ahead (as subsequent historical accounts will put it) of prevailing interpretations and changed the background in which interpretations are understood. Exceptional action gets ahead of theory, and theory, or other less formally recognized modes of political speech and persuasion, can get ahead of ordinarily accepted practice. But there is no way in which theory can get all the way ahead of practice and reach the final determination of what can make sense in political thought; it cannot ever, in advance, determine very securely what direction might count as "ahead." Very powerful political discourse can of course be proleptic and help to create the conditions it foresees. Liberal discourse itself has had considerable success in this, but it is a way that is markedly different from the ways in which liberalism typically sees itself, and there is good reason to think that its continued success, now, may require a better, more Wittgensteinian and, more important, Goethean self-understanding.

This returns us to human rights. There is, I said earlier, a universal paradigm of injustice. What in a given historical context will count as injustice will of course depend on what counts there as a legitimation of constraint of power used by the stronger, and this in turn involves questions of who is stronger and in what respects, of what counts as the interests of the weaker, and so forth. The most basic violations of human rights are indeed self-evident: they are abuses of power that almost everyone everywhere has been in a position to recognize as such. An extreme contrast with these are cases in which it is predictably contested, and a recognizable matter of political decision, what the exact limits of legitimate constraint may be; I suggested earlier that the control of pornography and setting boundaries between political expression and harassment fell into this class.

The most significant and difficult area falls between these extremes. This contains cases in which a style of legitimation that was accepted at one time is still accepted in some places but no longer accepted in others. These notably include, now, theocratic conceptions of government and patriarchal ideas of the rights of women. Should we regard practices elsewhere that express such conceptions as violations of fundamental human rights?

I must make clear that I am not raising here any relativist issue. The question does not involve the manifestly confused notion that these ideas might be somehow right for those that hold them and not for those who do not. Let us grant that such supposed legitimations have no sound support. The question is whether we must then think of these practices as violations of human rights. A short argument will say that they must be, as they involve coercion without legitimation. But this is a bit short. For one thing, there is an issue of how much manifest coercion is involved, and that is why the situation is worse in these re-spects if opponents of the theology are silenced or women are forced into roles they do not even think they want to assume. Simply the fact that this is so makes the situation more like the paradigm of injustice. How far it will have come to be like that paradigm is one of those matters of the historical environment which I have already mentioned. Up to a point, it may be possible for supporters of the system to make a decent case (in both senses of that helpful expression) that the coercion is legitimate. Somewhere beyond that point there may come a time at which the cause is lost, the legitimation no longer makes sense, and only the truly fanatical can bring themselves to believe it. There will have been no great change in the argumentative character of the legitimation or the criticisms of it. The change is in the historical setting in terms of which one or the other makes sense.

Much of this, of course, is equally true of a liberal regime taking steps against anti-liberal protestors. It is precisely because this is so that it is a crucial, and al-ways recurrent, matter of political judgment to determine how much rope a given set of protestors may be given. (A corollary of Goethe's saying is that there can be an important question of whose *Tat* should be *im Anfang*.)

Suppose, then, that the theocratic regime, or the subordinate roles of women, is still widely accepted in a certain society, more or less without protest. Then there is a further question: to what extent this acceptance, though it does not produce a genuine legitimation, nevertheless means that, as I put it earlier, it can be decently supposed that there is a legitimation. An important consideration, as the Frankfurt tradition has insisted, is how far the acceptance of these ideas can itself be plausibly understood as an expression of the power relations that are in question. It is notoriously problematic to reach such conclusions, but to the extent that the belief system can be reasonably interpreted as (to put it in im-probably extreme terms) a device for sustaining the domination of the more powerful group, to that extent the whole enterprise might be seen as a violation of human rights. Without such an interpretation, we may see the members of this society as jointly caught up in a set of beliefs which regulate their lives and are indeed unsound, but which are shared in ways that move the society further away from the paradigm of unjust coercion. In that case, although we shall have various things to say against this state of affairs, and although we see the decline of these beliefs as representing a form of liberation, we may be less eager to in-sist that this way of life constitutes a violation of human rights.

The charge that a practice violates fundamental human rights is ultimate, the most serious of political accusations. In their most basic form, violations of human rights are very obvious, and so is what is wrong with them. Moreover, in their obvious form, they are always with us somewhere. It is a mark of philosophical good sense that the accusation should not be distributed too inconsiderately, and in particular that theory should not lead us to treat like manifest crimes every practice that we reject on liberal principle, even if in its locality it can be decently supposed to be legitimate. It is also a question of political sense how widely the accusation should be distributed. As always, that consideration can cut both ways. It may be politically helpful in certain circumstances to exaggerate the extent to which a practice resembles the paradigms of injustice. As always in real political connections, there is a responsibility in doing such a thing: in order for the practice to come to be seen as resembling manifest crimes, it will almost certainly have to be made to change in actual fact so that more are committed.

Whether it is a matter of philosophical good sense to treat a certain practice as a violation of human rights and whether it is politically good sense cannot ultimately constitute two separate questions. This is because of the basic truth represented in Goethe's verse, that no political theory, liberal or other, can determine by itself its own application. The conditions in which the theory or any given interpretation of it makes sense to intelligent people are determined by an opaque aggregation of many actions and forces. A few of those actions are political actions. A few, a very few, may be the actions of theorists, whether acting politically, like Nino, or, like him and the rest of us, as theorists.

NOTES

1. I do not think, any more than he did, that my reasons for this, or the position that emerges, are the same as Rorty's.
2. Nino, *Ethics of Human Rights* (Oxford: Oxford University Press, 1991), 72–73.
3. Nino, *Ethics of Human Rights*, 139.
4. Nino, *Ethics of Human Rights*, 141.
5. Nino, *Ethics of Human Rights*, 36, 112 et seq.
6. Nino, *Ethics of Human Rights*, 112.
7. If Nino hung the circle from the idea of the moral, his project was formally similar to Hare, though it would not share a peculiarity of Hare's theory, that it is supposed to depend on a linguistic point about the word *moral*. On this, see Williams, "The Structure of Hare's Theory," in *Hare and Critics*, ed. Douglas Seanor and N. Fotion (Oxford: Clarendon Press, 1988).
8. Nino, *Ethics of Human Rights*, 139.
9. Nino, *Ethics of Human Rights*, 114.

10. Nino, *Ethics of Human Rights,* 139.

11. Nino, *Ethics of Human Rights,* 104.

12. I have argued this in "Wittgenstein and Idealism," reprinted in *Moral Luck* (Albany: State University of New York Press, 1993). On Wittgensteinian political philosophy, see "Left Wittgenstein," *Common Knowledge* (New York: Oxford University Press, 1992), I.

Chapter 4 Autonomy
and Consequences

Martin D. Farrell

Thomas Nagel has shown—in a way, I believe, that is compatible with Carlos Nino's thesis—the importance of some individual rights which go beyond those considered basic. And Bernard Williams has sustained—in a way, I am sure, that is incompatible with Nino's thesis—that the application of any political theory depends on some factual conditions.

I am not going to dispute their conclusions, because what I find in common to both papers is a gap: what is missing in them is the intellectual influence of their authors on the ethical theory of the man who prompted their remarks. Briefly, I will try to fill the gap.

Throughout his work Carlos Nino pervasively revealed himself to be—at least in appearance—an enemy of consequentialism. In *Ethics and Human Rights*, he addressed the ways in which the notion of causation undermined consequentialism. And in a later article he claimed that consequentialism is not a plausible moral theory.[1]

I do not believe, however, that Nino could be considered a deontologist, at least in the usual sense. According to Edwards's *Encyclopedia of Philosophy*, for example, a deontological theory of ethics is one that holds that at least some acts are morally obligatory regardless of their consequences for human weal or woe: let justice be done though the heavens fall.[2] More moderately, we may claim that in deontological systems certain features in the act itself have intrinsic value: there is something right about truth-telling and promise-keeping even when acting accordingly brings about a harm.[3] Nino was not a full-fledged deontologist, and did not rule out consequences with the same easiness as a moderate deontologist. He would indeed not hesitate to adhere to Rawls's idea that, in judging rightness, all ethical doctrines worth our attention take consequences into account and one that did not would simply be irrational and crazy.[4] Nino found it obvious that the assessment of some consequences of actions are relevant for their moral evaluation.[5]

If the deontologist/consequentialist distinction is an exhaustive one, Nino could be considered a consequentialist. But things are not of course so simple, because while the distinction is exhaustive in the sense that every norm is consequentialist or deontologist, it seems not to be so when we consider whole theories composed (as it is easy to see) of many norms. Let me also admit briefly that we can make another distinction. F. M. Kamm distinguishes between *consequentialism* and *nonconsequentialism* on the grounds that consequentialism is the view which determines the rightness or wrongness of acts on the basis of their consequences, while nonconsequentialism determines the rightness or wrongness of acts on grounds that include factors in addition to consequences. Nino would be a nonconsequentialist according to this classification, and would be also a nonconsequentialist according to Derek Parfit's classification, because, in that distinction, the central claim of consequentialism is that there is one ultimate moral aim—that outcomes be as good as possible—and Nino believed that moral purposes consist of something more than an interest in the outcome.[6]

There seems to be a good reason to include Nino among the defenders of consequentialism: it is his rejection of the distinction between the moral value of acts and omissions, usually made by deontologists. He claims that no distinctions should be made between active and passive behavior when acts and omissions cause the same result. The distinction would make use of a morally irrelevant factual difference and, therefore, there would be no substantial differences between the two behaviors.[7]

Nino, however, accepted that the duty not to kill is stronger than the duty to stop another person from killing, and he maintained that the distinction between doing and letting others do must not be confused with that between acts and omissions.[8] According to Nino it is not the distinction between acts and omissions, then, but the difference between not killing and failing to prevent others from killing that explains why he is reluctant to accept the utilitarian answer to Bernard Williams' well-known example of the botanical explorer who finds himself facing the dilemma of killing one Indian or refraining from such action, at the cost of a group of soldiers killing twenty Indians.[9] Williams claims that the difficulty in finding the right answer to the example lies in the distinction between my causing someone's death and having death be caused by somebody else as a consequence of what I do.[10]

To reject the distinction between acts and omissions does not entail the support of the utilitarian solution—killing one Indian, in this case—in complex ethical situations; in the former example that distinction is not relevant. Nevertheless, the utilitarian solution in the explorer's example does not raise objections even from those who rebuff the utilitarian tenets. Williams himself believes that the utilitarian answer to the alternative is probably right, even if he is not completely satisfied with the solution.[11]

Williams is concerned about the fact that utilitarianism can enjoin a person to forego his or her own project and decision, to acknowledge instead the decision which utilitarian calculation requires. Consequently, he argues that this relinquishment of our own choices is to alienate us (in a real sense) from our actions, and the source of our action, in our own convictions.[12] But, as Peter Railton noticed, there is another sort of alienation, not sufficiently discussed: individuals who cannot allow questions to arise about what they are doing from a broader perspective are in an important way cut off from their society and from the larger world.[13] Utilitarianism is frequently accused of not taking seriously the separation of persons, yet it would be equally plausible to say that their contenders do not take the bonds between persons seriously.

And it is also true that Williams's critique is limited to utilitarianism, that is, only to one possible form of consequentialism. If the failure to see that things other than subjective states have intrinsic value is a sort of alienation, we can choose a pluralistic approach—not any less consequentialist—in which several goods are viewed as intrinsically valuable, such as knowledge, autonomy, and respect.[14] But I am not adopting that stance in order to reconcile Nino's approach with consequentialism, for a simple reason: the main difficulty that Nino found in consequentialist ethics lay in the possible loss of the autonomy of the agent. This being so, it would be a trivial solution to adjust Nino's tenet to consequentialism by simply adopting a consequentialist theory for which autonomy is an intrinsically valuable good: indeed, any good can be adjusted to consequentialism simply by proposing that the good be maximized. I want to show that Nino's tenets can be adjusted to a consequentialist ethical theory which does not include autonomy among the goods to be maximized. Perhaps we can say it is a theory that does not include autonomy as the *only* good to be maximized. A pluralist theory, like that which proposes to maximize happiness, knowledge, and autonomy, not only has the advantage of including more intuitions about the constituents of the good, but also has the disadvantage of every pluralist theory, that is, that the values which the theory selects can be incomparable or incommensurable. Thus, I will try to adjust Nino's tenets to the requirements of a monist consequentialist theory. Obviously, utilitarianism is the better known monist consequentialist theory.

I do not sustain that Nino is a utilitarian, but I do believe that he would have accepted the utilitarian solution in Williams's example. (*A fortiori,* he would have adhered to a pluralist consequentialist theory, one in which autonomy is included as one of the goods to be maximized.) The interesting problem, in my opinion, consists of showing that concern for autonomy—the central concern in Nino's tenets—is not strong enough to override the power of a monist consequentialist theory (such as utilitarianism) which does not include autonomy as a good.

Nino found himself at odds with consequentialist ethics as a result of attaching supreme value to the autonomy of the agent. To understand fully this aspect of his belief, I will connect it with a topic introduced in contemporary philosophy—albeit with a different terminology—by Thomas Nagel in his book *The Possibility of Altruism,* and later developed in his Tanner Lectures and in *The View from Nowhere*: that of agent neutrality and agent relativity.[15]

An agent-neutral reason demands that we look for—impartially—the intrinsic good. General happiness will be the intrinsic good if we attach agent neutrality to the utilitarian theory. Yet we can adopt pluralistic consequentialism and, in this case, the agent-neutral reason will compel us—in an impartial way—to look for intrinsic goodness in, for example, happiness, knowledge, and autonomy.

There are two types of agent-relative reasons: reasons of autonomy and deontological reasons. Reasons of autonomy stem from desires, projects, commitments, and personal ties of the agent. The importance of such reasons derives from the fact that these desires, projects, and commitments contribute to the character of the agent.[16] These reasons limit the utilitarian calculus: when I am involved in a project that affects my life-plans, for example, I will leave aside the calculus of the intrinsic good. However, we cannot know beforehand if they limit *every* consequentialist calculus because that depends on the good—or goods—that the theory considers for maximization. Trivially, these reasons would not constrain a monist consequentialism, with autonomy as the only good to be maximized. But in this case the ethical theory doesn't need any agent-relative reason of autonomy: the agent-neutral reason is enough.

Deontological reasons stem from the claims of other persons not to be mal-treated in certain ways. According to Nagel, they are not agent-neutral reasons for everyone to want no one to be maltreated, but agent-relative reasons for each individual not to maltreat others. These reasons do not just limit the validity of utilitarian calculus: they simply suppress it. They are based on Williams's idea that each of us is specially responsible for our actions, rather than for what other people do.

The difference between these two kinds of reasons is quite clear: the reasons of autonomy are *permissions* while deontological reasons are *constraints* or *demands*. Suppose that I have adopted pacifism as a life-plan and that I am strongly opposed to harming any human being. The reasons of autonomy permit me to develop—within certain limits—this life-plan. But if I desire—as a pacifist—to minimize the death toll, then I must (or, at least, I can) kill one person in order to save ten. Deontological reasons, on the contrary, order me not to act in that case: I cannot kill, not even if by killing I minimize the death toll.

At first sight, it seems to be correct to identify agent-neutral reasons with consequentialism and agent-relative reasons with the different forms of deontologism. But it would be wrong to do so. Ethical egoism, for example, is a theory with both consequentialist and agent-relative reasons. It is consequentialist in the sense that an action is right or wrong according to its consequences for the agent: if the action promotes the happiness of the agent (in the case of an hedonist ethical egoism, for example), then the action is right. But the theory is interested in the consequences *for the agent*, not for human beings impartially considered. Agent x has a reason to do A if A enhances (even a little) x's intrinsic good, even when A (greatly) diminishes the intrinsic good of other people. Ethical egoism, therefore, is also based on agent-relative reasons.

In contrast, a theory is not deontologist because it accepts agent-relative reasons of autonomy, because, as we shall see, a theory of that kind does not suppress the calculus of consequences. We can accept consequentialism (although not of the utilitarian type) and accept, also, agent-relative reasons of autonomy (in the nontrivial sense of a consequentialism that does not have autonomy as the only good to be maximized). We can distinguish three types of reasons of autonomy: (a) neutral and consequentialist reasons, which intend to maximize autonomy for the greatest number; (b) relative and consequentialist reasons, which intend to maximize autonomy in each agent and (c) relative and deontological reasons, which intend to defend the right to autonomy. I have in mind here case (b).

Nino was concerned with the range of agent-neutral reasons and maintained that they presented some doubts and difficulties.[17] Quoting Nagel, he claimed that the value of autonomy elicited reasons directly related only to a specific life-plan, or—at least—related mainly to that plan. He believed, therefore, that an acceptable ethical theory must contain agent-relative reasons of autonomy.

This circumstance, I claim, does not render it necessary that we give up consequentialist ethics (or, more particularly, abandon a nonegoistic consequentialist ethics): agent-relative reasons of autonomy do not completely override the utilitarian calculus. I will analyze the utilitarian example, and establish whether the calculus of consequences still counts (against agent-relative reasons of autonomy) in an ethics in which the only agent-neutral reason is the impartial maximization of happiness. Obviously, if it counts in that theory, it counts in a pluralist ethics, in which autonomy is one of the goods to be maximized.

Which is the relation, then, between agent-neutral and agent-relative reasons? I believe that we can accept without much discussion that every ethics includes the *pro tanto* reason to promote the good analyzed by Shelly Kagan.[18] This being so, from a chronological point of view agent-neutral reasons surface earlier. But this is not the interesting relation, because we attempt to find a hierarchical relation between both types of reasons, not a chronological one.

When an agent-neutral reason is opposed to an agent-relative one, it seems obvious that the agent-relative reason must prevail, precisely because the goal of the agent-relative reason is to restrict the range of the agent-neutral reason.[19] If it were not this way, it would be useless to postulate the existence of agent-neutral reasons at all, when the theory has already accepted their existence. Let us look at the following example: if I help a relative (a son, for example) by giving him a preference, this attitude probably diminishes general happiness. There is an agent-neutral reason that tells me that it is wrong to act in this way. But I can reply to this objection invoking the existence of an agent-relative reason (flowing—perhaps—from my special obligations) that allows me to act in that way: it allows me to help my family even when this attitude diminishes general utility. (Obviously, this is the only interesting case to consider, because when in helping my family I also maximize general happiness, the case is covered by the agent-neutral reason.) If I therefore bring into operation an agent-relative reason under special circumstances, I am asserting that this reason has more weight than the agent-neutral one. If it were not so, I would not have invoked it.

It seems to follow that agent-relative reasons are superior in hierarchy to agent-neutral reasons. Utilitarianism, then, would be undoubtedly threatened when we allow agent-relative reasons of autonomy. The matter, however, is not so simple.

It is true that agent-relative reasons of autonomy seem to constrain the range of agent-neutral reasons and are thus of a higher hierarchy. But the important question is whether an agent-relative reason of autonomy *always* overrides an agent-neutral one. Suppose that I cause the death of ten people as a consequence of giving preferential treatment to a relative for trivial reasons (helping her organize her birthday party, for example); assume these people were in need of my help (they were drowning when I was supervising the baking of the cake). Can I plausibly invoke the agent-relative reason of autonomy, which allows me to help my family, to override the agent-neutral reason which commands me to maximize general happiness? I believe that the answer is that I cannot invoke successfully here the agent-relative reason of autonomy. Agent-relative reasons of autonomy are of a higher hierarchy than agent-neutral reasons but only *within certain limits,* and these limits are fixed by the calculus of consequences. Causing a slight inconvenience to the same ten people involved in the former example does not constitute a reason to give up supervising the baking of the cake. The death of those people is obviously reason enough. Would a great disturbance to the same people be enough? There is no exact answer to this issue, because this is a murky case impossible to sort out a priori on the basis of some general rule. We can say, as Kamm does, that a morally acceptable subjective view sometimes allows *some* more weight to be given to one's own concerns relative to those of others, but not just *any* weight.[20]

Note that the former argument recognizes two points: (a) that the agent-neutral reason that we are considering is the utilitarian reason to maximize general happiness, and (b) that there are occasions in which agent-relative reasons of autonomy override an agent-neutral reason.

About point (a), for those who stress the value of autonomy it is easier to accept the higher ranking of the agent-neutral reasons when autonomy itself is one of the goods to be maximized, as is the case in certain versions of pluralist consequentialism.

About point (b) I accept only hypothetically that sometimes the agent-relative reasons of autonomy override the utilitarian agent neutral reason; this hypothesis is adequate only to those who support the reasons of autonomy.[21] My goal is to show that, even for those who accept agent-relative reasons of autonomy, the utilitarian calculus of consequences is important and sometimes establishes the higher rank of the agent-neutral reason. This is not to deny that a theory that accepts agent-relative reasons of autonomy is not an orthodox utilitarian theory.

Up to this point, I have been dealing with the relation between agent-neutral reasons and agent-relative reasons of autonomy. I have not yet discussed another major issue, the relation between neutral reasons and deontological reasons. I cannot simply imagine an argument to justify the existence of deontological reasons. Moreover, these types of reasons do not in my view have any role in Nino's theory. First and foremost, deontological reasons do not help to maximize the autonomy of the agent, which would be an outcome of consequentialism that troubled Nino. Deontological reasons are not *permissions* to act but *constraints* on the behavior of the agent. They command that one not kill, for example, even when killing would diminish the death toll; deontological reasons seem to prevent the fulfillment of the theory's own ends.

No constraint would help to develop the life-plan of an agent (except, of course, self-imposed constraints). Nino's view can accept, therefore, agent-relative reasons of autonomy without feeling compelled to subscribe to deontological reasons. Scheffler has shown the truth of what he labels the "asymmetry thesis": although it is possible to identify an underlying principled rationale for an agent-centered prerogative (i.e., agent-relative reasons of autonomy), it is not possible to identify any comparable rationale for agent-centered restrictions.[22]

Thus, Nino's ethical principles include agent-relative reasons of autonomy, but do not include deontological reasons. To accept agent-relative reasons of autonomy, perhaps Nino might have taken into account that utilitarianism is intuitively plausible at a general level, but has intuitive difficulties when it is applied in particular cases. And to reject deontological reasons, perhaps he might have taken into account that deontologism is intuitively plausible in specific cases but has intuitive difficulties when generalized. As Edith Wharton says in *The Age of Innocence,* the worst of doing one's duty is that it apparently makes one unfit for doing anything else.

We have, then an ethical theory that, without rejecting agent-neutral reasons as the basis of the consequentialist calculus, adds to them the agent-relative reasons of autonomy. In certain cases these reasons of autonomy are limits to the consequentialist calculus (at least in the theories for which autonomy is not the only good to be maximized), but they do not restrict the calculus in *all* cases. In certain circumstances the agent-relative reasons of autonomy can not override the utilitarian agent-neutral reason.

A theory of this kind is a long way away from extreme or moderate deontologism. It is not, however, an orthodox utilitarian theory, nor even an orthodox consequentialist theory, because Nino believed that—at least in certain cases— an action should be valued for more than its consequences. It cannot be considered an orthodox consequentialist theory, then, even in the case in which autonomy is the only good to be maximized.

It would be a mistake to try to label the theory with precision. I want to point out only that the main concern of the theory lies in its interest for the autonomy of the agent, and therefore needs to incorporate agent-relative reasons of autonomy to constrain the utilitarian calculus. Sometimes autonomy limits the utilitarian calculus but—in the last resort—it is the calculus of consequences that constrains the exercise of autonomy. To be concerned with autonomy is not to be unconcerned with consequences. Let this be the lesson of the ethical theory of Carlos Nino.

NOTES

1. Carlos S. Nino, *Etica y derechos humanos* (Buenos Aires: Astrea, 1989), 336–337, and "Consecuencialismo: Debate ético y jurídico," *Telos,* 1, no. 1, 96.
2. Robert G. Olson, "Deontological Ethics," in Paul Edwards (ed.), *The Encyclopedia of Philosophy* (New York: Macmillan, 1972), 2:343.
3. Louis P. Pojman, *Ethical Theory* (Belmont, Calif.: Wadsworth, 1989), 157 and 225.
4. John Rawls, *A Theory of Justice* (Cambridge, Mass.: Harvard University Press, 1971), 30.
5. Nino, "Consecuencialismo," 96.
6. F. M. Kamm, *Morality, Mortality* (Oxford: Oxford University Press, 1993), 76. Derek Parfit, *Reasons and Persons* (Oxford: Clarendon Press, 1984), 24. In contrast, R. M. Hare believes that the distinction between deontological and teleological theories is a false one. He sustains that it is not possible to distinguish between a moral judgment made on the grounds of the effects of an action and one made on the ground of the character of the action itself; it is possible to distinguish only between different sorts of intended effects. R. M. Hare, *Freedom and Reason* (Oxford: Oxford University Press, 1978, orig. pub. 1963), 124.
7. Carlos S. Nino, "¿Dá lo mismo omitir que actuar?" *La Ley,* 1979 C, sec. doctrina, 810 and 814.
8. Nino, "Consecuencialismo," 86–87.
9. Bernard Williams, "A Critique of Utilitarianism," in J. J. C. Smart and Bernard Williams, *Utilitarianism: For and Against* (Cambridge: Cambridge University Press, 1973), 98.
10. Williams, "A Critique of Utilitarianism," 117.
11. Williams, "A Critique of Utilitarianism," 117.
12. Williams, "A Critique of Utilitarianism," 116.
13. Peter Railton, "Alienation, Consequentialism, and the Demands of Morality," *Philosophy and Public Affairs,* 13, no. 2 (1984), 151.
14. Railton, "Alienation," 148–149.

15. Thomas Nagel, *The Possibility of Altruism* (Princeton: Princeton University Press, 1970); "The Limits of Objectivity," in Sterling McMurrin (ed.), *The Tanner Lectures on Human Values,* vol. 1 (Cambridge: Cambridge University Press, 1980), and *The View from Nowhere* (Oxford: Oxford University Press, 1986).

16. Bernard Williams, *Moral Luck* (Cambridge: Cambridge University Press, 1981), 5–14.

17. Nino, "Consecuencialismo," 75.

18. Shelly Kagan, *The Limits of Morality* (Oxford, Clarendon Press, 1989), 16–17.

19. I say "to restrict" because I am considering here only the agent-relative reasons of autonomy.

20. Kamm, *Morality, Mortality,* 153.

21. Shelly Kagan, for example, would disagree with my conclusions on grounds that I will not address here. See *The Limits of Morality.*

22. Samuel Scheffler, *The Rejection of Consequentialism* (Oxford, Clarendon Press, 1982), ch. 4.

Chapter 5 On Philosophy
and Human Rights

Elaine Scarry

In his book on elegy, Peter Sacks looks at elegiac poems from the Greeks through Spenser, Milton, Shelley, Hardy, and Yeats. Sacks observes how often and closely "the elegist will try to imitate the admired qualities" of the person who has died: at the center of these poems is the work of "elegiac emulation."[1] Elegiac emulation has clearly shaped the essays in this book, for they are framed by the set of subjects to which Carlos Nino devoted himself—human rights, deliberative democracy, the problem of punishment. The work of elegiac emulation is also, more specifically, visible in the chapters by Thomas Nagel and Bernard Williams. Unlike the Greek elegist, they have not written in alternating dactylic hexameters and pentameters. But the list of subject matters originally included in the early elegy sounds not wholly out of place with the contents of their essays. Elegiac verses, Sacks tells us, "could contain a fairly broad range of topics, including exhortatory martial epigrams, political philosophy, commemorative lines, or [here one thinks particularly of Nagel] amatory complaints."[2]

Philosophy's obligation to address actual violations of human rights is the question posed by the life and writings of Carlos Nino; and it is also the question that Thomas Nagel and Bernard Williams have framed as central. Both philosophers directly speak to Carlos Nino as though he were present. Nagel sets in place a framing situation in which we must imagine, as the premise of his paper, a group of people dedicated to remedying violations of rights in their own countries, impatient with the work of contemporary philosophy; he asks us to see his chapter as philosophy's account of itself in return. In other words, the most basic aspiration of Carlos Nino—the bringing together of philosophy and activism—structures the essay. This framework, in turn, carries over into Bernard Williams's chapter where he explicitly allies himself with those imagined conferees, recommending that philosophy give up its attention to imposter rights and attend instead to the foundational ones.

Within this framing structure of elegiac emulation, however, the two papers go on to contest the kinship of philosopher and activist, the partnership of philosophy and basic rights. Contestation or debate is central to both realms and was, as Williams reminds us, especially revered by Carlos Nino. It is this debate that I will briefly address.

Nagel's essay contains a memorable sentence that states, with stunning concision, his skepticism about the relation of activism and philosophy: "unfortunately the flagrant violation of the most basic human rights is devoid of philosophical interest."[3] Williams disagrees: in fact he is startled by, and attempts to clarify, Nagel's claim. Yet Williams himself reinforces the scepticism in two ways. The first is the one he explicitly calls attention to, his wish to decouple the discussion of rights from justifications of liberal philosophy. The second is the fact that he sees these rights as self-evident. What distinguishes foundational rights from pseudo rights is that the first are "self-evident" and the second are "predictably contested."[4] These features are not incidental to the rights in question: they are central. We recognize a foundational right by the fact that it is self-evident; we recognize an impostor right by the fact that it is predictably contested. A right is a clear right; and conversely an unclear right is no right at all.

In making this claim, Williams, like Nagel, might seem to be introducing some skepticism about philosophy's relation to human rights since if basic rights are self-evident, they perhaps require no assistance from philosophic discussion and debate. (I would note here the small paradox that Nagel explicitly acknowledges that the foundational rights are not self-evident, yet holds their violation to be devoid of philosophic interest; Williams believes they are self-evident, yet is more sympathetic to their inclusion within philosophy.) At any rate, the basic outcome is to introduce scepticism and to require us to try to state why, on the contrary, violations of human rights press us to philosophy.

What might it mean to claim that human rights are devoid of philosophic interest or to argue that important human rights are self-evident? It might mean this. Human rights are enshrined in many practices. We rely on them. No one has to provide justifications. Williams, for example, shows us what is wrong with a Kantian justification. We rely on moral notions that are too strong: the Kantian view of rights is anchored in moral agency, but this, whether normative or empirical, has variations in it, thereby implying variability in our eligibility to be protected by rights. In the end, in order to know who we are as bearers of rights, we have to look not to these moral notions but to practices such as citizenship and related institutions.

But this explanation is precarious, for it would leave us—at the moment of a lapse in rights—in the position of having to point for protection to the fact that such rights are enshrined elsewhere; and this reliance on the practice of others could be instantly dismissed by our oppressors as ignoring the lessons of "cultural relativism." Further, it would be odd to argue that rights can be understood in terms of practice since it is so often a failed practice that brings them to our attention. Nagel's provocative sentence is, after all, phrased in terms of failed practice: he does not merely say "foundational rights are devoid of philosophical interest"; he says, "the flagrant violation of the most basic human rights is devoid of philosophical interest."

Nagel calls into question, but in the end confirms, the relation between lapsed practice and the need for philosophic address. "One could be pardoned," he observes, "for thinking that the philosophic interest of an issue of human rights is inversely proportional to its real-life importance"; and no doubt most of us would agree with him that, for example, the injuries in political imprisonment are much greater than the injuries on either side of the hate speech or pornography heartaches. But his essay itself confirms that "philosophic interest" is proportional to real-life importance since the rights he puts in front of us are among the ones that are, in our own culture, in immediate danger of being damaged or lost. The vividness and energy of the account seem to come from his sense of their violation in the real world. He refers to the "repressive impulse," speaks of finding himself "outraged" and of having a "sense of illegitimacy" out of proportion to harm. What makes these rights worthy of philosophical interest seems to be first, their continuity with basic rights; and second, the fact that they are, at the very moment, insufficiently enshrined in practice. Is it, then, their greater subtleness, their greater complexity and need for sorting out, that give them more philosophical interest than the foundational rights; or is that philosophical interest ignited by the very lapse in practice that in other countries, and in the United States in other decades, has made the foundational rights appear so full of philosophical interest? Isn't it, in other words, the very lapse in practice that announces the inherent subtleness and need for sorting out?

Even, then, if it is the case that "rights ordinarily are enshrined in practice, we rely on them, no one has to justify them," it is an odd twist on this to say "the justification for human rights is that we rely on them." It is true that rights are fundamentally proleptic: they eliminate injuries that have not yet happened. But they come into being because of harms that have already occurred or are perceived to be about to occur. Theory and practice here have a relation analogous to the one Hanna Pitkin observes in her account of consent. The great treatises on consent, she writes, have always been "essays in advocacy" since they have come into being to address concrete political crises when either the freedoms or the obligations embedded in consent have become obscure.[5] So, too, rights may be seen as distilled, single-sentence formulations of philosophical essays in advocacy occasioned by a now forgotten moment in their history when they were insufficiently enshrined in everyday practice.

A second way of understanding the claim that rights are devoid of philosophical interest, or the counterpart claim that rights are self-evident and hence in need of no philosophical justification, is to say that even in the midst of lapsed practice, no one ever tries to justify that lapse. No one ever tries to say that the infliction of torture is just. Bernard Williams's own account of slavery in ancient Greece might provide another illustration: "From the beginning," he writes, "the arbitrariness of slavery was recognized."[6]

But there are six responses to this argument that need to be held steadily in view. First, lapses in rights *are* sometimes held to be just. It would simply be wrong on the facts to say that no one has ever tried to describe slavery as a "positive good" or tried, however preposterously, to claim moral rightness for a regime that tortures. Because most of the fundamental rights are presently enshrined in practice, it can be hard to re-enact in one's imagination the condition of being non-self-evident. An example, however, is provided by the present lapse in the Second Amendment. The disappearance of the right to bear arms is widely tolerated because the principle of justice it condenses has become lost to view. The amendment is distributional and democratic: it seeks to guarantee a distribution of authorization over military power to a wide population in order to prevent a centralization of military authority and a consequent deformation of the polis. The setting aside of this right is repeatedly "justified" on the circular grounds that the right is "mysterious" or "muddled" or "baffling": in other words, the loss of the right is justified on the grounds that the justification of the right has become lost to view. Its absence is even seen as increasing the "justness" of our world: the disappearance of the right to bear arms is wrongly associated in many people's minds with a disappearance of guns and what could be more just than a disappearance of guns?[7]

A second response to the claim that no one ever tries to justify lapses in rights is to notice that even where no one sees the lapse as "just," there often remain surrounding questions in need of philosophical clarification. Even when, for example, slavery in the ancient world was perceived as a clear wrong, it was simultaneously seen as "necessary." The antagonistic relation between "necessity" and "justice" has required over the centuries a constant sorting out, especially since the first has so often been used to bypass the second, not only in the ancient world but in many others.

A third response to the claim is a version of the second. Our sense that no one ever tries to justify a lapse in rights may come from a peculiar feature of rights: the debates that surround the attempts to give rights an institutional or doctrinal location often lack the symmetrical two-sidedness that we ordinarily find in intellectual, moral, or political disagreement. For example, the American Bill of Rights, the first ten amendments to the United States Constitution, exist only because of heated debates during the ratification of the constitution and a consequent recognition on the part of the framers that without the amendments the Constitution might not pass. Those debates confirm the key contribution of philosophical inquiry and argument; at the same time, however, the oppositional side of the debate did not precisely take the form of anyone standing up to press that a lapse in free speech or jury trial would be just. The side antagonistic to the inclusion of rights argued that a specification of rights was actually a contraction of the Constitution's protection since it seemed to leave unprotected any rights that were not specified; they also argued that such specifications, should they turn out to be needed, could be included at a later point, rather than prior to ratification. But the exponents of the Bill of Rights did not confine their own arguments to the overtly symmetrical issues of specificity and time; the best arguments on behalf of the immediate, specific, and explicit inclusion of rights in the Constitution turned out to be arguments about the justness of the rights, even though the opponents did not precisely appear to be contesting their justness. Again in the twentieth century, the inclusion of rights in the newly formed constitutions of countries in Africa or South America has often entailed nonsymmetrical debates in which one side urges the justness of human rights against opponents who urge the noninclusion of the rights not on the manifestly preposterous ground that the rights are inherently unjust or on the ground that their absence will somehow be just but on the ground that their inclusion will make the new country culturally indebted to the west or to the north.[8]

A fourth response is to return to the label "self-evident" and look more closely at its limits. As noticed early, only during periods when rights are fully enshrined do they seem self-evident; the moment their practice is interrupted, their self-evident quality also seems to be interrupted. But at the moment when the right is most clear, how clear is it really? How close does "the self-evident" ever come to "the fully intelligible" or to "the fully available to articulation"? T. M. Scanlon writes, "It sometimes seems that to invoke a right, particularly one in our familiar pantheon of civil and political liberties, is to appeal to a discrete moral principle whose validity can be apprehended just by thinking about it, without recourse to complicated reasoning. . . . But this impression fades when we discover that it is extremely difficult even to give a coherent statement of any of our familiar rights."[9] Even, then, during their moments of greatest clarity, rights require the labor of philosophic description; how much more do they require it during periods of obscurity.

A fifth response is to move from solitary rights to rights as a group. Even if each right, considered in isolation, achieved full lucidity, there would still be the need for a coherent account of the entire array. Should rights be understood as individual or distributive? Are they universal or culturally relative? If a right is universally available across the surface of the earth, does it (as has been repeatedly asserted in recent years) bring about a uniformity in that world population, or does it instead (by placing no requirements on the attributes it is attached to) encourage the greatest possible diversity? Why is it that one right sometimes magnifies, and at other times competes with, a second right: is there some philosophically coherent way of sorting out these patterns of reciprocal magnification and diminution?

A sixth response is to question whether our starting point has been correct: is it the case that contemporary philosophy abstains from deliberating about fundamental rights? Bernard Williams and Thomas Nagel center their accounts of ethics in matters of individual agency; adjacent to these philosophical discussions are those of others who approach such matters through the avenue of public morality ("what are the principles by which society should be organized?") such as John Rawls, T. M. Scanlon, Amartya Sen, Stuart Hampshire, legal and constitutional philosophers such as Owen Fiss, Ronald Dworkin, and Akhil Amar, and such earlier writers as H. L. A. Hart. These two adjacent bodies of writing—one that takes individual agency as its starting point and another that begins with questions about public arrangements—together constitute what might have been thought of by Carlos Nino as a fairly robust commitment on the part of philosophy to the kinds of injuries he worried about. His insistence on having Bernard Williams, Thomas Nagel, Owen Fiss, Ronald Dworkin, and T. M. Scanlon present during the trials and revision of the Argentinian constitution seems a direct expression of that conviction.

Finally, it might make most sense to understand the central assertions of Nagel's and Williams's essays as proleptic. It ought to be the case (let it one day be the case) that rights are self-evident, so self-evident as to be in need of no philosophical address, so self-evident as to be even without philosophical interest. Human rights would come to have the quality of "claritas" that was long ago attributed to beauty. Williams's account of the self-evident not as a word describing our cognitive relation to rights but as a feature emanating from the rights themselves resembles the quality of "claritas" that once was perceived to reside in, to emanate from, that which was beautiful. Beauty did not wait for the beholder to discover it; it actively sought the observer out; it was a "call" or "greeting" emanating from the thing. Like claritas, the "evident" is—as its etymological roots remind us[10]—that which has the power of "making itself seen," that which has clearness, that which is self-ratifying; and like claritas with its call, its greeting, the root "vide" in "evident" is connected to the word "visit": the self-evident seeks us out, it comes to see us, suggesting a sense of rights as things whose rightness or justness would arrive in our perceptual field without our ever having to seek them out. In the meantime, and for some time to come, they will no doubt require us to seek them out.

NOTES

My thanks to Andreas Eshete for ongoing conversations about rights in theory and practice.

1. Peter M. Sacks, *The English Elegy: Studies in the Genre from Spenser to Yeats* (Baltimore: Johns Hopkins University Press, 1985), 270.

2. Sacks, *The English Elegy*, 2.

3. Since Thomas Nagel's writings are frequently read by people who work to address lapses in human rights, it seems tempting to ignore this sentence; but the sentence is written in a way that prohibits its being easily ignored.

4. In fact, Bernard Williams has three categories: "the self-evident," "the predictably contested," and "the manifestly confused."

5. Hanna Pitkin, "Obligation and Consent—I," 59 *American Political Science Review* no. 4 (1965), 990.

6. Bernard Williams, *Shame and Necessity* (Berkeley: University of California Press, 1993), 109.

7. The right to bear arms has lapsed during a historical period (second half of the twentieth century) when the number of the country's military armaments has skyrocketed. For

an elaboration, see E. Scarry, "War and the Social Contract: Distribution, Nuclear Policy, and the Right to Bear Arms," *University of Pennsylvania Law Review*, Spring 1991, 1257–1316.

8. The sense that the adoption of an invention makes one indebted to its inventor (or earliest user) is an odd one given the fact that our widespread use of other brilliant inventions—wheels and alphabets and numerical systems with zero as place holder—has not seemed to make any of us oppressively indebted to their original inventors.

9. T. M. Scanlon, "Human Rights as a Neutral Concern," in *Human Rights and U.S. Foreign Policy: Principles and Applications,* ed. Peter G. Brown and Douglas MacLean (Lexington, Mass.: D.C. Heath, 1979), 84.

10. On the etymology of "evident," see C. T. Onions, ed., *The Oxford Dictionary of English Etymology;* Robert K. Barnhart, ed., *The Barnhart Dictionary of Etymology;* Eric Partridge, ed., *Origins: A Short Etymological Dictionary of Modern English;* and Ernest Klein, *A Comprehensive Etymological Dictionary of the English Language.*

Part Three **Nation-Building,
Constitutionalism, and Democracy**

Chapter 6 The Moral Reading
and the Majoritarian Premise

Ronald Dworkin

CONSTITUTIONAL CONFUSION

There is a particular way of reading and enforcing a political constitution that I call the moral reading. Most contemporary constitutions declare individual rights against the government in very broad and abstract language, like the First Amendment of the United States Constitution, which provides that Congress shall make no law abridging "the freedom of speech." The moral reading proposes that we all—judges, lawyers, citizens—interpret and apply these abstract clauses on the understanding that they invoke moral principles about political decency and justice. The First Amendment, for example, recognizes a moral principle—that it is wrong for government to censor or control what individual citizens say or publish—and incorporates it into American law. So when some novel or controversial constitutional issue arises—about whether, for instance, the First Amendment permits laws against pornography—people who form an opinion must decide how an abstract moral principle is best understood. They must decide whether the true ground of the moral principle that condemns censorship, in the form in which this principle has been incorporated into American law, extends to the case of pornography.

The moral reading therefore brings political morality into the heart of constitutional law.[1] But political morality is inherently uncertain and controversial, so any system of government that makes such principles part of its law must decide whose interpretation and understanding will be authoritative. In the American system judges—ultimately the justices of the Supreme Court—now have that authority, and the moral reading of the Constitution is therefore said by its critics to give judges absolute power to impose their own moral convictions on the public. I shall shortly try to explain why that crude charge is mistaken. I should make plain first, however, that there is nothing revolutionary about the moral reading in practice. So far as American lawyers and judges follow any coherent strategy of interpreting the Constitution, they already use the moral reading.

That explains why both scholars and journalists find it reasonably easy to classify judges as "liberal" or "conservative": the best explanation of the differing patterns of their decisions lies in their different understandings of central moral values embedded in the Constitution's text. Judges whose political convictions are conservative will naturally interpret abstract constitutional principles in a conservative way, as they did in the early years of this century, when they wrongly supposed that certain rights over property and contract are fundamental to freedom. Judges whose convictions are more liberal will naturally interpret those principles in a liberal way, as they did in the halcyon days of the Warren Court. The moral reading is not, in itself, either a liberal or a conservative charter or strategy. It is true that in recent decades liberal judges have ruled more statutes or executive orders unconstitutional than conservative judges have. But that is because conservative political principles for the most part either favored or did not strongly condemn the measures that could reasonably be challenged on constitutional grounds in those decades. There have been exceptions to that generalization. Conservatives strongly disapprove, on moral grounds, affirmative action programs which give certain advantages to minority applicants for universities or jobs, and conservative justices have not hesitated to follow their understanding of what the moral reading required in such cases.[2] That reading helps us to identify and explain not only these large-scale patterns, moreover, but also more fine-grained differences in constitutional interpretation that cut across the conventional liberal-conservative divide. Conservative judges who particularly value freedom of speech, or think it particularly important to democracy, are more likely than other conservatives to extend the First Amendment's protection to acts of political protest, even for causes that they despise, as the Supreme Court's decision protecting flag-burners shows.[3]

So, to repeat, the moral reading is not revolutionary in practice. Lawyers and judges, in their day-to-day work, instinctively treat the Constitution as expressing abstract moral requirements that can be applied to concrete cases only through fresh moral judgments. As I shall argue later in this essay, they have no real option but to do so. But it would indeed be revolutionary for a judge openly to recognize the moral reading, or to admit that it is his or her strategy of constitutional interpretation, and even scholars and judges who come close to recognizing it shrink back, and try to find other, usually metaphorical, descriptions of their own practice. There is therefore a striking mismatch between the role the moral reading actually plays in American constitutional life and its reputation. It has inspired all the greatest constitutional decisions of the Supreme Court, and also some of the worst. But it is almost never acknowledged as influential even by constitutional experts, and it is almost never openly endorsed even by judges whose arguments are incomprehensible on any other understanding of their responsibilities. On the contrary, the moral reading is often dismissed as an "extreme" view that no really sensible constitutional scholar would entertain. It is patent that judges' own views about political morality influence their constitutional decisions, and though they might easily explain that influence by insisting that the Constitution demands a moral reading, they never do. Instead, against all evidence, they deny the influence and try to explain their decisions in other—embarrassingly unsatisfactory—ways. They say that they are just giving effect to obscure historical "intentions," for example, or just expressing an overall but unexplained constitutional "structure" that is supposedly explicable in nonmoral terms.

This mismatch between role and reputation is easily explained. The moral reading is so thoroughly embedded in constitutional practice, and is so much more attractive, on both legal and political grounds, than the only coherent alternatives that it cannot readily be abandoned, particularly when important constitutional issues are in play. But the moral reading nevertheless seems intellectually and politically discreditable. It seems to erode the crucial distinction between law and morality by making law only a matter of which moral principles happen to appeal to the judges of a particular era. It seems grotesquely to constrict the moral sovereignty of the people themselves—to take out of their hands, and remit to a professional elite, exactly the great and defining issues of political morality that the people have the right and the responsibility to decide for themselves.

That is the source of the paradoxical contrast between mainstream constitutional practice in the United States, which relies heavily on the moral reading of the Constitution, and mainstream constitutional theory, which wholly rejects that reading. The confusion has had serious political costs. Conservative politicians try to convince the public that the great constitutional cases turn not on deep issues of political principle, which they do, but on the simpler question of whether judges should change the Constitution by fiat or leave it alone.[4] For a time this view of the constitutional argument was apparently accepted even by some liberals. They called the Constitution a "living" document and said that it must be "brought up to date" to match new circumstances and sensibilities. They said they took an "active" approach to the Constitution, which seemed to suggest reform, and they accepted John Ely's characterization of their position as a "noninterpretive" one, which seemed to suggest inventing a new document rather than interpreting the old one.[5] In fact, as we shall see, this account of the argument was never accurate. The theoretical debate was never about whether judges should interpret the Constitution or change it—almost no one really thought the latter—but rather about how it should be interpreted. But conservative politicians exploited the simpler description, and they were not effectively answered.

The confusion engulfs the politicians as well, however. They promise to appoint and confirm judges who will respect the proper limits of their authority and leave the Constitution alone, but since this misrepresents the choices judges actually face, the politicians are often disappointed. When Dwight Eisenhower, who denounced what he called judicial activism, retired from office in 1961, he told a reporter that he had made only two big mistakes as President—and that they were both on the Supreme Court. He meant Chief Justice Earl Warren, who had been a Republican politician when Eisenhower appointed him to head the Supreme Court, but who then presided over one of the most "activist" periods in the Court's history, and Justice William Brennan, another politician who had been a state court judge when Eisenhower appointed him, and who became one of the most liberal and explicit practitioners of the moral reading of the Constitution in modern times.

Presidents Ronald Reagan and George Bush were both profound in their outrage at the Supreme Court's "usurpation" of the people's privileges. They said they were determined to appoint judges who would respect rather than defy the people's will. In particular, they (and the platform on which they ran for the presidency) denounced the Court's 1973 *Roe v. Wade* decision protecting abortion rights, and promised that their appointees would reverse it. But when the opportunity to do so came, three of the justices Reagan and Bush had appointed between them voted, surprisingly, not only to retain that decision in force, but to provide a new legal basis for it that more evidently adopted and relied on a moral reading of the Constitution. The expectations of politicians who appoint judges are often defeated in that way, because the politicians fail to appreciate how thoroughly the moral reading, which they say they deplore, is actually embedded in constitutional practice. Its role remains hidden when a judge's own convictions support the legislation whose constitutionality is in doubt—when a justice thinks it morally permissible for the majority to criminalize abortion, for example. But the ubiquity of the moral reading becomes evident when some judge's convictions of principle—identified, tested, and perhaps altered by experience and argument—bend in an opposite direction, because then enforcing the Constitution must mean, for that judge, telling the majority that it cannot have what it wants.

Senate hearings considering Supreme Court nominations tend toward the same confusion. These events are now thoroughly researched and widely reported by the media, and they are often televised. They offer a superb opportunity for the public to participate in the constitutional process. But the mismatch between actual practice and conventional theory cheats the occasion of much of its potential value. The hearings provoked by President Bush's nomination of Judge Clarence Thomas to the Supreme Court are a clear example. Nominees and legislators all pretend that hard constitutional cases can be decided in a morally neutral way, by just keeping faith with the "text" of the document, so that it would be inappropriate to ask the nominee any questions about his or her own political morality. It is ironic that Justice Thomas, in the years before his nomination, gave more explicit support to the moral reading than almost any other well-known constitutional lawyer has; he insisted that conservatives should embrace that interpretive strategy and harness it to a conservative morality. Any endorsement of the moral reading—any sign of weakness for the view that constitutional clauses are moral principles that must be applied through the exercise of moral judgment—would be suicidal for the nominee and embarrassing for his questioners. In recent years, only the hearings that culminated in the defeat of Robert Bork seriously explored issues of constitutional principle, and they did so only because Judge Bork's opinions about constitutional law were so obviously the product of a radical political morality that his convictions could not be ignored. In the confirmation proceedings of now Justices Anthony Kennedy, David Souter, Thomas, Ruth Bader Ginsburg, and Stephen Breyer, however, the old fiction was once again given shameful pride of place.

The most serious result of this confusion, however, lies in the American public's misunderstanding of the true character and importance of its constitutional system. As I have argued elsewhere, the American ideal of government not only under law but under principle as well is the most important contribution our history has given to political theory. Other nations and cultures realize this, and the American ideal has increasingly and self-consciously been adopted and imitated elsewhere. But we cannot acknowledge our own contribution, or take the pride in it, or care of it, that we should.

That judgment will appear extravagant, even perverse, to many lawyers and political scientists. They regard enthusiasm for the moral reading, within a political structure that gives final interpretive authority to judges, as elitist, antipopulist, antirepublican, and antidemocratic. That view rests, as we shall see, on a popular but unexamined assumption about the connection between democracy and majority will, an assumption that American history has in fact consistently rejected. When we understand democracy better, we see that the moral reading of a political constitution is not antidemocratic but, on the contrary, is practically indispensable to democracy. I do not mean that there is no democracy unless judges have the power to set aside what a majority thinks is right and just. Many institutional arrangements are compatible with the moral reading, including some that do not give judges the power they have in the American structure. But none of these varied arrangements is in principle more democratic than others. Democracy does not insist on judges having the last word, but it does not insist that they must not have it. I am already too far ahead of my argument, however. I must say more about what the moral reading is before I can return to the question of why it has been so seriously misunderstood.

THE MORAL READING

The clauses of the American Constitution that protect individuals and minorities from government are found mainly in the so-called Bill of Rights—the first several amendments to the document—and the further amendments added after the Civil War. (I shall sometimes use the phrase "Bill of Rights," inaccurately, to refer to all the provisions of the Constitution that establish individual rights, including the Fourteenth Amendment's protection of citizens' privileges and immunities and its guarantee of due process and equal protection of the laws.) Many of these clauses are drafted in exceedingly abstract moral language. The First Amendment refers to the "right" of free speech, for example, the Fifth Amendment to the process that is "due" to citizens, and the Fourteenth to protection that is "equal." According to the moral reading, these clauses must be understood in the way their language most naturally suggests: they refer to abstract moral principles and incorporate these by reference, as limits on government's power.

There is of course room for disagreement about the right way to restate these abstract moral principles, so as to make their force clearer for us, and to help us to apply them to more concrete political controversies. I favor a particular way of stating the constitutional principles at the most general possible level. I believe that the principles set out in the Bill of Rights, taken together, commit the United States to the following political and legal ideals: government must treat all those subject to its dominion as having equal moral and political status; it must attempt, in good faith, to treat them all with equal concern; and it must respect whatever individual freedoms are indispensable to those ends, including but not limited to the freedoms more specifically designated in the document, such as the freedoms of speech and religion. Other lawyers and scholars who also endorse the moral reading might well formulate the constitutional principles, even at a very general level, differently and less expansively than I just have, however, and though this essay is meant to explain and defend the moral reading, not my own interpretations under it, I should say something about how the choice among competing formulations should be made.

Of course the moral reading is not appropriate to everything a constitution contains. The American Constitution includes a great many clauses that are neither particularly abstract nor drafted in the language of moral principle. Article 11 specifies, for example, that the President must be at least thirty-five years old, and the Third Amendment insists that government may not quarter soldiers in citizens' houses in peacetime. The latter may have been inspired by a moral principle: those who wrote and enacted it might have been anxious to give effect to some principle protecting citizens' rights to privacy, for example. But the Third Amendment is not itself a moral principle: its *content* is not a general principle of privacy. So the first challenge to my own interpretation of the abstract clauses might be put this way: What argument or evidence do I have that the equal protection clause of the Fourteenth Amendment (for example), which declares that no state may deny any person equal protection of the laws, has a moral principle as *its* content though the Third Amendment does not?

This is a question of interpretation or, if you prefer, translation. We must try to find language of our own that best captures, in terms we find clear, the content of what the "framers" intended it to say. (Constitutional scholars use the word "framers" to describe, somewhat ambiguously, the various people who drafted and enacted a constitutional provision.) History is crucial to that project, because we must know something about the circumstances in which people spoke to have any good idea of what they meant to say in speaking as they did. We find nothing in history, however, to cause us any doubt about what the framers of the Third Amendment meant to say. Given the words they used, we cannot sensibly interpret them as laying down any moral principle, even if we believe that they were inspired by one. They said what the words they used would normally be used to say: not that privacy must be protected, but that soldiers must not be quartered in houses in peacetime. The same process of reasoning about what the framers presumably intended to say when they used the words they did yields an opposite conclusion about the framers of the equal protection clause, however. Most of them no doubt had fairly clear expectations about what legal consequences the Fourteenth Amendment would have. They expected it to end certain of the most egregious Jim Crow practices of the Reconstruction period. They plainly did not expect it to outlaw official racial segregation in school; on the contrary, the Congress that adopted the equal protection clause itself maintained segregation in the District of Columbia school system. But they did not say anything about Jim Crow laws or school segregation or homosexuality or gender equality, one way or the other. They said that "equal protection of the laws" is required, which plainly describes a very general principle, not any concrete application of it.

The framers meant, then, to enact a general principle. But which general principle? That further question must be answered by constructing different elaborations of the phrase "equal protection of the laws," each of which we can recognize as a principle of political morality that might have won their respect, and then by asking which of these it makes most sense to attribute to them, given everything else we know. The qualification that each of these possibilities might be recognizable as a political *principle* is absolutely crucial. We cannot capture a statesman's efforts to lay down a general constitutional principle by attributing to him something neither he nor we could recognize as a candidate for that role. But the qualification will typically leave many possibilities open. It was once debated, for example, whether the framers intended to stipulate, in the equal protection clause, only the relatively weak political principle that laws must be enforced in accordance with their terms, so that legal benefits conferred on everyone, including blacks, must not be denied, in practice, to anyone.

History seems decisive that the framers of the Fourteenth Amendment did not mean to lay down only so weak a principle as that one, however, which would have left states free to discriminate against blacks in any way they wished so long as they did so openly. Congressmen of the victorious nation, trying to capture the achievements and lessons of a terrible war, would be very unlikely to settle for anything so limited and insipid, and we should not take them to have done so unless the language leaves no other interpretation plausible. In any case, constitutional interpretation must take into account past legal and political practice as well as what the framers themselves intended to say, and it has now been settled by unchallengeable precedent that the political principle incorporated in the Fourteenth Amendment is not that very weak one, but something more robust. Once that is conceded, however, then the principle must be something *much* more robust, because the only alternative, as a translation of what the framers actually *said* in the equal protection clause, is that they declared a principle of quite breathtaking scope and power: the principle that government must treat everyone as of equal status and with equal concern.

I have provided substantive examples in other writings that give more detail to that sketchy explanation of the role of history and language in deciding what the Constitution means. But even this brief discussion has mentioned two important restraints that sharply limit the latitude the moral reading gives to individual judges. First, under that reading constitutional interpretation must begin with what the framers said, and, just as our judgment about what friends and strangers say relies on specific information about them and the context in which they speak, so does our understanding of what the framers said. History is therefore plainly relevant, but only in a particular way. We turn to history to answer the question of what they intended to *say*, not the different question of what *other* intentions they had. We have no need to decide what they expected to happen, or hoped would happen, in consequence of their having said what they did, for example; their purpose, in that sense, is not part of our study. That is a crucial distinction. We are governed by what our lawmakers said—by the principles they laid down—not by any information we might have about how they themselves would have interpreted those principles or applied them in concrete cases.

Second, and equally important, constitutional interpretation is disciplined, under the moral reading, by the requirement of constitutional *integrity*.[6] Judges may not read their own convictions into the Constitution. They may not read the abstract moral clauses as expressing any particular moral judgment, no matter how much that judgment appeals to them, unless they find it consistent in principle with the structural design of the Constitution as a whole, and also with the dominant lines of past constitutional interpretation by other judges. They must regard themselves as partners with other officials, past and future, who to-

gether elaborate a coherent constitutional morality, and they must take care to
see that what they contribute fits with the rest. (I have elsewhere said that judges
are like authors jointly creating a chain novel in which each writes a chapter that
makes sense as part of the story as a whole.)[7]

Even a judge who believes that abstract justice requires economic equality
cannot interpret the equal protection clause as making equality of wealth, or collective ownership of productive resources, a constitutional requirement, because
that interpretation simply does not fit American history or practice, or the rest
of the Constitution.

Nor could judges plausibly think that the constitutional structure commits
any but basic, structural political rights to their care. They might think that a
society truly committed to equal concern would award people with handicaps
special resources, or would secure convenient access to recreational parks for
everyone, or would provide heroic and experimental medical treatment, no matter how expensive or speculative, for anyone whose life might possibly be saved.
But it would violate constitutional integrity for judges to treat these mandates
as part of constitutional law. Judges must defer to general, settled understandings about the character of the power the Constitution assigns them. The moral
reading asks them to find the best conception of constitutional moral principles—the best understanding of what equal moral status for men and women
really requires, for example—that fits the broad story of America's historical
record. It does not ask them to follow the whisperings of their own consciences
or the traditions of their own class or sect if these cannot be seen as embedded
in that record. Of course judges can abuse their power—they can pretend to observe the important restraint of integrity while really ignoring it. But generals
and presidents and priests can abuse their powers, too. The moral reading is a
strategy for lawyers and judges acting in good faith, which is all any interpretive
strategy can be.

I emphasize these constraints of history and integrity, because they show how
exaggerated is the common complaint that the moral reading gives judges absolute power to impose their own moral convictions on the rest of us. Macaulay
was wrong when he said that the American Constitution is all sail and no anchor,[8] and so are the other critics who say that the moral reading turns judges
into philosopher-kings. Our constitution is law, and like all law it is anchored
in history, practice, and integrity. Most cases at law—even most constitutional
cases—are not hard cases. The ordinary craft of a judge dictates an answer and
leaves no room for the play of personal moral conviction. Still, we must not exaggerate the drag of that anchor. Very different, even contrary, conceptions of a

constitutional principle—of what treating men and women as equals really means, for example—will often fit language, precedent, and practice well enough to pass these tests, and thoughtful judges must then decide on their own which conception does most credit to the nation. So though the familiar complaint that the moral reading gives judges unlimited power is hyperbolic, it contains enough truth to alarm those who believe that such judicial power is inconsistent with a republican form of government. The constitutional sail is a broad one, and many people do fear that it is too big for a democratic boat.

WHAT IS THE ALTERNATIVE?

Constitutional lawyers and scholars have therefore been anxious to find other strategies for constitutional interpretation, strategies that give judges less power. They have explored two possibilities. The first, and most forthright, concedes that the moral reading is right—that the Bill of Rights can be understood only as a set of moral principles. But it denies that judges should have the final authority themselves to conduct the moral reading—that they should have the last word about, for example, whether women have a constitutional right to choose abortion or whether affirmative action treats all races with equal concern. It reserves that interpretive authority to the people. That is by no means a contradictory combination of views. The moral reading, as I said, is a theory about what the Constitution means, not a theory about whose view of what it means must be accepted by the rest of us.

This first alternative offers a way of understanding the arguments of a great American judge, Learned Hand. Hand thought that the courts should take final authority to interpret the Constitution only when this is absolutely necessary to the survival of government—only when the courts must be referees between the other departments of government because the alternative would be a chaos of competing claims to jurisdiction. No such necessity compels courts to test legislative acts against the Constitution's moral principles, and Hand therefore thought it wrong for judges to claim that authority. Though his view was once an open possibility, history has long excluded it; practice has now settled that courts do have a responsibility to declare and act on their best understanding of what the Constitution forbids.[9] If Hand's view had been accepted, the Supreme Court could not have decided, as it did in its *Brown* decision in 1954, that the equal protection clause outlaws racial segregation in public schools. In 1958 Hand said, with evident regret, that he had to regard the *Brown* decision as wrong, and he would have had to take the same view about later Supreme

Court decisions that expanded racial equality, religious independence, and personal freedoms such as the freedom to buy and use contraceptives. These decisions are now almost universally thought not only sound but shining examples of our constitutional structure working at its best.

The first alternative strategy, as I said, accepts the moral reading. The second alternative, which is called the "originalist" or "original intention" strategy, does not. The moral reading insists that the Constitution means what the framers intended to say. Originalism insists that it means what they expected their language to do, which as I said is a very different matter. (Though some originalists, including one of the most conservative justices now on the Supreme Court, Antonin Scalia, are unclear about the distinction.)[10] According to originalism, the great clauses of the Bill of Rights should be interpreted not as laying down the abstract moral principles they actually describe, but instead as referring, in a kind of code or disguise, to the framers' own assumptions and expectations about the correct application of those principles. So the equal protection clause is to be understood as commanding not equal status but what the framers themselves thought was equal status, in spite of the fact that, as I said, the framers clearly meant to lay down the former standard not the latter one. The *Brown* decision crisply illustrates the distinction. The Court's decision was plainly required by the moral reading, because it is obvious now that official school segregation is not consistent with equal status and equal concern for all races. But the originalist strategy, consistently applied, would have demanded the opposite conclusion, because, as I said, the authors of the equal protection clause did not believe that school segregation, which they practiced themselves, was a denial of equal status, and did not expect that it would one day be deemed to be so. The moral reading insists that they misunderstood the moral principle that they themselves enacted into law. The originalist strategy would translate that mistake into enduring constitutional law.

That strategy, like the first alternative, would condemn not only the *Brown* decision but many other Supreme Court decisions that are now widely regarded as paradigms of good constitutional interpretation. For that reason, almost no one now embraces the originalist strategy in anything like a pure form. Even Robert Bork, who remains one of its strongest defenders, qualified his support in the Senate hearings following his nomination to the Supreme Court—he conceded that the *Brown* decision was right, and said that even the Court's 1965 decision guaranteeing a right to use contraceptives, which we have no reason to think the authors of any pertinent constitutional clause either expected or would have approved, was right in its result. The originalist strategy is as indefensible in principle as it is unpalatable in result, moreover. It is as illegitimate to substitute a concrete, detailed provision for the abstract language of the equal protection clause as it would be to substitute some abstract principle of privacy for the concrete terms of the Third Amendment, or to treat the clause imposing a minimum age for a President as enacting some general principle of disability for persons under that age.

So though many conservative politicians and judges have endorsed originalism, and some, like Hand, have been tempted to reconsider whether judges should have the last word about what the Constitution requires, there is in fact very little practical support for either of these strategies. Yet the moral reading is almost never explicitly endorsed, and is often explicitly condemned. If neither of the two alternatives I described is actually embraced by those who disparage the moral reading, what alternative do they have in mind? The surprising answer is: none. Constitutional scholars often say that we must avoid the mistakes both of the moral reading, which gives too much power to judges, and of originalism, which makes the contemporary Constitution too much the dead hand of the past. The right method, they say, is something in between which strikes the right balance between protecting essential individual rights and deferring to popular will. But they do not indicate what the right balance is, or even what kind of scale we should use to find it. They say that constitutional interpretation must take both history and the general structure of the Constitution into account, as well as moral or political philosophy. But they do not say why history or structure, both of which, as I said, figure in the moral reading, should figure in some further or different way, or what that different way is, or what general goal or standard of constitutional interpretation should guide us in seeking a different interpretive strategy.[11]

So though the call for an intermediate constitutional strategy is often heard, it has not been answered, except in unhelpful metaphors about balance and structure. That is extraordinary, particularly given the enormous and growing literature of American constitutional theory. If it is so hard to produce an alternative to the moral reading, why struggle to do so? One distinguished constitutional lawyer who insists that there must be an interpretive strategy somewhere between originalism and the moral reading recently announced, at a conference, that although he had not discovered it, he would spend the rest of his life looking. Why? I have already answered that question. Lawyers assume that the disabilities that a constitution imposes on majoritarian political processes are antidemocratic, at least if these disabilities are enforced by judges, and the moral reading seems to exacerbate the insult. If there is no genuine alternative to the moral reading in practice, however, and if efforts to find even a theoretical statement of an acceptable alternative have failed, we would do well to look again at that assumption. I shall argue, as I have already promised, that it is unfounded.

I said earlier that the theoretical argument among constitutional scholars and judges was never really about whether judges should change the Constitution or leave it alone. It was always about how the Constitution should be interpreted. Happily, in spite of the politicians' rhetoric, that is now generally recognized by constitutional scholars, and it is also generally recognized that the question of interpretation turns on a political controversy, because the only substantial objection to the moral reading which takes the text seriously, is that it offends democracy. So the academic argument is widely thought to be about how far democracy can properly be compromised in order to protect other values, including individual rights. One side declares itself passionate for democracy and anxious to protect it, while the other claims to be more sensitive to the injustices that democracy sometimes produces. In many ways, however, this new view of the debate is as confused as the older one. I shall argue for seeing the constitutional argument in entirely different terms: as a debate not about how far democracy should yield to other values, but about what democracy, accurately understood, really is.

THE MAJORITARIAN PREMISE

Democracy means government by the people. But what does that mean? No explicit definition of democracy is settled among political theorists or in the dictionary. On the contrary, it is a matter of deep controversy what democracy really is. People disagree about which techniques of representation, which allocation of power among local, state, and national governments, which schedule and pattern of elections, and which other institutional arrangements provide the best available version of democracy. But beneath these familiar arguments over the structures of democracy there lies, I believe, a profound philosophical dispute about democracy's fundamental *value* or *point*, and one abstract issue is crucial to that dispute, though this is not always recognized. Should we accept or reject what I shall call the majoritarian premise?

This is a thesis about the fair *outcomes* of a political process: it insists that political procedures should be designed so that, at least on important matters, the decision that is reached is the decision that a majority or plurality of citizens favors, or would favor if it had adequate information and enough time for reflection. That goal sounds reasonable, and many people, perhaps without much reflection, have taken it to provide the essence of democracy. They believe that the complex political arrangements that constitute the democratic process should be aimed at and tested by this goal: that the laws the complex democratic process enacts and the policies it pursues should be those, in the end, that the majority of citizens would approve.

The majoritarian premise does not deny that individuals have important moral rights that the majority should respect. It is not necessarily tied to some collectivist or utilitarian theory according to which such rights are nonsense. In some political communities, however—in Great Britain, for example—the majoritarian premise has been thought to entail that the community should defer to the majority's view about what these individual rights are, and how they are best respected and enforced. It is sometimes said that Britain has no constitution, but that is a mistake. Britain has an unwritten as well as a written constitution, and part of the former consists in understandings about what laws Parliament should not enact. It is part of the British constitution, for example, that freedom of speech is to be protected. Until very recently, it has seemed natural to British lawyers, however, that no group except a political majority, acting through Parliament, should decide what that requirement means, or whether it should be altered or repealed, so that when Parliament's intention to restrict speech is clear, British courts have no power to invalidate what it has done. That is because the majoritarian premise, and the majoritarian conception of democracy it produces, have been more or less unexamined fixtures of British political morality for more than a century.

In the United States, however, most people who assume that the majoritarian premise states the ultimate definition of and justification for democracy nevertheless accept that on some occasions the will of the majority should *not* govern. They agree that the majority should not always be the final judge of when its own power should be limited to protect individual rights, and they accept that at least some of the Supreme Court's decisions that overturned popular legislation, as the *Brown* decision did, were right. The majoritarian premise does not rule out exceptions of that kind, but it does insist that in such cases, even if some derogation from majoritarian government is justified, something morally regrettable has happened, a moral cost has been paid. The premise supposes, in other words, that it is always unfair when a political majority is not allowed to have its way, so that even when there are strong enough countervailing reasons to justify this, the unfairness remains.

If we reject the majoritarian premise, we need a different, better account of the value and point of democracy. Later I will defend an account which I call the constitutional conception of democracy—that does reject the majoritarian premise. It denies that it is a defining goal of democracy that collective decisions always or normally be those that a majority or plurality of citizens would favor if fully informed and rational. It takes the defining aim of democracy to be a different one—that collective decisions be made by political institutions whose structure, composition, and practices treat all members of the community, as individuals, with equal concern and respect. This alternate account of the aim of democracy, it is true, demands much the same structure of government as the majoritarian premise does. It requires that day-to-day political decisions be made by officials who have been chosen in popular elections. But the constitutional conception requires these majoritarian procedures out of a concern for the equal status of citizens, and not out of any commitment to the goals of majority rule. So it offers no reason why some nonmajoritarian procedure should not be employed on special occasions when this would better protect or enhance the equal status that it declares to be the essence of democracy, and it does not accept that these exceptions are a cause of moral regret.

The constitutional conception of democracy, in short, takes the following attitude to majoritarian government. Democracy means government subject to conditions—we might call these the "democratic" conditions of equal status for all citizens. When majoritarian institutions provide and respect the democratic conditions, then the verdicts of these institutions should be accepted by everyone for that reason. But when they do not, or when their provision or respect is defective, there can be no objection, in the name of democracy, to other procedures that protect and respect them better. The democratic conditions plainly include, for example, a requirement that public offices must in principle be open to members of all races and groups on equal terms. If some law provided that only members of one race were eligible for public office, then there would be no moral cost—no matter for moral regret at all—if a court that enjoyed the power to do so under a valid constitution struck down that law as unconstitutional. That would presumably be an occasion on which the majoritarian premise was flouted, but though this is a matter of regret according to the majoritarian conception of democracy, it is not according to the constitutional conception. Of course, it may be controversial what the democratic conditions in detail really are, and whether a particular law does offend them. But, according to the constitutional conception, it would beg the question to object to a practice assigning those controversial questions for final decisions to a court, on the ground that that practice is undemocratic, because that objection assumes that the laws in question respect the democratic conditions, and that is the very issue in controversy.

I hope it is now clear that the majoritarian premise has had a potent—if often unnoticed—grip on the imagination of American constitutional scholars and lawyers. Only that diagnosis explains the near unanimous view I described: that judicial review compromises democracy, so that the central question of constitutional theory must be whether and when that compromise is justified. That opinion is the child of a majoritarian conception of democracy, and therefore the grandchild of the majoritarian premise. It provokes the pointless search I described, for an interpretive strategy "intermediate" between the moral reading and originalism, and it tempts distinguished theorists into constructing Ptolemaic epicycles trying to reconcile constitutional practice with majoritarian principles.

So a complex issue of political morality—the validity of the majoritarian premise—is in fact at the heart of the long constitutional argument. The argument will remain confused until that issue is identified and addressed. We might pause to notice how influential the majoritarian premise has been in other important political debates, including the pressing national discussion about electoral campaign reform. This discussion has so far been dominated by the assumption that democracy is improved when it better serves the majoritarian premise—when it is designed more securely to produce collective decisions that match majority preferences. The unfortunate Supreme Court decision in *Buckley v. Valeo,* for example, which struck down laws limiting what rich individuals can spend on political campaigning, was based on a theory of free speech that has its origins in that view of democracy.[12] In fact the degeneration of democracy that has been so vivid in recent elections cannot be halted until we develop a more sophisticated view of what democracy means.

In most of the rest of this essay, I shall be evaluating arguments for and against the majoritarian premise. I shall not consider, however, but only mention now, one plainly inadequate argument for it that I fear has had considerable currency. This begins in a fashionable form of moral skepticism which insists that moral values and principles cannot be objectively true, but only represent powerful concatenations of self-interest or taste, or of class or race or gender interest. If so, the argument continues, then judges who claim to have discovered moral truth are deluded, and the only fair political process is one that leaves power to the people. This argument is doubly fallacious. First, since its conclusion, favorable to the majoritarian premise, is itself a moral claim, it contradicts itself.

Second, for reasons I have tried to explain elsewhere, this fashionable form of skepticism is incoherent.

In fact the most powerful arguments for the majoritarian premise are themselves arguments of political morality. They can be distinguished and grouped under the three eighteenth-century revolutionary virtues—equality, liberty, and community—and it is these more basic political ideas that we must now explore. If the premise can be sustained, this must be because it is endorsed by the best conception of at least one and perhaps all of these ideals. We must go behind democracy to consider, in the light of these deeper virtues and values, which conception of democracy—the majoritarian conception which is based on the majoritarian premise or the constitutional conception which rejects it—is sounder. But we shall first need another important distinction, which I shall make now.

WE THE PEOPLE

We say that in a democracy government is by the people; we mean that the people collectively do things—elect leaders, for example—that no individual does or can do alone. There are two kinds of collective action, however—statistical and communal—and our view of the majoritarian premise may well turn on which kind of collective action we take democratic government to require.

Collective action is statistical when what the group does is only a matter of some function, rough or specific, of what the individual members of the group do on their own, that is, with no sense of doing something as a group. We might say that yesterday the foreign exchange market drove down the price of the dollar. That is certainly a kind of collective action: only the combined action of a large group of bankers and dealers affect the foreign currency market in any substantial way. But our reference to a collective entity, the currency market, does not point to any actual entity. We could, without changing our meaning, make an overtly statistical claim instead: that the combined effects of individual currency transactions were responsible for the lower price of the dollar at the latest trade.

Collective action is communal, however, when it cannot be reduced just to some statistical function of individual action, when it presupposes a special, distinct, collective *agency*. It is a matter of individuals acting together in a way that merges their separate actions into a further, unified, act that is together *theirs*. The familiar but emotionally powerful example of collective guilt provides a useful illustration. Many Germans (including those born after 1945) feel responsible for what Germany did during World War II, not just for what other Germans did. Their sense of responsibility assumes that they themselves are connected to the Nazi terror in some way, because they belong to the nation that committed those crimes. Here is a more pleasant example. An orchestra can play a symphony, though no single musician can, but this is not a case of merely statistical collective action because it is essential to a successful orchestral performance not just that each musician plays some appropriate score, timing his performance as the conductor instructs, but that the musicians play as an orchestra, each intending to make a contribution to the performance of the group, and each taking part in a collective responsibility for it. The performance of a football team can be communal collective action in the same way.

I have already distinguished two conceptions of democracy: majoritarian and constitutional. The first accepts and the second rejects the majoritarian premise. The difference between statistical and communal collective action allows us to draw a second distinction, this time between two readings of the idea that democracy is government by "the people." (I shall shortly consider the connection between these two distinctions.) The first reading is a statistical one: that in a democracy political decisions are made in accordance with the votes or wishes of some function—a majority or plurality—of individual citizens. The second is a communal reading: that in a democracy political decisions are taken by a distinct entity—the people *as* such—rather than by any set of individuals one by one. Rousseau's idea of government by general will is an example of a communal rather than a statistical conception of democracy. The statistical reading of government by the people is much more familiar in American political theory. The communal reading sounds mysterious, and may also sound dangerously totalitarian. If so, my reference to Rousseau will not have allayed the suspicion. I shall argue in the next two sections, however, that the supposedly most powerful arguments for the majoritarian premise presuppose the communal reading. They presuppose it but also betray it.

DOES CONSTITUTIONALISM UNDERMINE LIBERTY?

The majoritarian premise insists that something of moral importance is lost or compromised whenever a political decision contradicts what the majority of citizens would prefer or judge right if they reflected on the basis of adequate information. We must try to identify that moral cost. What is lost or compromised? Many people think that the answer is equality. I shall consider that apparently natural answer shortly, but I begin with a different suggestion, which is that when constitutional disabling provisions, like those found in the Bill of Rights, limit what a majority can enact, the result is to compromise the community's freedom.[13]

That suggestion plainly appeals to what Isaiah Berlin and others have called positive as distinct from negative liberty, and what Benjamin Constant described as the liberty of the ancients as distinct from that of the moderns. It is the kind of freedom that statesmen and revolutionaries and terrorists and humanitarians have in mind when they insist that freedom must include the right of "self-determination" or the right of the "people" to govern themselves. Since the suggestion that constitutional rights compromise freedom appeals to positive rather than negative liberty, it might be said to pit the two kinds of liberty against each other. Constitutionalism, on this view, protects "negative" liberties, like free speech and "privacy," at the cost of the "positive" freedoms of self-determination.

This means, however, that this argument from liberty we are considering must be based on a communal rather than a statistical reading of government by the "people." On the statistical reading, an individual's control over the collective decisions that affect his life is measured by his power, on his own, to influence the result, and in a large democracy the power of any individual over national decisions is so tiny that constitutional restraints cannot be thought to diminish it enough to count as objectionable for that reason. On the contrary, constraints on majority will might well expand any particular individual's control of his own fate. On the communal reading, however, liberty is a matter not of any relation between government and citizens one by one, but rather of the relation between government and the whole citizenry understood collectively. Positive liberty, so understood, is the state of affairs when "the people" rule their officials, at least in the final analysis, rather than vice versa, and that is the liberty said to be compromised when the majority is prevented from securing its will.

I discuss this defense of the majoritarian premise first because it is emotionally the most powerful. Self-determination is the most potent—and dangerous—political ideal of our time. People fervently want to be governed by a group not just to which they belong, but with which they identify in some particular way. They want to be governed by members of the same religion or race or nation or linguistic community or historical nation-state rather than by any other group, and they regard a political community that does not satisfy this demand as under tyranny, no matter how otherwise fair and satisfactory it is.

This is partly a matter of narrow self-interest. People think that decisions made by a group most of whose members share their values will be better deci-sions for them. The great power of the ideal lies deeper, however. It lies in half-articulate convictions about when people are free, because they govern them-selves, in spite of the fact that in a statistical sense, as individuals, they are not free, because they must often bend to the will of others. For us moderns, the key to this liberty of the ancients lies in democracy. As John Kenneth Galbraith has said, "When people put their ballots in the boxes, they are, by that act, inocu-lated against the feeling that the government is not theirs. They then accept, in some measure, that its errors are their errors, its aberrations their aberrations, that any revolt will be against themselves."[14] We think we are free when we ac-cept a majority's will in place of our own, but not when we bow before the doom of a monarch or the ukase of any aristocracy of blood or faith or skill. It is not difficult to see the judiciary as an aristocracy claiming dominion. Learned Hand described judges who appeal to the moral reading of the Constitution as "a bevy of Platonic guardians," and said he could not bear to be ruled by such a body of elites even if he knew how to select those fit for the task.[15]

But powerful as the idea of democratic self-governance is, it is also deeply mys-terious. Why am I *free*—how could I be thought to be governing *myself*—when I must obey what other people decide even if I think it wrong or unwise or un-fair to me and my family? What difference can it make how many people must think the decision right and wise and fair if it is not necessary that *I* do? What kind of freedom is that? The answer to these enormously difficult questions be-gins in the communal conception of collective action. If I am a genuine mem-ber of a political community, its act is in some pertinent sense my act, even when I argued and voted against it, just as the victory or defeat of a team of which I am a member is my victory or defeat even if my own individual contribution made no difference either way. On no other assumption can we intelligibly think that as members of a flourishing democracy we are governing ourselves.

That explanation may seem only to deepen the mystery of collective self-government, however, because it appeals to two further ideas that seem dark themselves. What could *genuine* membership in a political community mean? And in what sense can a collective act of a group also be the act of each mem-ber? These are moral rather than metaphysical or psychological questions: they are not to be answered by counting the ultimate constituents of reality or dis-covering when people feel responsible for what some group that they belong to does. We must describe some connection between an individual and a group that makes it *fair* to treat her—and *sensible* that she treat herself—as responsi-ble for what it does. Let us bring those ideas together in the concept of moral membership, by which we mean the kind of membership in a political community that engages self-government. If true democracy is government by the people, in the communal sense that provides self-government, then true democracy is based on moral membership.

In this section we are considering the argument that the moral cost incurred when the majoritarian premise is flouted is a cost in liberty. We have now clarified that argument—we must understand it to mean that the people govern themselves when the majoritarian premise is satisfied, and that any compromise of that premise compromises that self-government. But that majoritarianism does not guarantee self-government unless all the members of the community in question are moral members, and the majoritarian premise acknowledges no such qualification. German Jews were not moral members of the political community that tried to exterminate them, though they had votes in the elections that led to Hitler's chancellorship, and the Holocaust was therefore not part of their self-government, even if a majority of Germans would have approved it. Catholics in Northern Ireland, nationalists in the Caucasus, and separatists in Quebec all believe that they are not free because they are not moral members of the right political community. I do not mean that people who deny moral membership in their political community are always right. The test, as I said, is moral, not psychological. But they are not wrong just because they have an equal vote with others in some standing majoritarian structure.

When I described the constitutional conception of democracy earlier, as a rival to the majoritarian conception that reflects the majoritarian premise, I said that the constitutional conception presupposes democratic conditions. These are the conditions that must be met before majoritarian decision-making can claim any automatic moral advantage over other procedures for collective decision. We have now identified the same idea through another route. The democratic conditions are the conditions of moral membership in a political community. So we can now state a strong conclusion: not just that positive liberty is not sacrificed whenever and just because the majoritarian premise is ignored, but that positive liberty is enhanced when that premise is rejected outright in favor of the constitutional conception of democracy. If it is trite that self-government is possible only within a community that meets the conditions of moral membership, because only then are we entitled to refer to government by "the people" in a powerful communal rather than a barren statistical sense, we need a conception of democracy that insists that no democracy exists unless those conditions are met.

What are the conditions of moral membership, and hence of positive freedom, and hence of democracy on the constitutional conception? I have tried to describe them elsewhere, and will only summarize my conclusions here.[16] There are two kinds of conditions. The first set is *structural:* these conditions describe the character the community as a whole must have if it is to count as a genuine political community. Some of these structural conditions are essentially historical. The political community must be more than nominal: it must have been established by a historical process that has produced generally recognized and stable territorial boundaries. Many sociologists and political scientists and politicians would add further structural conditions to that very limited one: they would insist, for example, that the members of a genuine political community must share a culture as well as a political history: that they must speak a common language, have common values, and so forth. Some might add further psychological conditions: that members of the community must be mainly disposed to trust one another, for example.[17] I shall not consider the interesting issues these suggestions raise here, because our interest lies in the second set of conditions.

These are *relational* conditions: they describe how an individual must be treated by a genuine political community in order that he or she be a moral member of that community. A political community cannot count anyone as a moral member unless it gives that person a *part* in any collective decision, a *stake* in it, and *independence* from it. First, each person must have an opportunity to make a difference in the collective decisions, and the force of his or her role—the magnitude of the difference he or she can make—must not be structurally fixed or limited in ways that reflect assumptions about his or her worth or talent or ability, or the soundness of his or her convictions or tastes. It is that condition that insists on universal suffrage and effective elections and representation, even though it does not demand that these be the only avenues of collective decision. It also insists on free speech and expression for all opinion, not just on formal political occasions, but in the informal life of the community as well.

It insists, moreover, on interpreting the force of freedom of speech and expression by concentrating on the role of that freedom in the processes of self-government, a role that dictates different answers to several questions—including the question of whether campaign expenditure limits violate that freedom—than a majoritarian conception of democracy would.

Second, the political process of a genuine community must express some bona fide conception of equal concern for the interests of all members, which means that political decisions that affect the distribution of wealth, benefits, and burdens must be consistent with equal concern for all. Moral membership involves reciprocity: a person is not a member unless she is treated as a member by others, which means that they treat the consequences of any collective decision for her life as equally significant a reason for or against that decision as are comparable consequences for the life of anyone else. So the communal conception of democracy explains an intuition many of us share: that a society in which the majority shows contempt for the needs and prospects of some minority is illegitimate as well as unjust.

The third condition—of moral independence—is likely to be more controversial than these first two. I believe it essential, however, in order to capture an aspect of moral membership that the first two conditions may be interpreted to omit. The root idea we are now exploring—that individual freedom is furthered by collective self-government—assumes that the members of a political community can appropriately regard themselves as partners in a joint venture, like members of a football team or orchestra in whose work and fate all share, even when that venture is conducted in ways they do not endorse. That idea is nonsense unless it can be accepted by people with self-respect, and whether it can be depends on which kinds of decisions the collective venture is thought competent to make. An orchestra's conductor can decide, for example, how the orchestra will interpret a particular piece: there must be a decision of that issue binding on all, and the conductor is the only one placed to make it. No musician sacrifices anything essential to his control over his own life, and hence to his self-respect, in accepting that someone else has that responsibility, but it would plainly be otherwise if the conductor tried to dictate not only how a violinist should play under his direction, but what standards of taste the violinist should try to cultivate. No one who accepted responsibility to decide questions of musical judgment for himself could regard himself as a partner in a joint venture that proposed to decide them for him.

That is even more plainly true in the political case. People who take personal responsibility for deciding what kind of life is valuable for them can nevertheless accept that issues of justice about how the different and sometimes competing interests of all citizens should be accommodated must be decided collectively, so that one decision is taken as authoritative for all. There is nothing in that proposition that challenges individual responsibility to decide what life to live given the resources and opportunities that such collective decisions leave. So he can treat himself as bound together with others in a joint effort to resolve such questions, even when his views lose. But it would be otherwise if the majority purported to decide what he should think or say about its decisions, or what values or ideals should guide how he votes or the choices he makes with the resources it assigns him. Someone who believes in her own responsibility for the central values of her life cannot yield that responsibility to a group even if she has an equal vote in its deliberations. A genuine political community must therefore be a community of independent moral agents. It must not dictate what its citizens think about matters of political or moral or ethical judgment, but must, on the contrary, provide circumstances that encourage them to arrive at beliefs on these matters through their own reflective and finally individual conviction.

EQUALITY?

Although the argument from liberty is emotionally the most powerful of the arguments that might be made for the majoritarian premise, an argument from equality is more familiar. The dimension of equality in question is presumably political equality, because there is nothing in majoritarianism that could be thought automatically to promote any other form of equality, particularly not economic equality. True, if a society's economic structure is pyramidal, with progressively more people at progressively lower economic levels, then universal suffrage and majoritarian decisions might well push toward greater economic equality. But in the United States, and in other advanced capitalist countries where the profile of distribution is now very different, people in the majority often vote to protect their own wealth against the demands of those worse off than they are.

So the argument that equality is compromised when the majoritarian premise is ignored must appeal to some concept of political equality. But which concept this is depends on which of the two readings of collective action we have in mind. If we take government by "the people" to be only a statistical matter, then the equality in question is the political equality of citizens taken one by one. Such equality was certainly denied before women were permitted to vote, and it was compromised by the electoral system in Victorian Britain, which in effect gave university graduates extra votes. But what metric do we use in making those judgments? What *is* political equality according to the statistical concept of collective political action?

Perhaps surprisingly, we cannot capture political equality if we define it as equality of political *power,* because we have no interpretation of "power" that would make equality of power even an attractive, let alone an attainable, ideal.[18] Suppose we take political power to be a matter of impact, understood in the following way: my political impact, as a citizen of the United States, is a matter of how far my favoring a particular decision, just on its own, increases the antecedent likelihood of that being the collective decision, making no assumptions about what opinion any other citizen has or forms. Impact cannot be equal in a representative democracy: it must inevitably make a greater difference to the antecedent probability of a trade measure being approved that any particular senator favors it than that I do. In any case, impact does not capture any intuitively appealing concept of political power, because impact is insensitive to what is the most important source of unequal political power in modern democracies, which is the inequality of wealth that allows some people vast opportunity to influence public opinion. Ross Perot and I have only one vote each, but he can buy massive amounts of television time to persuade others to his opinion, and I cannot buy any.

This might suggest an improved account: that political power is a matter not of impact but of influence, understood as my overall power to affect political decisions, taking into account my power to affect the opinions of others. But equality of influence is plainly an unattractive—as well as unrealizable—goal. We do not want wealth to affect political decisions, but that is because wealth is unequally and unfairly distributed. We certainly do want influence to be unequal in politics for other reasons: we want those with better views, or who can argue more cogently, to have more influence. We could not eliminate differential influence from such sources without savage transformations of our whole society, and these would mean the end, not the triumph, of deliberation in our politics.

We must begin again. Political equality, on the statistical model of collective action, must be defined as a matter not of power but of the kind of *status* I discussed in connection with the conditions of democratic self-government. Male-only suffrage and university votes were inegalitarian because they presupposed that some people were worthier or better fit to participate in collective decisions than others. But mere political authority—the power attached to political office for which all are in principle eligible—carries no such presupposition. That is why the special power of political officials does not destroy true political equality, and it does not matter, for that point, whether or not the officials are directly elected. Many officials who are appointed rather than elected wield great power. An acting ambassador to Iraq can create a Gulf War and the chairman of the Federal Reserve Board can bring the economy to its knees. There is no inegalitarian premise of status—no supposition of first- and second-class citizenship—in the arrangements that produce this power. Nor is there any inegalitarian premise in the parallel arrangements that give certain American judges, appointed and approved by elected officials, authority over constitutional adjudication.

So the statistical reading of collective political action makes little sense of the idea that political equality is compromised whenever majority will is thwarted. And that idea is silly anyway if we have the statistical reading in mind. In a large, continental democracy, any ordinary citizen's political power is minuscule on any understanding of what political power is, and the diminution of that individual power traceable to constitutional constraints on majority will is more minuscule still. The egalitarian argument for the majoritarian premise seems initially more promising, however, if we detach it from the statistical reading of collective action and recast it from the perspective of the communal reading. From that perspective, equality is not a matter of any relation among citizens one by one, but rather a relation between the citizenry, understood collectively as "the people," and their governors. Political equality is the state of affairs in which the people rule their officials, in the final analysis, rather than vice versa. This provides a less silly argument for the proposition that judicial review or other compromises of the majoritarian premise damage political equality. It might be said that when judges apply constitutional provisions to strike down legislation that the people, through their representatives, have enacted, the people are no longer in charge.

But this argument is exactly the same as the argument considered in the last section: it appeals, once again, to the ideals of political self-determination. Positive liberty and the sense of equality that we extracted from the communal understanding of "we the people" are the very same virtues. (That is hardly surprising, because liberty and equality are, in general, aspects of the same ideal, not, as is often supposed, rivals.)[19] The objections I described in the previous section, which are fatal to any attempt to ground a majoritarian premise in positive liberty, are also decisive against the same argument when it cries equality instead.

COMMUNITY?

In recent years opponents of the moral reading have begun to appeal to the third revolutionary virtue—community (or fraternity)—rather than to either liberty or equality. They argue that because the moral reading assigns the most fundamental political decisions to an elite legal profession, it weakens the public's sense of community and cheats it of its sense of common adventure. But "community" is used in different senses, to refer to very different emotions or practices or ideals, and it is important to notice which of these is in play in this kind of argument. It is patently true, as philosophers since Aristotle have agreed, that people have an interest in sharing projects, language, entertainment, assumptions, and ambitions with others. A good political community will of course serve that interest,[20] but many people's interest in community will be better served by other, nonpolitical communities such as religious and professional and social groups. The disabling clauses of the American Constitution do not limit or impair people's power to form and share such communities; on the contrary, some constraints, like the First Amendment's protection of association and its prohibition against religious discrimination, enhance that power. The communitarians and others who appeal to community to support the majoritarian premise have something rather different in mind, however. They have in mind not the general benefits of close human relations, which can be secured in many different forms of community, but the special benefits that they believe follow, both for people as individuals and for the political society as a whole, when citizens are actively engaged in political activity in a certain spirit.

That is not the spirit recommended by a different tradition of political scientists who regard politics as commerce by other means, an arena where citizens pursue their own advantage through political action groups and special interest politics. Communitarians think that this "interest-group republicanism" is a perversion of the republican ideal. They want people to participate in politics as moral agents promoting not their own partisan interests but rival conceptions of the public good. They suppose that if genuine deliberative democracy of that kind can be realized, not only will collective decisions be better, but citizens will lead better—more virtuous, fulfilled, and satisfying—lives.

Communitarians insist that this goal is jeopardized by judicial review, particularly when judicial review is as expansive as the moral reading invites it to be. But they rely on a dubious though rarely challenged assumption: that public discussion of constitutional justice is of better quality and engages more people in the deliberative way the communitarians favor if these issues are finally decided by legislatures rather than courts. This assumption may be inaccurate for a large number of different reasons. There is plainly no necessary connection between the impact that a majoritarian process gives each potential voter and the influence that voter has over a political decision. Some citizens may have more influence over a judicial decision by their contribution to a public discussion of the issue than they would have over a legislative decision just through their solitary vote. Even more important, there is no necessary connection between a citizen's political impact or influence and the ethical benefit she secures through participating in public discussion or deliberation. The quality of the discussion might be better, and her own contribution more genuinely deliberative and public spirited, in a general public debate preceding or following a judicial decision than in a political battle culminating in a legislative vote or even a referendum.

The interaction between these different phenomena—impact, influence, and ethically valuable public participation—is a complex empirical matter. In some circumstances, as I just suggested, individual citizens may be able to exercise the moral responsibilities of citizenship better when final decisions are removed from ordinary politics and assigned to courts, whose decisions are meant to turn on principle, not on the weight of numbers or the balance of political influence. Although the political process that leads to a legislative decision may be of very high quality, it very often is not, as the recent debates in the United States about health care reform and gun control show. Even when the debate is illuminating, moreover, the majoritarian process encourages compromises that may subordinate important issues of principle. Constitutional legal cases, by contrast, can and do provoke a widespread public discussion that focuses on political morality. The great American debate about civil rights and affirmative action, which began in the 1950s and continues today, may well have been more deliberative because the issues were shaped by adjudication, and the argument over *Roe v. Wade,* for all its bitterness and violence, may have produced a better understanding of the complexity of the moral issues than politics alone would have provided.

I put the suggestion that judicial review may provide a superior kind of republican deliberation about some issues tentatively, as a possibility, because I do not believe that we have enough information for much confidence either way. I emphasize the possibility, nevertheless, because the communitarian argument simply ignores it, and assumes, with no pertinent evidence, that the only or most beneficial kind of "participation" in politics is the kind that looks toward elections of representatives who will then enact legislation. The character of recent American elections, and of contemporary national and local legislative debate and deliberation, hardly makes that assumption self-evident. Of course we should aim to improve ordinary politics, because broad-based political activity is essential to justice as well as dignity. (Rethinking what democracy means is, as I said, an essential part of that process.) But we must not pretend, when we evaluate the impact of judicial review on deliberative democracy, that what should happen has happened. In any case, however, whether great constitutional issues provoke and guide public deliberation depends, among much else, on how these issues are conceived and addressed by lawyers and judges. There is little chance of a useful national debate over constitutional principle when constitutional decisions are considered technical exercises in an arcane and conceptual craft. The chances would improve if the moral reading of the Constitution were more openly recognized by and in judicial opinions.

I do not mean, of course, that only judges should discuss matters of high political principle. Legislatures are guardians of principle too, and that includes constitutional principle.[21] The argument of this section aims only to show why the ideal of community does not support the majoritarian premise, or undermine the moral reading, any more effectively than do liberty and equality, the two senior members of the revolutionary brigade. We must set the majoritarian premise aside, and with it the majoritarian conception of democracy. It is not a defensible conception of what true democracy is, and it is not America's conception.

WHAT FOLLOWS?

In a decent working democracy, like the United States, the democratic conditions set out in the Constitution are sufficiently met in practice so that there is no unfairness in allowing national and local legislatures the powers they have under standing arrangements. On the contrary, democracy would be extinguished by any general constitutional change that gave an oligarchy of unelected experts power to overrule and replace any legislative decision they thought unwise or unjust. Even if the experts always improved the legislation they rejected—always stipulated fairer income taxes than the legislature had enacted, for example—there would be a loss in self-government that the merits of their decisions could not extinguish. It is different, however, when the question is plausibly raised whether some rule or regulation or policy itself undercuts or weakens the democratic character of the community, and the constitutional arrangement assigns *that* question to a court. Suppose the legislature enacts a law making it a crime for someone to burn his or her own American flag as an act of protest.[22] Suppose this law is challenged on the ground that it impairs democratic self-government, by wrongly constricting the liberty of speech, and a court accepts this charge and strikes down the law. If the court's decision is correct—if laws against flag-burning do in fact violate the democratic conditions set out in the Constitution as these have been interpreted and formed by American history—the decision is not antidemocratic, but, on the contrary, improves democracy. No moral cost has been paid, because no one, individually or collectively, is worse off in any of the dimensions we have now canvassed. No one's power to participate in a self-governing community has been lessened, because everyone's power in that respect has been increased. No one's equality has been compromised, because equality, in the only pertinent sense, has been strengthened. No one has been cheated of the ethical advantages of a role in principled deliberation if he or she had a chance to participate in the public discussion about whether the decision was right. If the court had not intervened—if the legislature's decision had been left standing—everyone would have been worse off, in all the dimensions of democracy, and it would be perverse to regard that as in any way or sense a democratic victory. Of course, if we assume that the court's decision was wrong, then none of this is true. Certainly it impairs democracy when an authoritative court makes the wrong decision about what the democratic conditions require—but no more than it does when a majoritarian legislature makes a wrong constitutional decision that is allowed to stand. The possibility of error is symmetrical. So the majoritarian premise is confused, and it must be abandoned.

These are important conclusions. They show the fallacy in the popular argument that since judicial review of legislation is undemocratic, the moral reading, which exacerbates the damage to democracy, should be rejected. But it is crucial to realize the limits of our conclusions. We do not yet have a positive argument in *favor* of judicial review, either in the form that institution has taken in the United States or in any other form. We have simply established a level playing field on which the contest between different institutional structures for interpreting the democratic conditions must take place, free from any default or presupposition whatsoever. The real, deep difficulty the constitutional argument exposes in democracy is that it is a procedurally *incomplete* scheme of government. It cannot prescribe the procedures for testing whether the conditions for the procedures it does prescribe are met.

How should a political community that aims at democracy decide whether the conditions democracy requires are met? Should it have a written constitution as its most fundamental law? Should that constitution describe a conception of the democratic conditions in as great detail as possible, trying to anticipate, in a constitutional code, all issues that might arise? Or should it set out very abstract statements of the democratic conditions, as the American Constitution and many other contemporary constitutions do, and leave it to contemporary institutions to interpret these generation by generation? If the latter, which institutions should these be? Should they be the ordinary, majoritarian parliamentary institutions, as the British constitution has for so long insisted? Or should they be special constitutional chambers, whose members are elected but perhaps for much longer terms or in different ways than the ordinary parliamentarians are? Or should they consist in a hierarchy of courts, as John Marshall declared natural in *Marbury v. Madison*?

A community might combine these different answers in different ways. The United States Constitution, as we noticed, combines very specific clauses, about quartering soldiers in peacetime, for example, with the majestically abstract clauses this essay mainly discusses. It is settled in the United States that the Supreme Court does have authority to hold legislation invalid if it deems it unconstitutional. But of course that does not deny that legislators have a parallel responsibility to make constitutional judgments themselves, and to refuse to vote for laws they think unconstitutional. Nor does it follow, when courts have power to enforce some constitutional rights, that they have power to enforce them all. Some imaginative American constitutional lawyers argue, for example, that the power of the federal courts to declare the acts of other institutions invalid because unconstitutional is limited: they have power to enforce many of the rights, principles, and standards the Constitution creates, on this view, but not all of them.[23]

The moral reading is consistent with all these institutional solutions to the problem of democratic conditions. It is a theory about how certain clauses of some constitutions should be read—about what questions must be asked and answered in deciding what those clauses mean and require. It is not a theory about who must ask these questions, or about whose answer must be taken to be authoritative. So the moral reading is only part, though it is an important part, of a general theory of constitutional practice. What shall we say about the remaining questions, the institutional questions that the moral reading does not reach?

I see no alternative but to use a result-driven rather than a procedure-driven standard for deciding them. The best institutional structure is the one best calculated to produce the best answers to the essentially moral question of what the democratic conditions actually are, and to secure stable compliance with those conditions. A host of practical considerations are relevant, and many of these may argue forcefully for allowing an elected legislature itself to decide on the moral limits of its power. But other considerations argue in the opposite direction, including the fact that legislators are vulnerable to political pressures of manifold kinds, both financial and political, so that a legislature is not the safest vehicle for protecting the rights of politically unpopular groups. People can be expected to disagree about which structure is overall best, and so in certain circumstances they need a decision procedure for deciding that question, which is exactly what a theory of democracy cannot provide. That is why the initial making of a political constitution is such a mysterious matter, and why it seems natural to insist on supermajorities or even near unanimity then, not out of any conception of procedural fairness, but rather out of a sense that stability cannot otherwise be had.

The situation is different, however, when we are interpreting an established constitutional practice, not starting a new one. Then authority is already distributed by history, and details of institutional responsibility are matters of interpretation, not of invention from nothing. In these circumstances, rejecting the majoritarian premise means that we may look for the best interpretation with a more open mind: we have no reason of principle to try to force our practices into some majoritarian mold. If the most straightforward interpretation of American constitutional practice shows that our judges have final interpretive authority, and that they largely understand the Bill of Rights as a constitution of principle—if that best explains the decisions judges actually make and the public largely accepts—we have no reason to resist that reading and to strain for one that seems more congenial to a majoritarian philosophy.

NOTES

1. Some branches of legal theory, including the Realist and Critical Legal Studies movements of recent decades, emphasize the role of politics for a skeptical reason: to suggest that if law depends on political morality, it cannot claim "objective" truth or validity or force. I reject that skeptical claim, and have tried to answer it in other work. See, for example, Dworkin, *Law's Empire* (Cambridge, Mass.: Harvard University Press, 1986).

2. *Adarand Constructors, Inc. v. Pena,* 115 S. Ct. 2097 (1995).

3. *Texas v. Johnson,* 491 U.S. 397 (1989).

4. See Antonin Scalia, "Originalism: The Lesser Evil," *University of Cincinnati Law Review,* 57 (1980), 1175.

5. See John Hart Ely, *Democracy and Distrust: A Theory of Judicial Review* (Cambridge, Mass.: Harvard University Press, 1980). Ely's book has been very influential, not because of his distinction between interpretive and noninterpretive approaches to the Constitution, which is happily not much used now, but because he was a pioneer in understanding that some constitutional constraints can be best understood as facilitating rather than compromising democracy. I believe he was wrong in limiting this account to constitu-

tional rights that can be understood as enhancements of constitutional procedure rather than as more substantive rights. See my article "The Forum of Principle," in *A Matter of Principle* (Cambridge, Mass.: Harvard University Press, 1985).

6. For a general discussion of integrity in law, see Dworkin, *Law's Empire.*

7. See Dworkin, *Law's Empire,* 228.

8. Thomas Babington, Lord Macaulay, letter to H. S. Randall, May 23, 1857.

9. For a valuable discussion of the evolution of the idea of judicial review in America, see Gordon Wood, "The Origins of Judicial Review," *Suffolk University Law Review,* 22 (1988), 1293.

10. Justice Scalia insists that statutes be enforced in accordance with what their words mean rather than with what historical evidence shows the legislators themselves expected or intended would be the concrete legal consequences of their own statute. See Scalia, "Originalism." But he also insists on limiting each of the abstract provisions of the Bill of Rights to the force it would have been thought to have at the time of its enactment, so that, for example, the prohibition against "cruel and unusual punishments" of the Eighth Amendment, properly interpreted, does not forbid public flogging, though everyone is now agreed that it does, because such flogging was practiced when the Eighth Amendment was adopted. Scalia agrees that contemporary judges should not hold flogging constitutional, because that would seem too outrageous now, but he does insist that the due process clauses and equal protection clauses should not be used to strike down laws that were commonplace when these clauses were enacted. His position about constitutional law is consistent with his general account of statutory interpretation only if we suppose that the best contemporary translation of what the people who enacted the Eighth Amendment actually said is not that cruel and unusual punishments are forbidden, which is what the language they used certainly suggests, but that punishments that were then generally regarded as cruel and unusual were forbidden, a reading we have absolutely no reason to accept.

11. Some scholars have tried to define an "intermediate" strategy in a way that, they hope, does not require answers to these questions. They say that we should look not to the concrete opinions or expectations of the framers, as originalism does, nor to the very abstract principles to which the moral reading attends, but to something at an intermediate level of abstraction. Judge Bork suggested, for example, in explaining why *Brown* was right after all, that the framers of the equal protection clause embraced a principle general enough to condemn racial school segregation in spite of what the framers themselves thought, but not so general that it would protect homosexuals. But there is no nonarbitrary way of selecting any particular level of abstraction at which a constitutional principle can be framed except the level at which the text states it. Why, for example, should we choose, as the intermediate principle, one that forbids any discrimination between races rather than one that permits affirmative action in favor of a formerly disadvantaged group? Or vice versa?

12. *Buckley v. Valeo,* 424 U.S. 1 (1976). Later in this essay, I argue that democratic self-government can be achieved only through a political process that is deliberative in a way that allowing unlimited expenditure in political campaigns, particularly for political advertising on television, subverts. In another article, I argue that the *Buckley* decision

should therefore be reconsidered, as inconsistent with the best understanding of what American democracy is. See "The Curse of American Politics," *New York Review of Books,* October 17, 1996.

13. See, e.g., Jürgen Habermas, "Reconciliation through the Public Use of Reason: Remarks on John Rawls' Political Liberalism," *Journal of Philosophy,* 92 (March 1995), 109.

14. John Kenneth Galbraith, *The Age of Uncertainty* (Boston: Houghton Mifflin, 1977), 330.

15. Learned Hand, *The Bill of Rights* (Cambridge, Mass.: Harvard University Press, 1958), 73.

16. See *Law's Empire,* and "Equality, Democracy, and Constitution: We the People in Court," *Alberta Law Review,* 28 (1990), 324.

17. See Robert Putnam, *Making Democracy Work: Civic Traditions in Modern Italy* (Princeton: Princeton University Press, 1993).

18. The argument of the next few paragraphs is a summary of a longer argument in my article: "Equality, Democracy, and Constitution: We the People in Court."

19. See my article "What Is Equality? Part 3: The Place of Liberty." *Iowa Law Review,* 73 (1987), 1–54.

20. See my article "Liberal Community," *California Law Review,* 77 (1990), 479.

21. See Dworkin, *Law's Empire,* chap. 6.

22. See *Texas v. Johnson.*

23. See Lawrence G. Sager, "Fair Measure: The Legal Status of Underenforced Constitutional Norms," *Harvard Law Review,* 91 (1978), 1212, and Christopher L. Eisgruber and Lawrence G. Sager; "Why the Religious Freedom Restoration Act Is Unconstitutional," *NYU Law Review,* 69 (1994), 437.

Chapter 7 Constitutionalism, Democracy, and State Decay

Stephen Holmes

The hazy mirror with which philosophy reflects its times has cracked under the impact of the collapse of communism and the end of the Cold War. Basic concepts and norms, models and paradigms, anxieties and aspirations, have had to be and are being fundamentally challenged in light of the dizzying and unforeseen events of the past decade. As a Polish journalist recently remarked, in 1989 most of us thought that good had conquered evil (that we had achieved a liberal revolution). What we have instead is a return to Chicago in the 1920s.

The intellectual and moral shock of this sort of turnabout has still not been fully absorbed, over there or over here. Nonetheless, a significant transformation of ideas and values has occurred. Previously idealized social patterns, such as markets and community, are gradually acquiring new and not entirely positive reputations. Both instrumental-monetized exchange and emotional-moral solidarity, both border-crossing arms smuggling and border-smashing tribalisms, now rouse new worries in the public mind. The fire sale of the Soviet military inventory, not to mention the unregulated market in ground-to-air missiles, it is fair to say, cause as much apprehension as Bosnia-style subgroup loyalty gone insane.

So what are the main lessons that transitology, in its current form, can teach political theorists? What do we learn when a system of power crumbles, and a state of nature with highly educated and understandably apprehensive inhabitants emerges, right before our eyes? More concretely, what can constitutional and democratic theorists learn from the unthinkable collapse of state institutions, especially in Russia, but also throughout the postcommunist world? What will the study of criminalization and tribalization, kleptocracy and territorial unraveling, do to our basic categories and questions?

It is still too soon to answer this question in a confident manner. But a number of conceptual reorientations or subtle shifts of emphasis in both constitutional and democratic theory can already be perceived.

CONSTITUTIONALISM AND ANARCHY

First, the common assumption that the basic fundamental function of any liberal constitution is to *prevent tyranny,* fueled by the political struggle first against Hitler and then against Stalin and his successors, is bound to fade into the background when the most dire and pressing social problems are caused by state decay. The totalitarian state has vanished from the horizon, but basic rights are not yet firmly in place. Indeed, as the above-cited Polish journalist suggested, the aftermath of communism's fall may resemble anarchy more than freedom. In Russia especially, the central authority's capacity to tax and to conscript and to feed the military is increasingly doubtful. Demoralized or corrupt police cannot enforce bans on carrying guns. The state has lost its Weberian monopoly on violence. A minimally effective Weberian bureaucracy has hardly begun to be built. After having suffered under decades of Communist Party autocracy, decent people at first had a difficult time switching gears and focusing on a very different threat, on the catastrophic consequences of state collapse. But in both Russia and Eastern Europe this fundamental shift of emphasis has long since occurred.

And it has also begun to occur in the West as well, for the important reason that state decay in the territory of the former USSR cannot be contained in its consequences, but will also profoundly affect most of the world. For one thing, it has made the Russian government into an unreliable diplomatic partner, able to sign treaties and exchange fountain pens but unable, not just unwilling, to keep its word. For another, it has also thrown into question both civilian control of the armed forces and the military's own internal chain of command. But crippled state capacities are dangerous for other reasons as well. An infirm and incompetent state that cannot monitor its food providers for cholera, for instance, that cannot keep track of its stockpiles of anthrax and plutonium, that cannot react promptly to another Chernobyl, that cannot control its increasingly porous borders—presents a global threat to security, and one which obviously cannot be handled by traditional methods of balancing or deterrence.

(To reinforce the point that the dangers and opportunities of postcommunism are seldom what they first seem, let me parenthetically note that state decay has ambiguous political effects. For instance, if the Russian-Ukrainian border were a *real* territorial frontier, instead of a blurry zone separating quasi states, with quasi currencies and quasi armies, tensions in the region would be much worse. Similarly, when Hitler seized power, he was able to take over a well-functioning and obedient state bureaucracy, while if eccentric nationalist and Duma member Vladimir Zhirinovsky somehow captured the Kremlin he would not necessarily control the other side of the street, which implies that territorial unraveling makes a reversion to authoritarianism unlikely anytime soon. Finally, if Kiev could effectively enforce its discriminatory language law privileging Ukrainophones, the backlash among Russophones would be much more resentful than it is. In other words, the practical tolerance of Ukraine's language policy represents a kind of "liberalism from weakness." In other words, some postcommunist countries may have institutionalized a civic-territorial rather than ethnic definition of citizenship by default.)

Despite such intriguing ambiguities, we can expect that the shocking experience of state decay and its aftermath will bring political theory (first in the postcommunist East, then in the West) back to an appreciation of the double function of constitutionalism, stressed by Kant and Madison, among others, but temporarily eclipsed by the twin totalitarian experiences of the twentieth century. A constitution must simultaneously prevent tyranny *and anarchy*. It must allow the government to rule the ruled, but without allowing it to abuse its power. Of course, the prevention of anarchy has not been entirely neglected in Western constitutional theory, as should be obvious from the French stress on *securité juridique* and the German principle of *Vertrauensschutz,* or the protection of legitimate expectations. But it has not been in the forefront of constitutional theory, as it is now likely to become, as the implications of state weakness after communism become more visible and more alarming.

Not only will negative constitutionalism, the theory that liberal-democratic constitutions are primarily designed to prevent tyranny, be supplemented by positive constitutionalism, or a stress on the power-creating and power-channeling functions of constitutional law. This predictable shift of attention will also inevitably cause us to rethink basic philosophical questions, such as the source of the binding authority of the constitution itself.

From a contemporary Russian perspective, a well-functioning constitution (minimally) must contain rules designed to settle conflicts without violence and to select leaders to make collectively binding decisions. Russia has a paper constitution, but its capacity to regulate the political game is questionable at best. Failure at institutionalizing fully the current Russian constitution, ratified in December 1993, is reflected in continued public uncertainty that President Boris Yeltsin's successor, if the incumbent were to die in office, would be chosen according to the written rules of succession. In any case, inhabitants of a weak and decaying state naturally look to their constitution as a source of stability in a hyperfluid situation. Why else did Russians, between 1991 and 1993, pour such energies into a mere "piece of paper"? And they had a point, however utopian their aspirations. A constitution does not merely, or even primarily, protect rights, however desirable that may be. More urgently, it organizes decision-making and establishes a clear system of political roles. If the main purpose of constitutionalism were to curb state power, constitutions would be practically redundant in most of the postcommunist world of weak states. The reason why interest in constitution-making in postcommunist societies was so unexpectedly intense in the beginning of the 1990s is that constitution-making is a form or aspect of *state-building,* and the most serious problem facing postcommunist societies is the construction or reconstruction of a reliable system of rules and roles for settling disputes without violence, inhibiting the wholesale embezzlement of state assets, and solving collective problems in an intelligent and publicly acceptable way.

WEAK-STATE PLURALISM

Another category currently being rethought is pluralism. Under postcommunism, as J. F. Brown has remarked, the open society has turned into an open sewer. Wild West lawlessness, brigands and gangsters, clan-based and nationality-based mafias, fanatical religious cults and nationalist paramilitary groups represent a distinctly illiberal form of unregulated pluralism. A civil society, by contrast, is characterized by *nonpredatory relations among strangers.* With this definition in mind, we can say that the new Russian pattern of weak-state pluralism represents the triumph of "uncivil society." It is populated by shady characters who benefit handsomely from unclear rules (when rules are unclear, bribes must flow), and who therefore have a strong vested interest in the postponement of a constitutional settlement. Instead of voluntary organizations that press their interests on the government, competitively and according to publicly known rules, we have secretive organizations that buy and extort privileges from underpaid or unpaid public employees. The corrupt state is therefore the counterpart to the uncivil society. The massive involvement of officials in embezzlement and smuggling is only natural, of course, when the state is insolvent and "the private sector" can easily disgorge suitcases full of hard currency. (All this suggests that postcommunism, with its pathological symbiosis of the new "mafiosi" and the old apparat, should force us to a better conceptualization of the mutually reinforcing state/society relations characteristic of liberal regimes. A preliminary thought, which obviously needs elaboration, is that when the state, the only available social institution that can systematically defend the interests of the weak, is "privatized"—when it becomes wholly, rather than merely partially, a tool of the strong—liberal state/society relations cannot emerge.)

THE RESOURCE-DEPENDENCY OF RIGHTS

Another unmistakable lesson of postcommunism is the degree to which rights protection depends on state capacities. Statelessness means rightlessness. People without states, such as Vietnamese or Caribbean boat people, or those who live in societies where state authority has collapsed or gone into steep decline, have few or no effective rights. The legal codification of rights has little meaning when political authorities lack enforcement powers. As a consequence, a constitution that does not organize effective government will wholly fail to protect rights. This has been a lesson long in learning for some human rights advocates who have devoted their careers to a militant campaign against the overmighty state. Rights, quite obviously, are an enforced uniformity. Equality before the law cannot be secured over a vast territory without an effective, centralized bureaucratic organization. For rights to exist in practice we do not need a terrorist, land-grabbing police-state, but we do need some kind of state (a liberal state).

Rights cannot be trumps because they depend essentially on scarce resources, extracted from society by state authorities and strategically applied where most needed. The resource-dependency of a liberal rights regime becomes undeniably clear when we inspect the weakness of rights enforcement in a resource-strapped state. Even negative rights will not be protected in an insolvent country, as is shown by the case of a Polish criminal court that was sued for failing to pay its rent. Less frivolously, we can all imagine how well protected rights are likely to be in a society where local police departments are fundamentally unmonitored from above, as in Russia today. (The procuracy, which once fulfilled this function under party supervision, is no longer doing its job.) This case shows that rights protection is a problem of complex institutional design and resource allocation, not merely building judicially tended "limits" around the government and its agents. To create an institutionally independent subunit within each local police department that is immune to bribes and threats and responsible for monitoring the illegal and corrupt behavior of fellow policemen is no easy matter, and it cannot be achieved without the coercive extraction and intelligent reallocation of considerable resources, neither of which, unfortunately, are likely to occur in Russia today.

Two more examples can be cited. Rights will not be protected if, to take a hypothetical case, German firms were to truck dangerous industrial waste into Poland and bury it there by night without either the German or Polish governments knowing that it happened. Here again, state weakness (in this case, state ignorance or blindness) makes rights enforcement impossible. One of the main lessons political theorists can learn from the postcommunist experience, in fact, is the tenuousness of the distinction, common in Western discussion, between welfare rights and classical liberal rights. The distinction seems commonsensical in the West largely because our societies are so fabulously wealthy and the earmarking of social resources for the guarantee of negative rights is politically uncontested. In resource-poor societies with ambitions to imitate the West, the distinction between welfare rights and classical liberal rights seems much less obvious. Both types of rights depend on scarce resources, first of all. For instance, constitutional guarantees of "good health" are derisory when the state cannot afford to clean up the water and air, or when public hospitals have no gasoline for their ambulances (as once happened, for instance, in Vilnius), and where the best doctors leave the country to practice their profession abroad under minimally decent conditions. But the right to litigate (a classical liberal right, not a welfare right), is similarly degraded by a lack of resources. Take the case of liability for medical malpractice. Laws on the books in postcommunist societies—Hungary is an example—make it possible to sue doctors for compensatory damages. But these laws are next to useless where judicial dockets are impossibly crowded, where there is no service for reliably hand-delivering written judgments (normal overworked postal carriers are given the job), where hospitals cannot even buy antibiotics much less pay compensation, where there is no insurance system ready and able to pay. Injured patients win court cases but cannot recover. In this way, they learn to despise the worthless currency of liberal rights.

A final way in which rights enforcement hinges upon administrative competence and the artful allocation of scarce social resources should be mentioned here. The problem of criminality, especially gang warfare and extortion by threats of violence, is chronic everywhere in the postcommunist world. And it is clear that, psychologically, citizens lose interest in legal restrictions on the discretion of lethally armed policemen in crime-intensive environments. To put this in bookish but pertinent terms, the Hobbesian problem has to be solved before the Lockean solution looks attractive. If citizens will tolerate police brutality as long as the crime rate is high, then a full-fledged rights regime will emerge only in those societies where the crime rate (that is, the ordinary citizen's fear of bodily harm) is kept below a certain level. Or, to formulate the same point another way, rampant criminality is one of the central obstacles to the rise of rights consciousness in postcommunist societies. It is additionally dangerous because skillful demagogues can use popular frustration with anarchical conditions to mobilize political support in the streets. Here again, rights are a matter of institutional architecture and resource allocation. In postcommunist societies, especially given the lack of historical traditions, rights consciousness will never emerge unless the police achieve a minimal level of effective control. And this is a question of scarce social resources effectively applied.

LIBERALISM AND PUBLIC GOODS

A stateless society is not a civil society, as gangland killings make clear. One reason why both unregulated markets and blood communities have recently fallen under a cloud is that both have dangerously uncivil consequences when released from ameliorating forms of political and social restraint. But the contribution of state power to civil society is not exhausted by rights protection, law enforcement, and social discipline. Civil society cannot exist unless a liberal state can extract social resources and use them, under democratic scrutiny, to supply other essential public goods (besides safety at home and on the streets). In the Russian case, for instance, the state must rebuild the nation's infrastructure (its educational, medical, judicial, and transportation systems) and repair or mitigate the country's ecological catastrophe. Among the other public goods that the liberal state must provide to make liberal pluralism, as distinct from illiberal pluralism, possible are the following: a system of titles and deeds, a clear and enforceable condominium law (so that someone fixes the elevators), and confidence that contracts will be enforced and that violations of patent law and trespass law will be punished.

Civil society also presupposes a relatively consistent government that does not alter tax, banking, customs, and investment regulations like a drunken sailor. If consistency is a form of state strength, then liberal pluralism requires a strong state. The state also has to have stature and authority if it is going to broker ongoing agreements between labor and capital with the aim of preventing a destabilizing wage-price spiral. In this context, we can define one aspect of state strength in the following way. While a weak government takes demands sequentially and caves into pressures for subsidies until the cash register is empty, a strong government gathers all demands, figures out which are the most important, and delivers a package to satisfy, at least in part, the most powerful supplicants. In line with this model, it takes a strong state to produce the public good most hotly debated everywhere in the postcommunist world, that is, stable currency. Only a state that is strong in this sense can resist the temptation to print money to fulfill its incontinent promises.

A SIMPLE SOLUTION TO THE PARADOX
OF SELF-BINDING

The December 1993 ratification of the current Russian constitution was the result of a massive falsification of votes. In reality, too few people voted to reach the 50 percent threshold legally required. But when this problem was revealed by a Yeltsin-appointed committee, the general reaction in Moscow was indifference. One might attribute this attitude to a low level of "constitutional culture," but it can be interpreted in another way. Given the extent of Russian society's problems, the pedigree of the new constitution is a trivial detail. *What makes a constitution legitimate is not its source but its consequences.* Postcommunist constitution-making will drive this lesson home. A democratic constitution will be legitimate, will be publicly accepted and survive, if it makes decent and effective government possible. If it does not do this, it will not be legitimate, no matter how impeccable its ratification. Constitutional theorists who have secularized the timeless will of God into the ex ante will of the people and rooted the legitimacy of the constitution in the initial consent of a ratifying public have misunderstood the logic of democracy. For democratic voting is inevitably retrospective, in constitutional politics as in normal politics. The constitution is ratified not in a prior ceremonial plebiscite, but by being voluntarily used, over time, to organize successfully public deliberation and decision-making.

According to a Russian proverb, "the law is like the tongue of a wagon, it will go which ever way you turn it." Those who cite this proverb usually mean to lament the low level of respect for law in Russian history and the tendency to see law as a mere tool. They often go on to attribute the fast and loose attitude of Russian politicians toward their own constitution to this same inherent anarchism in the Russian soul.

There may be some merit to this stress on inherited psychological habits, but I prefer a different explanation for casualness with which constitutions are sometimes treated under postcommunist conditions. First, when societies are in tremendous flux, it is very unlikely that bargains struck one day will seem reasonable the next. Institutional rigidity in times of rapid change will produce unpredictability, not predictability, as Juan Linz has explained, because social pressures will force political actors to abandon an obsolete framework entirely. And anyway, how can we respect a bargain made yesterday when we know that it was designed to trick our political opponents who, it so happens, have now utterly vanished from the scene? More generally, it is very difficult to formulate a clear rule for settling conflicts among important groups when groups are dissolving and reforming kaleidoscopically every few months.

But my main point is that what determines a people's willingness to live under a constitutional order is not their advanced or retrograde cultural level, but the practical consequences of the constitution. Indeed, an instrumental attitude toward constitutional law is the right attitude. Constitutions are tools, instruments of government. That, by and large, is the postcommunist view, and it is correct. The problem occurs only when political rivals each try to use the constitution as a weapon to destroy one another. If all major political actors see themselves as being in the same boat, and having common problems to resolve (and the conditions for this collective self-perception need to be discussed) then an instrumental attitude toward constitutional law will be a stabilizing factor.

Unlike lower-order law, which is binding because enforced from above, constitutional law, in a democratic state, is a law that the people imposes on itself. This intellectual construction raises the paradox of self-binding. How is democratic constitutionalism possible, if the power to bind includes the power to loose? The way to solve this paradox is to dissolve it. Groups and individuals will submit themselves voluntarily to enforceable restrictions if they perceive these restrictions as possibility-creating. If the game seems worth playing, people will voluntarily abide by the rules. A democratic public will accept a constitutional order, judicially enforced, not because of ancestor worship but because this system produces tolerably good government.

Prohibitions on political censorship, for example, are meant to improve the government's capacity to adapt, innovate, and learn, to confront important

problems before they get out of hand and to question the way public issues have
been framed in the past. A democratic constitution is an enabling rather than
disabling device. It strives to organize government in such a way as to improve
the thoughtfulness and fact-mindedness of public deliberation. Take freedom
of speech and freedom of the press. A democratic people will accept rigid restrictions on majority discretion (for instance, the majority can never prevent
its decisions from being publicly criticized) not because this rule comes from
heaven or tradition, but because it is the best means yet discovered for improving the quality of collective decisions, for avoiding stupid choices that everyone
will live to regret, and for bringing out the excellence of democracy. A secular
people does not want the bare right to decide. It also wants to make good decisions. Therefore, it will "bind itself" (not merely its representatives) to a free-
speech regime because it knows that such a system can help transform the un-
enlightened into the enlightened will of the people. Note also that a liberal
constitution will also be accepted if it gives important social groups and actors
a reasonable voice in the decision-making process, for procedural fairness
enhances the likelihood that losers will comply voluntarily with government
decisions.

One important disadvantage of theories that locate the legitimacy of the constitution in its source rather than in its consequences lies in their effect on the
self-understanding of constitutional courts. Given the enormous practical problems faced by postcommunist societies, some of which can be solved only by energetic political action, it will be unfortunate if constitutional courts refuse to
identify with the goals of the political branches—to solve society's problems—
and see themselves as a breed apart, custodians of higher values which executives
and legislatures fail to appreciate or understand. To put the relationship between
unelected courts and elected parliaments in a proper perspective, it helps to notice that the "rights" that courts defend, far from having been inscribed unam-
biguously and unalterably in constitutional stone, are always elaborated and re-
shaped by a long and unending political process in which parliaments play a
central role.

TERRITORIALITY AND MEMBERSHIP

The postcommunist era has also raised the question of politically sustainable
borders, a subject almost never discussed in Western democratic theory, but no
less crucial for that. The norms of minority rule and equality before the law, obviously enough, can come into force only after territorial borders have been laid

down and an answer has been given to the question of who is a member of the community. And while these norms depend on a prior definition of membership and territoriality, they can do nothing to justify the latter. Democracy and legal equality are dependent on conditions they cannot create (which is one reason they are so fragile and historically rare). The empty-handedness or empty-headedness of classical liberalism in this domain is nicely revealed by the paradoxical assertion that borders are meaningless, from a humanistic point of view, and therefore should be treated as inviolable. A universalistic ideology cannot deal comfortably or frankly with the need for exclusivity characteristic of every liberal state.

Postfascist constitution-making was much easier than postcommunist constitution-making because, to take the West German case, questions of borders and membership were decided by the victorious powers and did not have to be worked out politically. When problems of such magnitude are placed on the public agenda, liberal democracy has a major problem of self-presentation. For there are no just borders, and border disputes cannot be resolved democratically. The need to settle the border question, therefore, brings home to everyone the limited capacities of the democratic and rule-of-law formulas for the solution of public problems.

Along similar lines, one of the most disturbing lessons of the transition has been this: the way justice is defined depends on who holds effective political power. Why has private property, considered "unjust" under the communists, suddenly become "just" under the new regime? The simplest and most obvious answer is that power has changed hands. Similarly, the current allocation of property rights in Bohemia is widely acknowledged to be a product of brute force and ethnic cleansing, not of the voluntary transfer of legal title. And nomenklatura privatization ensures that property rights are associated by most people not with elementary justice but with the shady deals of scoundrels and crooks. (The subordination of rights to power also comes across quite clearly, although inadvertently, in the expressionless reaction met by Estonian visitors to Washington who naively explain that the only just solution in their country is for the original settlers to take back all the land.)

We cannot expect American understandings of basic rights to be transferred easily to a society where private holdings are so conspicuously unjust. A rights-based regime is morally implausible in such a setting. Private property can be justified in postcommunist societies only by its consequences, by the advances in social productivity that accrue to all or most citizens. The legitimacy of the system cannot rest on a sense of unquestioning awe before the sacred institution of private property, but only on the conviction, spread to the public through political discussions, that private property has social benefits, even for the weakest members of society. So, in postcommunist conditions, democratic discussion is a necessary condition for the institutionalization of private rights,

Finally, as Charles Tilly and others have shown, the traditional European method for state-building has been war-making. But it is obviously crucial for the development of liberal democracy in postcommunist societies that states are built without war. How this magical trick can occur is yet unclear. But constitutions, laying down mutually beneficial rules of the game, should surely play a central role. In any case, a relatively benign international environment, the absence of great predator empires on the march, and the fact that current borders, however weakly legitimate, are no longer perceived as wounds, gives the states of Eastern Europe, at least, more time than they have ever had to develop the basic institutions of sovereign power.

A NOTE ON COMMUNITY

In such a setting it would be natural for state-builders to rely on national or ethnic identification as a source of allegiance or willingness to obey. This possibility has attracted worldwide attention because nation-building, with its stress on ethnic homogeneity, is incompatible with the creation of multinational states. (And multinational states are the only alternative to ethnic cleansing in this demographically mingled part of the world.)

From this difficult process, as I said at the outset, political theorists should learn to re-evaluate the crucial concept of community and its relation to liberal ideals. Communitarians often present membership as a form of cultural and emotional richness unknown to advocates of free markets and the rule of law. But the conflict between state-building and nation-building in the postcommunist world has a different implication. It suggests that community is not always an enrichment, but rather sometimes an impoverishment. As Juan Linz, has argued, human beings are perfectly comfortable with multiple loyalties and memberships. They can be both Russophone and members of the Ukrainian state without suffering an identity crisis or any other psychological disorder. What communitarians (or nationalists) want, from this perspective, is not to have rich identity but, on the contrary, to kill all loyalties but one, or perhaps to subordinate all final loyalties to one superloyalty that drowns out the rest. This, at least, is what the experience of forced denationalizations suggests. *Intolerance for dual loyalty,* a common enough human sentiment, is the heart of the communitarian project, at least in its most extreme incarnation, and the ultimate basis of the communitarian animus against liberal political arrangements. Instead of eliminating the causes of social conflicts (by creating ethnic homogeneity), liberalism tries to cope with its effects (by creating mechanisms for public bargaining). There is nothing in this solution that dictates the liquidation of cultural identifications. As John Rawls has argued, citizens in a multi-ethnic state can share penultimate values (such as freedom of religion) even while they differ about ultimate values (specific religions or atheism). Or, to continue with my example, they can be Russians culturally and Ukrainians politically. Close observation of the painful choice between the civic-territorial and the ethnic definitions of citizenship, it seems to me, will lend support to the importance of Rawls's simple formulation of how liberal constitutions must handle conflicting loyalties within a single state.

PUBLIC DELIBERATION IN WEAKENED STATES

As the problems of anarchy and ungovernability grow, pressure for a Hobbesian or strong-arm solution will also mount. Because the machinery of enforcement is in shambles, any imposed "order" must have widespread popular support for compliance. In other words, public officials will have to present their actions, in a persuasive way, as serving the public interest. But policies that ostensibly serve "the public interest" are usually biased in a number of ways, delivering surplus benefits to a few who have an interest in making a skewed scheme seem neutral.

Put differently, in conditions of anarchy (but not only there) public officials will impose a special kind of "order," one that just happens to serve their own privatistic interests, while it is sold to the citizenry as a public good. Because this pattern is inevitable, the core institutions of constitutional democracy are not the judicially protected private rights of conscience and autonomy, but the politically sustained communication rights meant to foster publicity and public discussion. These rights, and the institutions they make possible are so essential because they create forums (such as parliament and a pluralistic and free press) where claims by public officials to be pursuing the public good can be thrown continuously into question. All power-wielders prefer to act in secret rather than in public, and if allowed to do so will invariably begin to use public resources for private purposes. Given the needs for governance in all postcommunist societies, it is wholly impractical, even dangerous, to throw insurmountable legal barriers in front of political authorities. The only feasible method for introducing into politics some modicum of self-restraint is not judicial monitoring (courts will be rolled over easily), but publicity. This is a reasonable option in postcommunist societies because, in the lands of glasnost, communication rights, unlike most other rights, have achieved a high degree of institutionalization in a very short time. This cannot be done cheaply, but it remains affordable even in resource-strapped states. Publicity, be it noted, is not a matter of hot air, but an enormously powerful force, capable, for instance, of driving tough guys to commit suicide. A newspaper is not "just a piece of paper," nor is a constitution that helps newspapers stay independent. The positive effect of jury trials on the behavior of public procurators in Russia corroborates the shaping power of publicity. Hence, in my view, all hopes for the evolution toward constitutional democracy in the region hinge upon the reinforcement of the now-functioning institutions of public monitoring and discussion. That courts have an important role to play here is beyond question.

This thesis is strengthened when we recall the extent to which many "rights" are, in fact, politically extracted concessions. Not merely voting rights, but other rights as well (such as the right to strike), have been won when previously unprotected groups were able to deliver plausible threats of noncooperation. This consideration suggests that the following question should be asked whenever constitutional rights are enforced: Does the enforcement of constitutional rights produce not just winners, but also losers who can tell publicly reputable stories about the wrong or harm done to them? (Think about abortion rights in the United States.) When losers can tell such tales, then justice bleeds into politics. Here is where the function of publicity becomes important once again. We can assume that judges will feel that rights enforcement is apolitically neutral in cases where the loser group is too weak to cause trouble or where the winner group has overwhelming public support. In other cases, only a liberal regime of uninhibited publicity will give losers, who could otherwise subvert the entire system, an ongoing chance to voice their grievances in a forum that will (perhaps) be more welcoming than a supposedly neutral judiciary.

DEMOCRACY IN THE STATE OF NATURE?

The majority of citizens will soon lose interest in influencing government decisions if they see that these decisions are announced on the evening news but never implemented or even noticed by the responsible officials. So democracy is useless, and will be viewed as such, in a stateless society. But it gains in importance as public institutions begin to take shape.

A minimal constitution, as I have defined it, lays down a publicly known set of rules to settle conflicts without violence. To be realistic, this formula refers exclusively to conflicts between *important* social actors. Members of society with nothing to offer and no ability to threaten—those who, for whatever reason, lack the organizational capacity effectively to pursue their interests—are excluded from the minimal constitutional pact. According to this model, democratization is the process of inclusion whereby out-groups gradually become in-groups, dealing themselves into the constitutional bargain, extracting concessions (rights) in exchange for their useful cooperation. As the process of democratization advances (I am simplifying for clarity), certain members of the inner circle try to enhance their relative bargaining position by using the democratic formula of elections. To gain votes, in turn, they grant concessions not just to powerful lobbies, but to broad swaths of the electorate. In this way the citizenry at large gains not a fair share but at least a small share of the public resources extracted (from them) by the state.

This way of thinking about democratization is not entirely satisfactory, but under the special conditions in postcommunist societies it has an important advantage. If we introduce a concept of democracy of which there has never been a known example, there is probably something wrong with our concept. And if we hold up an image of democracy such that it is wholly unreachable given the scarce resources (including time and human capital) in a society, we will produce bitterness, not a willingness to work for some modest progress. With this in mind, I propose that we define constitutional democracy, in its initial postcommunist phase (which is, unfortunately, all that Russia can hope for at the moment), as a system of *moderated kleptocracy.* What postcommunist elites must learn is that they can steal from the public coffers for a *longer* period of time if they steal less in the short run. This sounds simple, but is harder than it seems, for time horizons tend to be severely curtailed in times of rapid and unpredictable social change. Put somewhat less cynically, democratization proceeds when self-enriching officials and privatistically oriented elites come to see the advantage to be gained if the citizenry at large is provided with some of (its own) public resources, instead of being left to freeze and starve.

THE CENTRALITY OF PARLIAMENT

The core institution of liberal democracy is not the constitutional court but the parliament. The study of administratively weak and chronically impecunious states makes this clear. The most difficult problem facing postcommunist societies is the creation of a government that can pursue effective reforms while re-

taining public confidence and remaining democratically accountable. For a variety of reasons, only a government that emerges from a parliamentary system can manage to combine legitimacy with effectiveness, representativeness with governability, public acceptance with successful strategies of economic reform. When resources are scarce, all policy decisions produce resentful losers whose cooperation is nevertheless needed if the policy is to be successfully implemented. A parliamentary system that gives a small voice to many parties and which allows losers to air their grievances and keep their plight before the public eye is an essentially legitimating device, one of the few available under conditions of public penury. (Resiliency, adaptability, and the capacity to innovate are also more likely to be found, for a variety of reasons, in an executive power that emerges from a parliamentary system.)

A well-run and highly visible legislative branch has a special role to play in societies where reformist governments are imposing unprecedented burdens on the population. Not only are citizens of postcommunist states being forced to accept great deprivations in standards of living, safety in the streets, and ideological certainty. They are also being compelled to conform their behavior to new and complicated rules of capitalist and competitive behavior that are hard for ordinary people to understand and follow. In communicating to a confused public, parliaments have an essential function to fulfill. Every reformist government needs a good deal of public cooperation, not merely public acquiescence (which could satisfy the czars and their communist successors). Parliament can help secure this cooperation or, to use Samuel Beer's phrase, it can "mobilize consent," especially between elections. Or, less ambitiously, the heat and light of parliamentary debate can be used to communicate the government's decisions to the public (and lower-rank officials) by filtering them through a partisan battle, which will surely attract more attention than a bureaucrat's posted decree.

If a well-functioning parliament is so vital, for this reason and others, then the greatest threat or obstacle to political reform in postcommunist societies is not the purported lack of a constitutional culture or ingrained contempt for rights, but rather *the spirit of antiparliamentarism*. As many surveys reveal, antiparliamentary feelings run deep throughout the region, and with good reason. Most members of Parliament are amateurs and opportunists. Unseemly scandals are continually coming to light. Absenteeism is rife and the entire nation can inspect the vacant rows on television. The original "forum" parties have hopelessly splintered, and lack of party discipline sometimes reaches clownish proportions. And, of course, parliamentary governments have had a very difficult time "delivering

the goods," producing economic prosperity while alleviating economic insecurity, providing capitalist wages together with socialist benefits.

In such a setting, it is crucial that constitutional courts do not try shortsightedly to aggrandize themselves by diminishing the status of the parliament in the public eye. Constitutional court justices should not, on the one hand, identify the basic social problem as "the tyranny of the majority" embodied in the legislative branch. And they should not, on the other hand, present themselves as the only true guardians of the interests of the people, for to overlegitimate the court in this way is, implicitly, to discredit the nascent idea of representation through periodic elections. The self-inflation of constitutional courts implies (as does a heavy reliance on popular referenda) that the voice of the people is not adequately expressed through the representative process. There is surely more than a grain of truth in such an insinuation. But constitutional courts, which will not survive if the systems in which they are embedded go down, should conceive of legislative development as one of their principal aims. The choice is not between crude Sejmocracy and the enlightened rule of law (administered by prestigious judges) but between politically sustainable parliamentarism and some combustible mixture of anarchy and tyranny. Judicial review is always selective, and judges learn on their own to select cases that will help them avoid making powerful enemies and preserve their own precious powers. But they should perhaps be nudged to use their discretion to minimize damaging the already weakened prestige of embattled legislatures as well. They should therefore use their limited credibility primarily to help reinforce the communication rights which have already begun to take root and which are so central to the long-term development of democratic political life.

From a constitutional perspective, another important function of parliament is also worth stressing. The Great Transformation of 1989 in Eastern Europe and 1991 in Russia was accompanied by a degree of public euphoria, but it was not instigated by mass mobilization, not even in Poland. It is impossible to say that the population at large *chose* the new political orders, or were psychologically prepared for the radicalness of the change. The consequence is that the basic choice of regime, and the constitution built upon it, must still be explained to the public. Only through a political process dominated by actors who know how to speak to ordinary citizens (as judges seldom do) can a revolution that dropped from the sky gain the kind of public acceptance it needs to endure.

Finally, parliamentary representation, if it is effective, preempts the emergence of nonparliamentary leaders who can build public support on the basis of nondemocratic and unelectoral forms of legitimacy. If citizens do not feel rep-

resented in parliament, they will eventually begin to shop around for other leaders to represent them. If public frustrations are not handled within the political
system, they will be handled outside. If "society" does not express itself in elections and the press, through labor unions, interest groups, and lobbies, it may
eventually resort to the streets. Extraparliamentary leaders, while unelected, can
gain support by making appeals to national pride, ethnic superiority, Christian
values, personal charisma, and so forth. Liberal "performance legitimacy" can
be formulated as follows: you obey us because, after having elected us, we help
you identify and solve your collective problems, provide public goods (clean
streets), improve public well-being, settle conflicts without violence, and introduce a small measure of fairness in the allocation of public resources. These goals
are very hard to achieve under present circumstances, which is why postcommunist societies may be vulnerable to the illiberal legitimacy formula: obey us
because we avenge historical wrongs, purge the alien element, and restore damaged national pride. (All leaders, elected or unelected, liberal or illiberal, promise
to protect citizens against "danger." Here is another reason for the centrality of
publicity to liberal politics, for only a regime of free-wheeling discussion can
provide the standing forums where the perhaps self-serving definition of "danger" offered by political leaders can be successfully queried and challenged.)

A CAUTIONARY REMARK ABOUT
MINORITY RIGHTS

Unfortunately, the centrality of parliament cannot be guaranteed by a well-
designed separation of powers and a self-effacing court alone. For parliament to
connect society and government, legitimacy and effectiveness, political parties
must exist. Parties are the vehicles through which society talks to public authorities, the organized channels without which representation and accountability are impossible. (Recall Adam Przeworski's definition of democracy: "a
system in which parties lose elections.") So far, however, political parties are a
largely missing element in postcommunist democratization. Societies in the region are just as weak as the states, which is why we see no signs of the classical
Huntingtonian problem, weak states being overtaxed by clamorous social demands. One reason postcommunist societies have been so docile or quiescent is
that they are not just demoralized, but also incredibly disorganized and shape-
less, even pulverized. Group identifications (apart from ethnic minorities and
criminal syndicates) are weak on all levels, which is why political strains associated with strong social heterogeneity have not yet emerged. There are rich and

poor, but the system of social stratification has not yet begun to gel. Hence, despite desperate conditions, there has been no labor unrest to speak of. Hence, the political battles between elites (such as the battle between Yeltsin and the former Supreme Soviet) have had no obvious relation to deeper social cleavages or conflicts. This pulverized condition makes the formation of strong political parties unlikely any time soon. An amorphous society, after all, is almost impossible to represent. Ongoing social chance is part of the problem. In the flux of the present, people are not sure where they will be in six months. It is very difficult, therefore, for them to band together with others to pursue their common interests. (For with whom do they have common interests?) It is no surprise then that Russian "political parties" are located exclusively in Moscow and St. Petersburg.

So my entire argument about the priority of parliaments over courts, of representation over rights, hinges upon the eventual development of a viable party system in postcommunist societies. This is undeniably an enormous problem with no obvious solution. But the same conditions which render party-formation difficult also give these countries and their leaders some breathing room. Panic would be out of place, so far, precisely because Stalinism and its aftermath created low-mobilization, dysphoric, heads-down societies. State weakness has let loose rats and wasps, but it has not (so far) unleashed social furies because of a palpable social numbness or lethargy. Citizens in postcommunist societies, speaking generally (the Yugoslav exception remaining to be explained), are difficult to galvanize for any cause, good or bad. And they suffer from massive dis-identification, which infuriates nationalists such as Solzhenitsyn.

This leads me to a final cautionary remark directed to the ardent and well-meaning seekers of rights, rights, and ever more rights. As Amos Twersky has shown, the unavailability of high-visibility culprits subsidizes patience with frustrating and onerous circumstances. People will peacefully put up with a lot if they can find no one to blame. (Perhaps we can call this "false necessity.") The Yugoslav tragedy was due, in part, to the ready availability to all parties of a blameworthy "other" on whom aggressions could be conveniently unleashed.

From this perspective, an amorphous society in which the sense of subgroup membership is low has an obvious advantage in times of trouble. Pulverization and lack of group identity make it difficult to pick out guilty parties whom one might blame for humiliating woes. (This is an alternative to Hannah Arendt's argument that social atomization produced fascism; on the contrary, atomism makes fascism unlikely, at least to the extent that fascism thrives on a shared mental picture of tightly knit and hideously guilty social groups.)

I introduce these admittedly overly general considerations only to make a concluding point about "minority rights." In resource-strapped societies, it is not necessarily wise to use the courts to enforce the rights of ethnic minorities. (I leave aside the moral problem that minority rights often grant unfair privileges to the self-appointed spokesmen and leaders of any minority group that is not organized in a democratic manner.) Militant advocates of minority rights may well suffer from the dangerous illusion that rights are apolitical, that is, that rights enforcement produces no loser groups capable of making trouble. But, as even a casual inspection of the postcommunist landscape reveals, this assumption is unsound. If a weakly legitimate quasi-democratic state extracts resources from a penurious society and (to please international monitors) loudly advertises its decision to spend a disproportionate amount of these resources on an ethnic minority, it risks producing an unpleasant backlash. Rights are expensive, and the allocation of public resources is a very ticklish issue in poor states with high literacy rates and well-developed systems of mass communication. The judicial enforcement of minority rights, under such conditions, may do something in the short run for the minority in question, but it will also dangerously raise the visibility of this minority in the envy-struck public eye. According to Twerskian logic, therefore, it may highlight an all-too-convenient scapegoat for the venting of public frustrations. If this is true, judicial sensitivity to minority rights may not necessarily be in the long-run interest of minorities. A judiciary system focused exclusively on individual rights might perform a more useful service, even for minorities. The question is enormously complicated, of course, but, ultimately the rights of minorities can be protected only if the political system manages to solve the most pressing social problems, including the reduction of social frustrations through economic growth. In the meantime, it is up to democratic leaders, in the arduous process of building party organizations from scratch and mobilizing political support, to convince their followers of the virtues of coexistence and self restraint. Judges, whose capacity to speak to common citizens, as I said, should not be exaggerated, can engrave minority rights on tablets of stone, but only parliamentary leaders can bring these rights to life.

Chapter 8 Constitutionalism and Democracy

Alberto Calsamiglia

Constitutions must prevent simultaneously tyranny and anarchy. In his contribution to this volume, Stephen Holmes focuses on the problem of the decay of the state from the point of view of the stability of the state. He claims that a society must address the Hobbesian problem before the Lockean solution looks attractive. I would like to suggest that the situation of anarchy or decay of the state is not always worse than the situation of tyranny under Hitler or Stalin. It can be argued that states are only legitimate if they provide stability and respect for human rights.

I assume that coordination of decision-making is a condition of legitimacy, but something else is needed. I strongly disagree with the assertion that we must first address Hobbes and establish any state structure and then turn to Locke for legitimacy. Stability can be ensured by dictatorship. Legitimacy can be achieved only if equality and basic needs are guaranteed to everybody. This is my universalistic claim.

When we speak about human rights, we have to study the major problems facing humanity: poverty, inequality, torture, and genocide. These problems exist everywhere, in both developing and developed countries alike. Some people assert that democratic systems have solved the main problem of legitimacy. They consider that postcommunist Eastern Europe can lead us to think about the decay of the state, but we can also examine the dynamics of state decay in well-established democracies. I will focus here on the problem of representation and human rights.

The year 1989 is an important one for democracy. Prior to 1989 democracy was challenged by communism, and nations were judged in the context of this bipolar conflict. There were two main political ideals: democratic and communist. The clash between these ideals created the Cold War. If we judge communism using the political standards of democracy, we will soon agree that democracy is a better system of government; democratic governments better provide and protect individual rights of the citizenry through the mechanisms of representation. After 1989, as Bruce Ackerman has pointed out, the framework has changed.[1] Democracy is no longer challenged by communism. The decline and destruction of the communist regimes has been spectacular, and there are few adherents today of communist ideals.

Since 1989, democracy has been challenged from within. If we begin to analyze the political ideals of democracy and the reality of democracy we will find many problems that remain to be solved. It can be argued that the path toward democracy has begun, but that it has not reached its main goals. Of course, many people were concerned about the fulfillment of democratic values prior to 1989, but the challenge came not only from the reality of their unfulfillment but also from the alternative values of communism.

THE PROBLEM OF REPRESENTATION

In modern theories of democracy, representation plays a secondary role in providing justification. The contramajoritarian principle has been accepted, and it has been used to create a system that prevents the tyranny of majorities.

Representation is a distinctive characteristic of democracy, and it has not been satisfactorily achieved in existing democracies. Marx claimed that popular sovereignty was a myth. He argued that Parliament was not the people in miniature, because not everyone was represented. He was correct, for in the nineteenth century people who could not read or write, people who could not pay taxes, and women did not have any political rights. Parliaments represented only the dominant class. Popular sovereignty was really male sovereignty, or bourgeois sovereignty, or both. The crux of Marx's criticism was that there was a difference between the people and their deputies in Parliament. Today, however, Marx's criticisms do not apply since democratic societies have evolved so that women, workers, people who cannot pay taxes, and people who cannot read have the right to vote and to be elected.

But the question still remains: is there a difference between the people and their representatives? In other words, are the mechanisms of representation that democracies have designed good enough to answer the most abstract and general of Marxist criticism? Is popular sovereignty the ultimate source of power and the foundation of legitimacy of the power of democracies? I think that the answer to these questions is no. First, if we look at the literature of contemporary political theory we see that one of its great achievements has been to design mechanisms to address the tyranny of the majority—popular sovereignty must be counterbalanced by other institutions that are not representative of the popular will.

Second, one of the most relevant sources of power today is information. Information allows people to make good choices. People who do not have access to information are discriminated in a way similar to those denied the vote a century ago. Without information, people choose irrationally. This is one reason that education is so important. If we analyze the information available to people when they vote, we can see that most of it has been manipulated by powerful people who design the agenda, define the issues, have full information, or have the money and power to create an efficient propaganda campaign.

Third, the people who are represented do not have the means to control the activities of their representatives. Edmund Burke's thesis that there is no possibility of an imperative mandate is accepted uncritically. In other words, the people cannot dismiss representatives who betray the ideas for which they voted. The relationship between the people and their representatives is very weak, and it is difficult to argue that real democracy is legitimated given the effect of this relationship on individual autonomy. The relationship between governed and governors is far from supporting the ideal of self-government according to which the governors are controlled by the governed. It is for this reason that coercion is justified in a democracy.

Fourth, elections take place in finite political divisions. The size and contours of these divisions can have many consequences in the role of representatives and the real value of the vote. It is possible to find in any democratic country that the vote of one person is worth more than the vote of another because electoral districts have different size populations but the same number of representatives. Problems are also raised by the timing of elections. This is a problem that history can explain but not justify. Dworkin's argument that there are practical problems, and that this rule of discrimination was not designed out of lack of respect, does not mean that in effect it does not lack respect for people.[2] And yet, Dworkin's argument—that there are practical problems in electoral systems which produce injustice—seems to recognize that there are people who are excluded. Dworkin suggests that this rule of discrimination must not be designed with lack of respect. But the discrimination exists. The fact that there are people without a voice affects the legitimacy of democracy. Defense of a dependent conception of democracy means that the best form of democracy is the one that produces substantial results and decisions that treat all members of the community with equal concern. Dworkin's theory seems sound only if there is a substantial value that justifies this restriction. History cannot justify the main value: equal concern.

Democracy continues to have problems with the mechanism of representation, and Marx's criticisms still require a better response than existing democratic political systems have been able to provide. One response is to rethink the relationship between democracy and representation. Representation is not the only source of democratic legitimacy. We misunderstand democracy if we equate it with representation. Representation is necessary, but not sufficient, for the achievement of democracy. Institutions are required to protect individual rights against the will of the majority, and those institutions cannot be controlled by that same majority. The introduction of such an institution presupposes a shortcoming of the system of legitimacy of democracy, and gives support to Plato's elitist theory arguing that the boat must be directed by the captain. If we accept this, then we must admit that the boat that is the state must be led by the elite that knows what is right and what is wrong. This argument suggests that there exist well-informed and clever people who can be the guardians of democracy and who define what is good and what is bad. Although this system might work very well, it is far from the central idea of democracy and from its central idea of self-government. Enlightened despotism is not a form of democracy. Perhaps the contramajoritarian principle can be reconstructed as a form of this enlightened despotism.

Another response is the development of a more substantial conception of democracy. Democracy is a system that not only translates individual preferences into collective preferences, but also creates a forum for discussion of the values that society accepts. We cannot separate the formal aspects of democracy—that is, representation and the majoritarian principle—from the core values of democracy. There are fundamental values that the mechanism of representation cannot change. The core values of democracy cannot be ignored if we want to design a mechanism of legitimacy for such a political system. The construction and reconstruction of these values is important for justifying democracy. Public dialogue is one of the elements that justifies it. The form of democracy, however, in this view is subordinated to the substantial value. This form of democracy has been called by Dworkin a dependent conception, in contrast to the detached conception of democracy, which is concerned only about the distribution of political power but not about results.

If we approach the problem this way, we can dismiss Marx's criticism by saying that Marx has questioned the legitimacy of democracy from the point of view of the mechanism of representation and not from the point of view of the substantial values that democracy claims. Of course, Marx identified substantial values of democracy of a different kind. Marx did not believe that pluralism, dialogue, and compromise could solve our main social problems. Democratic people think that through dialogue and the protection of rights, a social agreement can be constructed. Democracy avoids skepticism and violence.

To summarize, the conception of democracy that focuses on the mechanism of representation can be successfully challenged by Marx's observations of the problems of representation in practice. In addition, democracy is legitimated not merely through its formal mechanism, but also through the substantial values that it embodies.

INDIVIDUAL RIGHTS

If we agree that the system of legitimacy of democracy requires not only the formal mechanisms of representation, but also substantial values, then we need to develop a conception of individual rights and their protection.

Historically, individual rights have been conceptualized as natural rights. I do not like to speak in terms of natural rights because natural rights adherents argue that such rights cannot change with the passage of time. In fact, the main ideas of freedom and equality have dramatically changed in the last century. Individual rights are rights that can be conceptualized as universal: although they can change they are not dependent on the community to which an individual belongs. After 1989, and even during the 1970s, many argued that individual rights must be contextualized in communities. Postmodernism has suggested that an *opus artis* must be judged not by itself in an abstract and decontextualized way, but contextualized in its social and historical place. The consequence of this view for a theory of rights is that every community should define its own rights, and that the problem of individual rights should be contextualized for each community. This is the problem of nationalism. Nationalism rejects the historical universal nature of human rights and distinguishes between the citizen and the foreigner. Solidarity is a value only within the community. The foreigner does not belong to the community, and thus has no rights.

Marxism has sustained the value of universalism. Marx opposed the theory of natural rights because he thought they were formal, and that their application to different social classes resulted in injustices. Marx suggested that the language of rights be abolished because rights were not really universal. Marx was puzzled because he realized that by following formal rules injustice is possible, that justice is the primary goal of politics, and that justice is possible only if equality is guaranteed.

The claim of equality is the first claim of substantive democracy. The main external challenge to democracy now is fundamentalist nationalism, which rejects equality. This nationalism can be theocratic or it can derive from a poor conception of democracy that, because it does not use substantial values for its legitimation, is not concerned about the problems of the many people who do not have their basic needs met. The expanding circle of democracy means more social homogeneity and equality; it claims not only participatory ideals but also substantial ideals of equality and their application.

If we accept universalism in this way, it is extremely difficult to justify the establishment of strong immigration controls because everybody can claim certain basic rights. In fact, the end of communism has resulted in migrations of people who are not having their basic needs met. Opulent democratic countries cannot argue that they embody the ideals of democracy when they fail to meet the challenge of helping these people to meet their basic needs. Perhaps these migratory people are challenging the opulence of democratic countries, or perhaps the democratic republic has forgotten one of its valuable revolutionary aspects: universalism of the basic rights.

This claim may be criticized as utopian, but I cannot accept that the traditional method of state-building—that is, war-making—can justify decisions as to what belongs to the state and who has rights. The decay of the state is approaching the state of nature. It is extremely important to prevent anarchy as Holmes has pointed out; but the prevention of anarchy is not enough if legitimacy is our goal. We need to rethink our states if we want them to be legitimated. Without universal consideration and respect for new participants, there is no legitimacy.

NOTES

I am very grateful to Ronald C. Slye for editing and criticism and also to Victor Ferreres.

1. Bruce Ackerman, *The Future of Liberal Revolution* (New Haven: Yale University Press, 1992).

2. See, e.g., "What Is Equality? Part IV: Political Equality," *University of San Francisco Law Review* 22 (1987), 1; "Equality, Democracy, and Constitution: We the People in Court," *Alberta Law Review* 28 (1990), 324.

Chapter 9 Group Aspirations and Democratic Politics

Ian Shapiro

The question "Should groups have rights to self-determination?" is ill put. Proposed rights cannot be evaluated without reference to the contexts in which they are asserted or to the purposes for which they will be exercised. I believe a further constraint is also in order: that group-based aspirations be rendered compatible with democratic politics. Because this seems to be the most fundamental issue, I begin with it, turning second to questions of context and purpose, and concluding with some remarks on institutional redesign.

DEMOCRACY'S OBLIGATORY CONSTRAINT

In most countries of the modern world, democracy exhibits a non-optional character that other political ideals lack. In the United States, for instance, few would take seriously the proposition that the state may require people to be liberal or conservative, or religious or secular, but equally few would deny the proposition that they can be required to accept the results of appropriately functioning democratic procedures. We are thought free to despise the elected government, but not its right to *be* the government. Of course, different people understand different things by democracy, and every democratic order will be thought by some not to be functioning as it should, in the corrupt control of an illicit minority, or otherwise in need of repair. But the very terms of such objections to democracy affirm its obligatory character, because it is the malfunction or corruption of democracy that is being objected to. Christian fundamentalists may believe that they are acting on God's orders, but the fact that they claim to be a "moral *majority*" indicates that, as far as *political* legitimacy is concerned, they understand democracy's non-optional character. The more or less universal move toward democracy in the ex-Soviet world and much of Africa and Latin America tells a similar story: much as they might disagree over the meaning of democracy, and over how best to institutionalize it, the great majority accept its obligatory force.

This force stems from many roots. Part of it derives from the economic and military successes of twentieth-century democracies when compared to the going alternatives. Part of it derives from agitation by weak and dispossessed groups in undemocratic countries to better their circumstances, and their hope (perhaps, often, naïve) that democratization will help bring this about. And part of it derives from claims for more democratic governance of international institutions. The pressure that emanates from the leaders of many poor countries to democratize the United Nations and other international institutions implicitly affirms democracy's legitimacy. One can scarcely insist on democracy in international institutions without thereby conceding the validity of democratic principles; these then are enhanced willy-nilly in domestic political contexts.

Although democracy means many things to many people, most plausible accounts include two components: that people, collectively, are presumed entitled to an equal say in the decisions that affect them, and that opposition to currently prevailing policies is always legitimate. Traditionally, the first of these ideas finds expression in a default—but rebuttable—presumption in favor of majority rule, while the second is institutionalized in the idea of "loyal" opposition. Whatever the procedures by which a decision is arrived at, there must be mechanisms through which those who are dissatisfied with a particular outcome can seek change in the future, as long as they limit their opposition to producing a different decision rather than destroying the democratic order.

If democracy is understood as including these requirements, this leaves open the question, "How should democracy fit with group identities and aspirations?" In my view, the best way to think about democracy's place is as a subordinate, or conditioning, good.[1] Democracy functions best when it shapes the terms of our common interactions without thereby setting their course. Most of the things people value can be pursued in a variety of ways, and it is the challenge of democracy in the modern world to get people to pursue them—even to *want* to pursue them—in more rather than less democratic ways. Democracy should be thought of as omnipresent in that it appropriately shapes the pursuit of all goals in which power relations are implicated, but not as omnipotent. Doing things democratically is always important, but it should rarely, if ever, be the point of the exercise. People should be induced to pursue their goals democratically, but not to sacrifice those goals *to* democracy. The task is to get them to rise to the creative challenge this represents. It is an especially difficult challenge as far as group aspirations are concerned, because these so often do obliterate other considerations. Yet it is all the more urgent for that reason.

GROUP-BASED CLAIMS

From the perspective of a commitment to democratic politics, we can approach questions about the context and purpose of group-based claims. One way to do this is by thinking through examples. In the transition to democracy in South Africa between 1990 and 1994, two groups with intense desires for self-determination found those desires frustrated as the outgoing National Party (NP) government and the African National Congress (ANC) negotiated a pact, with the enthusiastic blessing of much of the world community. One was the Inkatha Freedom Party (IFP), the ethnic Zulu nationalist party with a significant though not decisive power base in Natal. In the old "divide-and-rule" days of apartheid South Africa, particularly the 1980s, the IFP had received strong support from the NP government in hopes of weakening the ANC, which had strong majority support among South Africa's black population. Before the transition began to become a reality, many—including IFP leader Mangosuthu Buthelezi—believed that if the government was to "cut a deal," it would be with the IFP, which would gain control of a substantially autonomous entity, if not an independent country, in Natal. This was, after all, consistent with the Afrikaner ideology of "separate development," and few believed that the NP would ever give up control over all of white South Africa to the ANC.

In the event, Buthelezi was as surprised as most observers at the developments that actually unfolded. Following failed "roundtable" negotiations at the Conference for a Democratic South Africa (CODESA) in 1990 and 1991, in mid-1992 the NP and ANC leaderships began negotiating a secret agreement on South Africa's transition to democracy. The IFP was completely excluded from these discussions, whereas it had been a principal player at CODESA. The reason was that the IFP had been one of the main stumbling blocks to an agreement there because they had no real interest in the negotiations' succeeding. Throughout, both the ANC and the NP were committed to maintaining the new democratic South Africa as a unitary state. Despite its propaganda about widespread support, the IFP knew what all other principals knew: That it would be a marginal player in such an order. The IFP's own polls told them that they would not even win a majority of the Zulu vote. Consequently, the IFP wanted an independent Zulu nation in Natal, or, failing that result, something as close to it as possible. They denounced the negotiations which resulted in the February 1993 NP-ANC agreement, began calling for a referendum on self-rule in Natal, and refused—almost to the end—to participate in the April 1994 elections. They hoped, forlornly as it turned out, that somewhere along the line they would be able to scuttle the transition.

In the last days before the election, making the best of it, the IFP added its name to the ballot. Its change of heart appears in retrospect to have resulted from the fact that President F. W. De Klerk (presumably with ANC approval) secretly transferred some three million acres of land to the control of Zulu king Goodwill Zwelitini in Natal. Until then Zwelitini had demanded the creation of a Zulu kingdom there with himself on its throne. This bribe was sufficient to buy him off, splitting him from Buthelezi and making any continued thought of opposition obviously fruitless, even to Buthelezi.[2] In the event, the ANC won 62.6 percent of the popular vote, the NP won 20.4 percent, and the IFP won 10.5 percent (about one-third of the Zulu vote nationally). In Natal, the IFP was declared to have won just over half the vote, despite widespread charges of electoral fraud and violence that the new government—perhaps wisely—decided not to pursue. This vote was sufficient to give the IFP 43 of the 277 seats in parliament and 3 of the 27 seats in Government of National Unity's new cabinet.[3]

A second group, also ethnically based with territorial national ambitions that had been obstructionist at CODESA and was marginalized in the subsequent negotiations, was the white right. Unlike the IFP, they were deluded about the degree of their support. White Afrikaners comprise 7.5 percent of the population (57.5 percent of the white population), yet the Afrikaner separatist Freedom Front (FF) won 2.2 percent of the vote in the April 1994 election, indicating that three out of four white Afrikaners voted for another party—the great majority for the NP.[4] Almost until the end the Freedom Front believed that the majority of white South Africans, as well as the military, would come to see the transition to majority rule as a calamity to be avoided and would turn to them.

In the last months before the elections they had tried to take a stand by supporting a black "homeland" leader in Boputaphuswana who also opposed the elections, only to be unceremoniously arrested by the army, which by this time was manifestly loyal to the transition. Although they continued (and continue) to call for the creation of an Afrikaner "volkstaat," they have ceased to be a serious force in South African politics.

Both Inkatha and the white right are politicized ethnic groups with national territorial ambitions, yet neither commands much sympathy outside their own constituency in South Africa, on the world stage, or even from intellectuals who champion rights of ethnic determination. The reasons why are instructive. The IFP has shown itself to be manifestly uninterested in democracy, both internally and in its dealings with other groups. Its arguments that a democratic national state is incompatible with "traditional" Zulu society conceal the fact that this society is highly authoritarian and manifestly oppressive of women. For this reason, King Goodwill's periodic claims for reinstatement of his "rightful" kingdom in what is now Natal—first taken from his forefathers by the British in the nineteenth century—win little support. In its dealings with others, the IFP has been warlike and instrumentalist, often bolstered, it should be said, before the transition by South Africa's apartheid government.

No doubt there is plenty of blame to go around as far as antidemocratic politics are concerned, and the NP and ANC historical records are scarcely without blemish in this regard. But Inkatha's opposition to democracy is foundational, even principled. Buthelezi is a member of the Zulu royal family, more interested in consolidating authority of traditional chiefs than any sort of electoral politics. By contrast, both the ANC and NP leaderships now accept democracy as the governing principle of the country. Despite their histories, and despite the continuing practices of "disloyal" opposition politics among some of their constituencies, they are publicly committed to making democracy work. Perhaps democracy is less threatening to them, perhaps they have come to believe that the alternatives to it are all, as Churchill said, worse. Whatever the reason, failures of democracy are, for them, failures to be accounted for, justified, rationalized, or explained away. By contrast, the IFP leadership makes no secret of the fact that its allegiance to democracy is contingent on events. They participated in the 1993 elections only when it became evident that they could not derail them, and they played a similar game of cat-and-mouse with the negotiations on the permanent constitution: refusing to participate unless virtual independence for Kwazulu/Natal was guaranteed, which in Buthelezi's mind included having its own army which would be under his personal command.[5]

If democrats have reasonably shed few tears for Inkatha's group-based ambitions, they have reasonably shed even fewer for those of the white right. Conservative ethnic Afrikaners opposed the democratization of South Africa at every turn, relying substantially on the ideology of separate development of the country's races. Yet the "bantustans" and "homelands" they made available to blacks were not remotely viable economic or political entities, comprising a tiny portion of South Africa's least well-endowed lands. Unsurprisingly, therefore, even in the heyday of apartheid it was envisaged that the white South African economy would be sustained by black migrant labor from these bantustans. One ironic consequence of the disingenuousness of the Afrikaners' nationalist commitment to separate development is their own geographical dispersion throughout South Africa today. It means that there is no viable territorial site for the volkstaat about which they have been talking since the transition became inevitable. The historical facts feed the suspicion that such a volkstaat would, in any case, be a platform for a relentless war of attrition against the new South Africa. The great majority of ethnic Afrikaner nationalists do not believe that it is legitimate, and they probably never will. In such circumstances, why should others defer to their ethnic and nationalist aspirations? Unlike Inkatha, they are not hostile to democracy within their own group. However, they are implacably hostile to the democratic South Africa with which they are at odds. They are "disloyal" rather than "loyal" opponents. At bottom, this is why their aspirations are fairly resisted by democrats.

Separatist demands from hostile groups are not always so easily dismissed, as is indicated by the more intricate problem of the Palestinian aspirations for national self-determination in part or all of what is now Israel. On balance, Palestinian political elites may be no less intolerant of Israeli religious and nationalist aspirations than the separatist Afrikaners are of the new South Africa. Unlike the separatist Afrikaners, however, in the present circumstances of Middle Eastern politics Palestinians are a dominated minority who are denied equal rights of democratic participation in the Israeli state that governs them. I do not mean to deny that Israelis have good reasons to fear Palestinians, given the history of the conflict, and it should be said that commitment to democracy (internal or external) is not obviously high on the agenda of either the PLO or Hamas. In such circumstances separation seems to be the only solution, a reality that was poignantly captured by one cartoon during the Intifada which depicted a prominent Likud politician saying to a foreign reporter: "Our policy concerning the Palestinians is simple. We will keep beating them until they stop hating us." Israel cannot fairly deny the separatist aspirations of a group that it has no intention ever of recognizing as equal citizens within the Jewish state (how could it?), yet it reasonably fears expansionist Palestinian aspirations that are every bit as potent as right-wing Jewish affirmations of the legitimacy of "greater" Israel. The "two-state solution" seems inescapable in this type of zero-sum circumstance, even if it carries a depressingly Solomonic air.

A small minority deny this, arguing instead for a secular unitary state in the entire region. But the histories that led both Jews and Palestinians to their circumstances of present mutual hostility render this unrealistic. Perhaps it would be better in some ultimate sense if the lessons of seventeenth-century England and Europe had led substantial numbers of the present power-brokers in the Middle East to see the virtues of religious disestablishment. Personally I wish that this were so. But that is not the present reality, and calling for it is reminiscent of the American senator who wondered aloud during the Suez Crisis why Jews and Arabs could not "settle their differences in a Christian fashion."

REENGINEERING IDENTITIES DEMOCRATICALLY

It might be said that there is a certain theoretical artificiality to my discussion of the preceding examples. They all involve groups that are in various respects distasteful to democratic sensibilities. As such, perhaps they do not capture much of what defenders of the legitimacy of group rights often have in mind. Such an assertion would be partly justified only: it invites the retort that theoretical literature on this subject is often starry-eyed in ignoring what can be at issue in actual movements that seek to vindicate group claims. That said, the intuition that one should not think only about group aspirations that stand in flat contradiction to democratic practices is sound. Indeed, I want to press it further by saying that, for democrats, the creative challenge is to try to structure things so that group-based claims for enhanced representation or self-determination express themselves in ways that are more rather than less compatible with democracy. To advance this view it is necessary to say something about the nature and sources of such claims. There seem to me to be three principal possibilities.

One is primordialist. If one thinks of identities as unalterable, then the appropriate political stance would be purely instrumental: find ways to prevent people from killing one another by channeling the destructive aspects of their fixed aspirations away from one another. In the "divided society" literature, such thinking often gives rise to consociationalism. The injunction is to devise systems of minority vetoes or other mechanisms that force leaders of different groups to work out a modus vivendi and govern as a "cartel of elites."[6] If the primordialists are right, such instrumental constitutional engineering makes sense. If they are wrong, as I have argued with Courtney Jung in the South African context that they are, then the primordialists become vulnerable to the charge that their remedy might produce the malady to which it is supposed to respond.[7] Consociational institutions can manufacture or exacerbate ethnic division.

An opposing view stems from the postmodern rejection of primordialism. Postmodernists contend that political identities are "socially constructed": they are malleable and evolve over time. On this view, there is nothing natural or necessary about ethnic, racial, and other group-based antipathies. They might have developed differently than they have, and they can change in the present and future. Although postmodern writers seldom get into the technicalities of how they believe this might be accomplished, it seems reasonable to assume that— on their view—forms of identity could develop that differ radically from those presently prevailing in the world. In particular, people might come to accept, perhaps even celebrate, differences that today are sources of mutual hatred.

Postmodernists can correctly point out that politicized identities evolve with time and circumstance. But to say that politicized identities are historically contingent does not entail that they are infinitely malleable; it does not even entail that forms of identity that need not have been mobilized, but have been, can subsequently be demobilized. This is more than the problem of getting the toothpaste back into the tube. The degree to which things are alterable may not vary with the extent to which they are socially constructed. Many features of the natural world, ranging from the temperature of our bath water to the genetic structure of our beings, can be altered by conscious human design. Socially constructed phenomena, by contrast, often defy all efforts at conscious human control. Markets are human constructions, yet we may be unable to regulate them so as to operate at full employment with no inflation. Ethnic hatred may be conceded to be learned behavior, yet we may have no idea how to prevent its being reproduced in the next generation. Postmodernists leap too quickly from the idea of social construction to that of alterability; at best the two are contingently related.

An intermediate view that is to me more plausible avoids the attendant difficulties of both primordialism and postmodernism. With apologies to philosophical purists it might be described as a brand of neo-Aristotelian naturalism. On this view, human beings are shaped by context and circumstance, but also constrained by their basic constitutions. These basic constitutions may themselves evolve, but at a given time and place they limit the possibilities of social construction. Human nature is always malleable but never infinitely so, and certain ways of shaping it are likely to be more effective than others. The interesting questions concern what the limits to this malleability are, and which forms of social construction are likely to be more satisfying and effective than others. At bottom these are empirical questions about which there is not a great deal of accumulated knowledge in the social sciences.[8] As a result, it is wise to work at the margins rather than the core, and to think about institutional redesign rather than a tabula rasa approach. Identities are fixed to some—usually unknown— degree, but they also adapt to circumstances, incentives, and institutional rules. The goal should be to reshape such constraints, where possible, so that at the margins identities evolve in ways that are more rather than less hospitable to democratic politics.

One mechanism through which this can be pursued is electoral systems. Since group-based hatred is often mobilized by political leaders in response to what they see as routes to power, it is important, as Donald Horowitz has argued, to shape the incentives for gaining power in ways that will produce a different result. What is needed in circumstances when such antipathies are strong (and assuming partition is not on the agenda), are systems that affect the behavior of elites from one group toward the grass-roots members of other groups.[9] This can be achieved in a variety of ways, all of which require politicians to compete for votes among politicized groups other than their own. The most obvious is a combination of coalition politics and heterogeneous constituencies. Horowitz describes a successful example of this kind from Malaysia, in which Malay and Chinese politicians were forced to rely in part on votes delivered by politicians belonging to the other ethnic group. The votes would not have been forthcoming "unless leaders could portray the candidates as moderate on issues of concern to the group that was delivering its votes across ethnic lines." In this type of situation, which Horowitz identifies as having operated for considerable periods (and then failed) in countries as different as Lebanon, Sri Lanka, and Nigeria, compromises at the top of a coalition are reinforced by electoral incentives at the bottom.[10]

Another possible device is geographical distribution requirements, such as the Nigerian formula for presidential elections employed in 1979 and 1983. The winning candidate had to get both the largest number of votes and at least 25 percent of the vote in two-thirds of the then-nineteen states of the Nigerian Federation. This type of system seems unlikely to work in countries like South Africa, however, given the territorial dispersion of politicized groups. In such circumstances, the two most promising candidates are proportional representation utilizing the single transferable vote system, and an alternative vote rule that also lists more than one ordered preference, but declares elected only candidates who receive a majority (rather than a plurality) of votes. Both systems require politicians to cater to voters' choices other than their first preferences, assuming heterogeneous constituencies, so that the politicians' incentives work in the appropriate moderating directions. Horowitz thinks this will be accentuated further by the alternative vote system, assuming that parties proliferate.[11]

Horowitz makes a convincing case that in many circumstances such vote-pooling systems are more likely to achieve interethnic political cooperation than systems that merely require seat-pooling by politicians in coalition governments, whether first-past-the-post or proportional. They are also superior, from a democratic point of view, to schemes like Lani Guinier's cumulative voting as devices for achieving viable group diversity in representation.[12] Cumulative voting gives each voter in a territory a number of votes equal to the number of representatives. If a state is to have eight congressional representatives, every voter would have eight votes that can be cast however they wish: all for one candidate or spread among several. If there are intense ethnic preferences, members of a minority group can cast all eight votes for the representative of their group; if not, they can distribute their votes among several representatives. This has advantages over racial gerrymandering, which (like consociationalism) can be accused of entrenching ethnic and racial differences and leading to balkanization rather than diversity. The cumulative voting approach responds to intense ethnic preferences that might exist in a population, but it does nothing to produce or reinforce them. Yet by the same token it does nothing to undermine or ameliorate potentially polarizing forms of aspirational difference. This is why it is inferior, from a democratic point of view, to systems that give aspiring political leaders active incentives to avoid mobilizing forms of identity that exacerbate cultural competition and to devise, instead, ideologies that can appeal across the divisions of such groups.

Giving leaders electoral incentives to avoid inflaming intergroup antipathies will not always work. Parties may proliferate within politicized groups in ways that undermine this dimension of the logic behind transferable vote schemes.[13] Furthermore, some of the worst of what often (misleadingly) gets labeled interethnic violence is actually intra-ethnic violence that results when different parties seek to mobilize support in the same ethnic group. Much of the South African violence that erupted in Natal after 1984 resulted when the United Democratic Front (UDF) was formed and challenged IFP support among Zulus there, and some of the worst violence among white nationalists resulted from comparable competition for the white nationalist vote.[14] There are limits to the degree that intra-ethnic competition of this sort can be ameliorated by transferable vote mechanisms. In theory they may have a positive effect. If parties have incentives to mobilize support in more than one ethnic constituency, they should avoid campaigning as ethnic parties more than they have to. In practice, however, parties like the IFP—whose raison d'être is ethnic—may have little scope to campaign on any other basis. Accordingly, they may resist, perhaps violently, any inroads into their "traditional" sources of support. For them it is at best a zero-sum game.

Whether this is likely to be the case can be difficult to predict. In the early 1990s, the NP transformed itself in a short time into a viable non-ethnic party (more than half of whose votes in the 1994 election came from nonwhites). They did this because its leaders came to believe that their alternatives were "adapt or die." In Canada, less apocalyptic thinking appears so far to have been sufficient to cause the leaders of ethnic parties to accept that their aspirations must triumph through a democratic process or not at all. By contrast, Bosnia and the Middle East reveal that sometimes even the likelihood—indeed, the certainty—of death is not sufficient to head off the pursuit of mutually incompatible group aspirations. Yet most people do not want to die. The challenge, for democrats, is to devise mechanisms that make it more likely that people will live in conditions of inclusive participation and nondomination. Group aspirations that by their terms cannot be realized within democratic constraints are to be resisted, but it is better to work for a world in which such aspirations will diminish. Getting rid of institutions that press in the opposite direction seems like a logical place to start.

NOTES

1. For elaboration, see my collection of essays, *Democracy's Place* (Ithaca, N.Y.: Cornell University Press, 1996), especially chaps. 5 and 8.

2. *New York Times,* May 24, 1994, A6.

3. Election results taken from *Foreign Broadcasting Information Service Daily Report,* May 6, 1994, 5. Cabinet portfolios from Associated Press wire, May 9, 1994.

4. *Foreign Broadcasting Information Service Daily Report,* May 6, 1994, 5, and Andrew Reynolds, "The Results," in Andrew Reynolds, ed., *Election '94 South Africa* (Cape Town: David Philip, 1994), 183–220. Population statistics computed from *South Africa 1994* (Parktown, Johannesburg: South Africa Foundation, 1994), 14–15.

5. See *New York Times,* January 7, 1996, 1, 12.

6. Arend Lijphart, "Consociational Democracy," *World Politics,* 4, no. 2 (January 1969), 213–215, 222.

7. See Courtney Jung and Ian Shapiro, "South Africa's Negotiated Transition: Democracy, Opposition, and the New Constitutional Order," *Politics and Society,* 23, no. 3 (September 1995), 269–308, and Ian Shapiro and Courtney Jung, "South African Democracy Revisited: A Reply to Koelble and Reynolds," *Politics and Society,* 24, no. 2 (June 1996), 237–247.

8. For elaboration, see my *Political Criticism* (Berkeley: University of California Press, 1990), chaps. 8 and 9.

9. Donald L. Horowitz, *A Democratic South Africa? Constitutional Engineering in a Divided Society* (Berkeley: University of California Press, 1991), 155. Generally, see his *Ethnic Groups in Conflict* (Berkeley: University of California Press, 1985).

10. Horowitz, *Democratic South Africa?* 154–155.

11. Horowitz, *Democratic South Africa?* 184, 166, 187–196.

12. For Guinier's proposals see her "The Triumph of Tokenism: The Voting Rights Act and the Theory of Black Electoral Success," *Michigan Law Review,* 89, no. 5 (March 1991), 1077–1154, and "(E)racing Democracy: the Voting Rights Cases," *Harvard Law Review,* 108, no. 1 (November 1994), 109–137. On the battle over her confirmation, see her *Tyranny of the Majority* (New York: Free Press, 1994).

13. For elaboration of these and related difficulties confronting Horowitz's proposals, see my "Democratic Innovation: South Africa in Comparative Context," *World Politics,* 46, no. 1 (October 1993), 145–147.

14. I am grateful to Courtney Jung for discussion of this point.

Part Four **Democracy and Deliberation**

Chapter 10 Creating the Conditions for Democracy

Irwin P. Stotzky

In the past two decades, many Latin American and Eastern European nations have been involved in a remarkable political experiment. The historically ubiquitous authoritarian regimes, usually in the form of military juntas and dictators, have gradually been replaced by constitutional democracies. This process—usually referred to as the transition from dictatorship to democracy—is, however, far from complete. Indeed, it remains much debated in concept and fragile in practice.

The expansion of interest in democracy in diverse parts of the world has given rise to the need to examine, in greater depth, the varied forms that law and institutions designed to promote human rights and government by and for the people can take. In particular, this wave of democratization has brought a renewed interest in justificatory theories and conceptions of democracy. These theories are crucial for creating the conditions and justifying institutional reforms, on both macro and micro levels, which may help turn the possibility of democracy into an actuality.

To generalize, the literature on democratic theory suggests two radically different approaches to justifying democracy. First, there are theories which attempt to carve out a sphere for the operation of politics in general, and democratic politics more particularly, in which moral issues are left uncontested or moral evaluation is suspended a priori because of a presupposition of the value of the political process.[1] In this view, the democratic process takes as given the interests and preferences of people, even when they are egotistic or even morally blameworthy. That process also takes as given the political actions of people and groups on the basis of those preferences. Democracy is seen as generating such a dynamic of collective action that it produces morally acceptable results. Thus, it is not necessary to modify the preferences of people in a morally virtuous direction.

These visions of democracy, of course, generally start from a pessimistic view of human nature and of the possibility of changing the self-interested inclinations of people. They attempt to present democracy as a system of collective interactions which makes the best of those self-interested inclinations. Moreover, this pessimistic view is also extended to the formation of factions and corporations. Although accepting the position that associations of people acting on the basis of their self-interest may be a threat to the rights of individuals, proponents of these views argue that the virtue of democracy lies in neutralizing but not dissolving the power of these factions or corporations through a series of mechanisms which force results that respect the rights of individuals.

In addition, proponents of these views frequently assume a skeptical or relativistic meta-ethical stand that demonstrates serious doubt about the existence of objective reasons for the determination that some people's preferences are immoral and therefore should be disqualified from consideration. This is not the whole of the matter. Those who espouse these views also claim that the pretension of discovering these so-called objective reasons generally leads to authoritarian political enterprises and to unacceptable interventions into people's private lives. Thus, under these views, democracy is valuable precisely because the dynamics of the system work toward the accommodation of everyone's preferences without judging their moral content. Nevertheless, the result of this morally neutral process is seen as morally valuable.

The second family of theories justifying democracy adopts the exact opposite approach to the capacity of democracy to transform the preferences and inclinations of people and, thus, to the insertion of the democratic process into the moral realm.[2] The virtue of democracy lies precisely in the inclusion of mechanisms that promote the transformation of people's original self-interested preferences into more altruistic and impartial ones. Democracy not only produces morally acceptable results, but produces them through the moralization of people's preferences, and perhaps even through the moralization of people themselves. This vision of democracy implies a much more optimistic view of human nature and of how it may be molded through social mechanisms according to some particular scheme of values. The approach toward factions and corporations is also radically different from the previous family of views. Indeed, the ambition of these visions of democracy is that a democracy may be able to dissolve those groupings of individuals on the basis of their self-interest. If this dissolution cannot be accomplished, a democracy may nevertheless attenuate to a large extent the power of these groups in favor of those of the isolated citizen, or of associations of citizens, on the basis of altruistic inclinations or at least impersonal values and ideologies.[3]

There are other differences between these competing theories of democracy. This second family of justifications of democracy is not, in general, relativistic or skeptical in meta-ethics. Unlike the first family of theories justifying democracy, this second family considers that there may be objective reasons for the morality of certain outcomes. It goes so far as to argue that the democratic process itself helps to determine the morally correct result, or at least it helps determine the knowledge needed to reach that result. In some manner, this second family also attempts to overcome the charge that this view of democracy may lead to a moral authoritarianism, and to models of democracy that are quite impervious to the recognition of liberal rights.

Carlos Nino took a firm and interesting stand on the justificatory bases for democracy that fit within this second family of justifications. He endorsed a unique and specific theory that assigns value to democracy based on a processing of preferences and puts the greatest emphasis on the practice of rational deliberation. His view relies on the virtue of democracy to transform people's self-interested preferences into more altruistic and impartial ones.

Carlos Nino's view further assumes that the method of turning people's selfish preferences into more impartial ones is that of collective deliberation—dialogue. Further, and most significant, Nino argues that collective deliberation has value in itself because it provides reasons for believing that the solution endorsed by that consensus agrees with what is prescribed by valid moral principles which, in turn, provide us with autonomous reasons to act. When democracy is conceived of in this way, there is an intrinsic relationship between democratic politics, the law which results from it, and morality.[4]

In this essay, I wish to develop some of Carlos Nino's wonderful insights about democracy and human rights by looking at some of the breathtaking difficulties of moving from dictatorship and authoritarianism to democracy in Haiti.

In the first part, I begin by explaining a preliminary conception of democracy. This conception is developed as a justification for democracy and thus as a basis for examining the Haitian dilemma. It is also useful for suggesting changes in the structures of that society which may allow the people of Haiti a serious opportunity to experience democracy.

In the second section, I examine some of the history of Haiti, and I describe and analyze the extremely difficult problems of making such a transition in the real conditions that confront the Haitian people. Next I suggest an alternative political economy that fits into my conception of democracy and that is necessary to the process of democratization in Haiti. The fourth section examines in more detail the problems associated with the consolidation of democracy on a macro level and suggests some institutional structures that may allow democratic processes to come closer to producing morally acceptable results in Haiti. The fifth part examines the micro-politics of habitual social interactions that must be overcome if democracy is to become a reality.

Finally, I discuss the complicated issues raised in holding individuals accountable for massive human rights violations. Examining these issues brings into sharp focus my conception of democracy and its application to many of the questions I analyze in this essay. Facing the question of whether and how to deal with those who have committed massive human rights violations should enlarge the Haitian people's vision, focus their attention on what the process of democratization can mean to their lives, and help change the institutional structures of that society. Dealing with these questions will begin the public discourse so necessary to a democratic society and to the positive transformation of the lives of the Haitian people.

A PRELIMINARY CONCEPTION OF DEMOCRACY

The democratic conception that I have in mind is an extremely broad one, explicitly a conception of a political, economic, and social order.[5] It is a conception of a social system in which public debate over the direction of social life is not only expected, but actively encouraged. I view democracy, in part, as a public forum for moral discourse, where principles rather than special interests prevail. I believe that the best means for countering the overpowering influence of special interests is to create a polity governed by universal and impersonal principles where individual citizens, who preserve the ability to adopt new interests and who are not necessarily identified with any special interest, make choices in a process of public justification and dialogue.[6] Implicit in this conception of democracy is the realization that the removal of existing barriers to free deliberation would not necessarily eliminate all grounds for political, social, and economic disagreement. Indeed, democracy can never be dedicated to an ideal of a perfectly harmonious community. That would, in any event, be an illegitimate utopian conception of democracy. The task of a democratic conception, therefore, is not to describe a social order in which all disputes would be trivial, or indicative of a failure to realize the principles of the order. Rather, the burden is to outline a political, social, and economic order in which disagreements over the direction of that order can be socially addressed through a process of free, equal, and collective deliberation.

In view of these considerations, it follows that the democratic order must satisfy several major requirements. The principles of that order must be clarified by describing the justification or principle of democratic legitimacy. Some description and explanation must then be given of a set of institutional requirements rooted in those fundamental principles. Finally, an account must be offered of the motivations that might lead people to support and maintain such institutions over time.

I have already suggested the requirements of the first condition. A democratic society is an ongoing order characterized in the first instance by a certain principle of justification—a principle that recognizes the legitimacy of democracy. This principle requires that sovereign individuals be free and equal in determining the conditions of their own association. This justificatory principle of democracy also requires that sovereignty be exercised by the participants in the order who are educated on the issues confronting society and thus have the ability to form rational judgments about the ends of social life. In addition, the democracy must ensure that the citizens are constrained in making those judgments only by the conditions necessary to preserve reasoned public deliberation, and that nothing actually determines the ends of social life other than the judgments arrived at by the members of the order. Moreover, the views of each member of the democracy must carry equal weight in public deliberation. Further, the principles of democratic legitimacy must not be prey to the intrusion of private power. Thus, material inequalities in resource allocations and control must be changed.[7]

Second, the satisfaction of this principle must be manifest or clearly visible to participants of the order in the actual workings of its institutions. This, in turn, provides one of the foundations for the stability of the democratic order over time. In addition, this general conception of democracy has consequences for the sorts of claims that members of a democratic order can make on one another and on the society as a whole. There are many such claims that can be made by free and equal participants in the exercise of sovereignty, but of particular importance is the claim of autonomy. Autonomy consists of the exercise of self-governing capacities, such as understanding, imagining, reasoning, valuing, and desiring. Free persons have and are recognized as having such capacities. In a political order dedicated to securing the conditions of free deliberation for its members, those members can legitimately expect of that order that it not only permit but also encourage the exercise of such capacities—that it permit and encourage autonomy. Further, to claim autonomy for oneself is to recognize the reciprocal and equally legitimate claims to autonomy by others.

In sum, the principle of legitimacy requires an ongoing order of mutually assured and encouraged autonomy in which political, social, and economic decisions are always based on the judgments of the members who are free and equal persons. It requires that the expression of self-governing capacities operate both within the formal institutions of government and in the affairs of daily life. Finally, it requires that the democratic order stably satisfy the conditions of equal freedom and autonomy that give it definition. Since the absence of material deprivation is a prerequisite for free and unconstrained deliberation, a basic level of material satisfaction, which would be more precisely specified through a free process of collective deliberation, should be provided for all members of the political order.

These conditions provide the basis for considering the more specific institutional arrangements and requirements of a democratic order. But elaborating these requirements is not an easy task. It cannot be done in any absolute sense. The institutional structure for a visionary democracy that justifies itself in the way I have elaborated it can only proceed in general outline. It must necessarily be experimental. Like Carlos Nino's conception of democracy, this democratic conception assumes a broad framework of social cooperation. How that framework will be expressed institutionally must necessarily vary under different cultural, psychological, and historical conditions.

Thus, in describing the institutional requirements of a democratic political order, my discussion must remain somewhat provisional and abstract. I cannot necessarily anticipate the variety of conditions under which democratic institutions might arise. Moreover, in describing these requirements in the real conditions of Haiti, the intricacies become even more complex and the discussion even more problematic. Nevertheless, these various institutional requirements within a democratic conception comprise a system—a set of constraints and conditions which are interrelated and which define a distinct social structure of coordination and power.

A DEMOCRATIC VISION FOR HAITI

At this point, I shall analyze the opportunities for applying these views of democracy to Haiti. At a minimum, a theory that justifies democracy through its epistemic value suggests the distance between an ideal model of democracy and the realities of Haitian society. It also suggests changes both in the macro-politics of institutional structure and in the micro-politics of social interactions that must take place if the misery of the Haitian people is to be alleviated. Following a short discussion of Haitian history, I analyze the major difficulties of making a transition to democracy. Finally, I suggest some institutional innovations that may help in the transition, particularly in light of these justificatory conceptions of democracy.

Some Historical Data

The history of Haiti is a tragic tale of political corruption and military violence. With the singular exception of one regime lasting from 1818 to 1843, Haiti has been marked by ceaseless coups, assassinations, and massive violations of human rights.[8] The only period of relative stability was between 1915 and 1934, when the United States Marines occupied the country to ensure American commercial privileges.[9] When the troops were finally removed, conventional hostilities with the Dominican Republic resumed.

Any notion of stability after the departure of U.S. troops was achieved through dictatorships. The most powerful and successful dictator was François "Papa Doc" Duvalier, who ruled between 1957 and his death in 1971 with an iron fist and the aid of a maniacal private security force known as the Tonton Macoutes.[10] Duvalier consolidated his power quickly and ruthlessly. He eviscerated individual liberties and political opposition with equal dispatch; indeed, more than 40,000 Haitians reportedly lost their lives as victims of official brutality.[11] Duvalier stole more than $500 million in foreign aid and taxes and put the money into personal accounts in Haiti and abroad. Officials at all levels of government, taking their cue from Duvalier, took part in similar acts of corruption.[12]

Duvalier remained in power for more than fourteen years, and in order to ensure a legacy of Duvalier control over the country, organized a referendum on

January 31, 1971, in which voters approved his nineteen-year old son, Jean-Claude ("Baby Doc"), as successor.[13] When his father died, Jean-Claude became "President for Life." He ruled in a manner as repressive as his father. In 1986, however, when the levels of economic disparities and political corruption reached ungovernable proportions, "Baby Doc" fled Haiti for exile in France.[14]

Following the Duvaliers came a series of political regimes that owed their survival to a large military caste operating with the indefatigable support of a small upper class.[15] None of these regimes, however, had the support of the Haitian people. Each ruled through the power of the gun.[16] The popular will was finally given formal expression in the elections of 1990.

The 1990 election of Jean-Bertrand Aristide—the first fully democratic election to take place in Haiti in nearly two hundred years—represented a unique opportunity for democracy to take root in Haiti.[17] Popular support for Aristide was overwhelming; he received two-thirds of the vote, giving him an unprecedented mandate for reform.[18] Equally impressive was the election process, which represented the culmination of an extraordinary international effort to launch Haiti on the path of democracy. Both the Organization of American States and the United Nations actively participated in helping Haitian officials assure the security and dignity of the election process.[19] Voter turnout was remarkably high; 75 percent of the eligible voters—approximately 2.7 million out of the 3.2 million registered voters—turned out to vote despite extremely difficult logistical problems in the rural areas of Haiti.[20] Moreover, the high illiteracy rate compounded the challenge of registering and voting.[21] Nevertheless, despite these problems, virtually all observers who monitored the voting claim that the election was fair and that voters experienced no intimidation.[22] In addition, the military helped assure that violence would not occur.[23]

This peaceful election soon gave way to violence. After several unsuccessful coup attempts, the military finally overthrew Aristide in September 1991.[24] The coup attempt not only was successful, but also resulted in a widely publicized reign of terror in Haiti.[25]

During its short tenure, however, the Aristide government took important steps to create a democracy by improving the rule of law in Haiti.[26] In one of his first official acts, President Aristide announced the retirement of senior military officials who had either been involved in past human rights violations or who had failed to punish those responsible for such abuses.[27] He also appointed several new public prosecutors and removed corrupt officials linked to the military.[28] Simultaneously, Aristide announced the creation of a human rights commission charged with investigating some of the most notorious human rights abuses committed in the past.[29]

The most significant step taken by Aristide to improve respect for the rule of law was the dissolution of the institution of rural section chiefs accountable to the military authorities.[30] These section chiefs had unfettered control over the lives of the peasants in the rural areas—where 75 percent of the population lives—and that unchecked power led to systematic disregard of human rights with complete impunity.[31] The Aristide government replaced the section chiefs' system with a system of rural police under the jurisdiction of the Ministry of Justice. It appointed a new corps of rural agents made up of individuals untainted by the abuses of the old system.[32]

But these reforms did not last long. The overthrow of the Aristide government resulted in the death and torture of thousands of innocent people that continued into Aristide's reinstatement to power in 1994.[33] Moreover, after the overthrow of Aristide, the military rapidly took steps to consolidate power. They named a civilian government, including an interim president, to complicate the return of Aristide.[34] They reversed each of the systemic changes made by the Aristide government and created a society ruled by fear and terror.

After years of serious but frustratingly unsuccessful international efforts to negotiate the restoration of the democratically elected Aristide government, in September 1994 U.S. President Bill Clinton made a televised address bluntly informing the Haitian military that it must relinquish power or it would be forced out.[35] In a last-ditch effort to avoid an invasion, Clinton asked former President Jimmy Carter, Senator Sam Nunn, and General Colin Powell to go to Haiti to negotiate the peaceful departure of the military.[36] On September 18, 1994, the Carter delegation reached an agreement with the Haitian military leaders. The agreement provided that U.S. forces would enter Haiti with the "close cooperation" of the Haitian military and police, under conditions of "mutual respect."[37] In addition, high-ranking military officers were to retire upon the enactment by Parliament of "a general amnesty . . . or [by] Oct. 15, whichever is earlier." Finally, sanctions were to be "lifted without delay in accordance with relevant U.N. resolutions."[38] Approximately two thousand U.S. troops entered Haiti the next day.[39] By the second week of October, approximately twenty thousand United States troops had arrived.[40]

On October 15, 1994, after three years of forced exile, Aristide triumphantly returned to Haiti.[41] He thus became the first democratically elected president overthrown by a coup d'état to be returned to power by the international community and to replace the very same dictators who overthrew him. His peaceful return seemingly marked a victory for the United States and the international community.[42] It promised an end to tyranny and represented an important preliminary step toward the creation of a lasting democracy.

The Difficulties of the Transition

On December 17, 1995, the Haitian people elected René Preval to succeed Aristide as Haiti's next President. He formally took office on February 7, 1996. This is the first time in the history of Haiti that power has been democratically passed from one regime to another. What difficulties does the current Haitian government face in attempting to create a democracy in Haiti? Haiti has never had a secure democratic government, and it is not clear that there are enough elements of civil society to provide a proper foundation for one within a length of time the U.S. public and international community would support. Indeed, if the international community decides to withdraw its financial and military support, the successors of the de facto military regime will still be there, and the country will still be split between a tiny elite and a vast poor majority. What, if any, alternatives exist? The answer begins with a focus on the very complex issues involved in any transition to democracy, especially one that may take place in Haiti.

There is a deeper meaning to the rejection by the Haitian people of the military coup leaders than is traditionally suggested. It is a revulsion against the lack of a public life that is little more than a weapon or disguise of private interests. But there is a caveat to offer. This rejection cannot succeed in its larger objectives without changes in the established structure and dominant ideas of Haitian society that remain far outside the realm of traditional Haitian politics and even outside international understanding of the problem.

This skewed perception is not, however, unique to Haiti. Rather, it is reflected in the institutional structures of many developing nations. For example, the dominant political regimes of the less developed economies, and even critics of these regimes, often start with the desire merely to imitate and import the institutional arrangements of the rich industrial democracies. They do this with the belief that from similar institutional devices similar economic and political consequences will result. Such imitation, however, has not led to these desired results. The failure of these efforts at emulation may nevertheless be useful to the development of new institutional structures. To put it another way, such efforts may end up driving these countries into an involuntary institutional experimentalism, which may shed light on the suppressed opportunities for transformation. So it is possible that if Haiti begins on this path, positive results may follow.

The path is, however, littered with deep potholes. Several prominent problems in the transition to democracy in Haiti must be successfully resolved if the transition is to succeed without great harm to masses of people. This is, of course, not an easy task. Institutional structures must be developed and secured. Economic and political stability must be assured. Corporatist social and political structures must be transformed so that the powerless get their fair share of the basic necessities of life. The rule of law must become paramount in the formal institutions and practices of government, and in the affairs of daily life.

These issues are more complicated than they first appear. Although these issues may be theoretically severable, they are also inextricably intertwined. The rule of law, for example, must be consolidated not only to protect human rights, but also to help secure a satisfactory level of economic, political, and social development. Moreover, an independent judiciary is crucial in the consolidation of the rule of law.

The role of an independent judiciary in the transition process is, of course, extremely complicated. One major obstacle is the fact that the institutional structures necessary for a viable democracy remain in varying stages of development. The transition to democracy is usually represented in one of two distinct stages. In the first stage of development, a country is attempting to adjust norms or institutions toward the strictures of the democratic rule of law. The institutional structures associated with a democratic government, such as an independent judiciary or competition between different political parties, must be developed. In the other stage of development, the democratic institutional structures exist in a developed form, but their stability is not completely secured.

Haiti is clearly in the first stage of development. The nation not only needs to develop institutions, it must also train a large number of people to run them. Even more ominous for the success of any possible transition to democracy in Haiti is the fact that Haiti's institutional structure, particularly its judicial structure, is less developed than virtually any nation that has attempted this precarious transition.

Moreover, social tensions and conflicts coercively interfere with the creation and development of viable institutional structures. For example, it is no exaggeration to state that Haiti has never had a system of justice. The Armed Forces of Haiti (the Forces Armées d'Haïti or FADH) systematically violated and ignored internationally and nationally recognized human rights in their treatment of civilians. Even to speak of a "Haitian system of justice," before the reinstatement of the Aristide government, dignifies the violence and brutal use of force by soldiers and attachés, the corruption of judges and prosecutors, and the anarchy of Haitian courtrooms and prisons.[43]

THE ABSENCE OF MATERIAL DEPRIVATION:
A FIRST STEP TOWARD DEMOCRACY

Because free and unconstrained deliberation and individual development and fulfillment requires the absence of material deprivation, a democratic society must provide a basic level of material satisfaction for all members of the political order. Further, to satisfy democratic values, the level of material satisfaction must be determined through a free process of deliberation among the people. Indeed, the expression of self-governing capacities must operate both within the formal institutional structure of government and in the affairs of social life. The democratic order must, in any endeavor, satisfy the conditions of equal freedom and autonomy that help define it. But how can a government fulfill these requirements in Haiti?

The overriding characteristic of the political life and political discourse of Latin American and other developing nations today is a frustrated desire to escape the choice between a nationalist-populist and a neoliberal project. The import substituting, protectionist style of industrialization, and the pseudo-keynesian public finance that accompanied it, seem to have exhausted their capabilities. The neoliberal alternative, however, is unable to service the real conditions of sustained economic growth. Moreover, if taken seriously, this neoliberal economy remains anathema to the very elites that pretend to champion it. There is an absence of an articulated and viable alternative to these rejected and unpromising options.

In political economic terms, a country like Haiti might develop such an alternative by moving toward the following goals (some of which are in the Aristide government's economic recovery plan):[44]

1. Initiation of a dramatic rise in and focusing of the tax rate, in order to take macroeconomic stabilization seriously. This would impose upon the privileged classes and regions of Haiti (of which there are very few) the costs of public investment in people and in infrastructure. It would, of course, be utterly unrealistic in Haiti to conceive of a sound financial system as one based upon a drastic lowering of governmental expenditure rather than upon raising and rationalizing taxes.

2. Creation of an "anti-dualist" political economy, attacking and overcoming the internal division of Haiti into two (or more) economies only weakly and hierarchically connected. What is needed, therefore, is the consolidation and development of a technological vanguard in both the public and private sectors and the use of this vanguard to lift up and transform the immense, backward second economy of Haiti.

3. The imposition of capitalism upon capitalists through the privatization of the private sector (i.e., real competition, real refusal of the capitalization of profits through the socialization of losses, real antitrust laws and enforcement, real markets in corporate control, real constraints upon nepotism and inheritance, real private responsibility for the costs of public investment). Moreover, the government must create and develop public companies and impose upon these companies a regime of decisive competition and independent financial responsibility.

4. A massive investment in people and infrastructure financed by taxes on the people with the goods. There must be a priority of such claims upon the budget, backed by procedural devices with executory force. In addition, there must be precedence of preventative public health, sanitation, and food supplementation over therapeutic medicine. Even more important, the people must be educated.

INSTITUTIONAL ORGANIZATION
AND THE TRANSITION PROCESS

In the organization of government, politics, and civil society, the alternative would take the following form: a public-law counterpart to the political economy I have just outlined, animated by the same concerns and moving toward the same goals. This raises questions about the significance and independence of the judiciary, but I do not believe that the problem is any different in Haiti or other developing nations than it is in any liberal democracy. When we say independence, we usually refer to independence from parties, politics, and sometimes even ideology. But serious obstacles to these ideas remain dominant in many developing nations, particularly one as underdeveloped as Haiti.

It is clear that the Haitian people, as well as many people in Eastern European and Latin American nations, have not internalized the significance and legitimacy of a constitutional system based on the rule of law. Moreover, the Haitian culture appears to be strongly resistant to the internalization of universal standards of achievement and competition necessary for an equitably functioning democracy. Rather, Haitians appear to have internalized a belief in the over-powering importance of status and connections, thus crippling the transition to a constitutional democracy. It is a sobering thought that the problems associ-ated with the transition to democracy in Haiti may be intractable. Is it possible to convince the military and economic elite that the moral bases of a democracy must be adhered to for their lives and their children's lives to improve?

The democratization process needs further elucidation. Setting aside the complex question of when a democracy has been consolidated, which I believe depends implicitly upon justificatory conceptions of democracy, the concept of consolidation presents difficult problems of its own.[45] Each of these problems, in turn, must be confronted and overcome if democracy is to take root. More-over, the idea of consolidation is intimately connected to the stability of a given political system, and it is plausible to argue that the latter is itself an arrange-ment—a dispositional property—which in turn depends upon certain predic-tions.

Yet predictions about the success of any political process, and particularly the process of change in Haiti, are problematic at best, and I thus do not intend to make such predictions. I do, however, wish to discuss briefly some of the most prominent challenges facing any consolidation of democracy and to look at these issues in the Haitian context. The claim that the transition to democracy in Haiti can succeed depends on predictions that these features are useful in formulating.

The first significant feature of the consolidation of democracy is the fact that the process of democratization in Haiti must take place during one of the worst political, social, and economic crises in the history of the nation. In general, this crisis manifested itself in extremely high rates of human rights abuses, includ-ing murders, disappearances, rapes, and tortures. Indeed, the number of polit-ical assassinations that took place during the military coup period (1991–1994) is estimated to be more than five thousand.[46] This crisis also manifested itself in enormously high rates of unemployment, unacceptably high increases in infant mortality, epidemics, and a variety of other social catastrophes.[47] This is not, of course, the whole of the matter. Haiti's human and material resources are either in such short supply or have been so degraded by poverty, illiteracy, malnutri-tion, disease, violence, corruption, overpopulation, rapid urbanization, defor-estation, and soil erosion as to raise serious questions about its continued sur-vival as a society and as an independent nation-state. There may be nothing on which to build.

The most difficult obstacle to democracy in Haiti, however, may be psychological and cultural. The tradition of a predatory, oppressive state has left Haitians deeply distrustful of government. Moreover, due to the colonization of Haiti by France and the protracted armed struggle for independence, and the almost twenty-year occupation of Haiti by the United States, Haitians remain deeply distrustful of foreigners.[48] In addition, Haiti's political culture has long idolized the use of force. Political disputes are often settled not by negotiation, but through violence, and respect for democratic procedures and obligations is minimal.

Furthermore, there is great uncertainty in the international community about whether the transition to democracy in Haiti may lead to changes in the economic and social structures necessary to create a new oligopolization of the economy.[49] They may be at odds with democratization, but if international aid is forthcoming, Haiti may be able to change its economic structure to create more efficient modes of production and thus benefit all sectors of society. But such a possibility requires massive changes in the Haitian economic, political, and social structure, as well as support from the international community.

A second prominent feature of the consolidation of democracy, and integrally connected to the first, is the clear fact that the corporatist political and social structure that characterizes Haiti must be transformed. This corporatism has been described as bi-frontal.[50] On the one hand, it serves the state by allowing it to control different sectors of civil society, and, on the other, it involves the establishment of cleavages of privilege and domination on the part of different social groups within the very structure of the state. The groups that form the constellation of corporative power in Haiti include the armed forces, the Catholic Church, the trade groups, a variety of civic organizations, and the economic elite. From 1991 to 1994, the armed forces in Haiti and their civilian front (attachés) assumed total power and completely violated and destroyed any semblance of democratic practices and institutions. Indeed, the military forces consolidated their rule by ruthlessly suppressing Haiti's once diverse and vibrant civil society. The military systematically repressed virtually all forms of independent associations in an attempt to deny the Haitian people any organized base for opposition to the brutal dictatorship. The aim appears to have been to push Haiti back into an atomized and fearful society reminiscent of the Duvalier era. The strategy appears to have been based on the assumption that even if Aristide returned to power, he would have great difficulty transforming his popularity into the kind of organized support necessary to exert civilian control over the army and to create a democratic institutional structure that could aid in that endeavor.[51]

The Church has played both positive and negative roles in the life of Haiti.

The organized Church has traditionally allied itself with the military and economic elite. Indeed, the Vatican was the only nation to officially recognize the political legitimacy of the military government of Haiti.[52] The Church has consistently opposed Aristide. But local churches have helped the people of Haiti by nurturing popular groups in the rural areas.

The trade unions have been weakened by increased unemployment and the reduction—sometimes adversely affecting parties normally allied with the government—of any state aid. They have also been decimated by the various trade embargos employed against the dictatorship during the coup period by the Organization of American States, the United Nations, and the United States.

Until the September 1991 coup, an incredibly diverse civil society existed. Haiti boasted a huge assortment of peasant associations, grass-roots development projects, trade unions, student organizations, church groups, and independent radio stations. In the rural areas, local groups, generally known as "popular organizations," formed literacy programs, rural development projects, and farming cooperatives, often with international support. Churches supported these efforts. Consequently, lay involvement in church activities increased dramatically. Some of these associations developed into political groups and began to address questions of land distribution, human rights abuses, and corruption. There was also a vibrant set of organized groups in urban areas. Politically active trade unions, professional, student, and women's organizations, and thousands of block associations and community groups flourished. A vibrant group of radio journalists provided a forum for organizational activities and denounced attacks on this independent civil society.

Thus, unlike many nations attempting to make the transition from dictatorship to democracy, Haiti's civil society was extremely advanced. Political parties, however, were among the least advanced parts of civil society. The strength of Haitian civil society was to be found in its diversity and breadth outside of electoral politics.

The great unknown factor is whether the previous dominant economic groups remain all powerful or have instead been reduced to puppets of the military. During most of Haiti's history, the military did the bidding of the elite classes by protecting their economic monopolies and brutally suppressing the vast majority of the poor. In turn, the rich paid off the dictators. But during the 1991 coup, the military took over the country's ports and airstrips, prospering in the illicit drug trade. Even more significant for the future of Haiti is the fact that the military increasingly prospered through its control of state monopolies, such as the telephone company. For example, Colonel Joseph Michel François (one of the Haitian military leaders) took over from the rich the old monopolies in flour, sugar, rice, and cement.[53] This caused some of the economic elite to support the Governors Island Agreement.[54] But the question remains: What will the economic elite do now that Aristide has served his term and the Haitian people have elected a successor president, René Preval?

Strongly interconnected in several ways with the two above described features of the process of democratic consolidation is a final one, which is extremely relevant to the transition process—the failure to fulfill the requirements of the rule of the law.[55] The serious consequences of the absence of the rule of law pervade Haiti. The failure to follow the rule of law inhibits any possible positive democratic development.

Members of the FADH and its paramilitary supporters systematically ignored basic human rights in their treatment of civilians. Moreover, internationally recognized human rights, which are frequently codified in Haitian law, were intentionally and persistently violated. The pattern of abuses included murder, torture, rape, and other blatant violations of the rule of law.[56] Corruption was rampant. There was simply no system of justice. These acts, of course, undermine the credibility of democratic institutions.

It is not the case, however, that Haiti lacks a comprehensive legal structure that would support a democracy. The blueprint for a democracy is set forth in the 1987 constitution, which the Haitian people overwhelmingly approved in a March 29, 1987, election. The constitution contains specific guarantees of personal liberty and political and civil rights.[57] It provides citizens with all of the basic freedoms associated with a democratic state: the right to life (Article 19), freedom of expression (Article 28), freedom of association and assembly (Article 31), freedom of the press (Article 28-1), and freedom of religion and conscience (Article 30). It also provides protection from prosecution, arrest or detention unless pursuant to law (Article 24-1). Article 276-2 expands these protections by providing that all international treaties ratified by Haiti are directly incorporated into Haitian law and supersede any conflicting domestic laws. This provision is significant because Haiti has ratified several international conventions.[58]

Despite these provisions, the Haitian judicial system remains in disarray. Most judicial officials fail to apply the law, because they are either corrupt or incompetent. The problem is even more deeply rooted. During the reign of the military, deeds of corruption by the highest government officials occurred daily. Yet judicial procedures were not helpful in investigating them. A United Nations special expert concluded in 1988 that: "The ordinary system of justice, organized along traditional lines . . . did not play its role. The cases of torture, ill treatment, and arbitrary detentions led to practically no checks on its part, no arrests, no proper investigations. . . . The independence of the judicial authorities is not safeguarded and their powers are very restricted . . . [T]hey have been unable to clear up any of the numerous crimes committed during the past few years."[59] These acts of corruption generally undermine the credibility of democratic institutions.

Perhaps even more destructive to the creation of a democracy than these acts of corruption has been the domination by the authoritarian military dictatorship over all other state powers and branches of government. For example, Article 263 of the Haitian constitution requires the separation of the police from the military, but during the coup period the police were under the control of the army.[60] In the rural areas, section chiefs, charged with performing police duties, were little more than gang leaders who reported to military officials rather than to civilian authorities.[61] They possessed absolute power in the region and were immune from civilian control. They imposed arbitrary taxes, arrested and murdered people, and had private armies. Some of them even maintained their own private prisons.

Haitian prisons were also controlled by the military. The prison conditions clearly constituted severe and systematic violations of Haitian law and international standards. There was overcrowding, poor food, and lack of access to water, medical care, and legal counsel.[62]

Moreover, the military dominated the civilian justice system to such an extent that it failed to investigate or identify those responsible for massive human rights violations. The judiciary was not independent. Judges were appointed and removed at the will of the military. Finally, the congressional branch of government had no power. It followed the dictates of the military.

The systematic violation of legal norms, however, has not been restricted to the de facto regime's military leaders or their supporting cast. Unfortunately, such behavior is a distinguishing mark of Haitian political and social life evident throughout its history. This failure to follow the rule of law is evident in both social practice and the actions of governmental bodies. And this tendency of unlawfulness does not infect only public officials; it pervades the general society. Indeed, this history of unlawfulness correlates with a general trend towards anomie in society as a whole. It manifests itself in such things as corruption in private economic activities, nonobservance of efficient economic norms, and noncompliance with the most basic rules of society. This general tendency toward illegality in public and social life normally appears in one of two ways. People in Haiti may adopt a "finalist attitude," where they agree with the goals of a rule but do not follow the commands of the rule. Conversely, they may adopt a "formalistic attitude," where they blindly comply with the commands of the rule but ignore its goals. Both of these attitudes are incompatible with, and thus contribute to, the continuing difficulty of securing adherence to the rule of law.

The problem is even more complicated. The tendency of unlawfulness in Haitian public and social life is often the product and the cause of collective action problems, such as those which have structures that game theory labels prisoner's dilemma, assurance game, chicken game, and so forth. Frequently, the combination of expectations, interests, possibilities of actions, and their respective pay-offs are such that the rational course of action for each individual participant in the process of political or social interaction is not to comply with a certain norm, despite the fact that general compliance with it would benefit everybody, or almost everybody. This kind of anomie may be called "dumb anomie," since it refers to situations in which the compliance with a certain norm would have led the social actors to a more Pareto-efficient result than what they obtain if they do not observe such norms.[63]

Moreover, dumb anomie is connected with the stunting of Haiti's economic and social development. First, there is a direct conceptual connection between this dumb anomie and failures in economic productivity. Indeed, dumb anomie is identified by the inefficient results of processes of interaction, including economic ones, which do not observe certain norms. Second, it is clear that anomie affects the process of capital accumulation. For example, when the behavior of people intervening in the process of production—even that of judges and governmental officials—is not sufficiently predictable, productive investments decline or claim disproportionate profits.

Therefore, it is critical for the life of the Haitian nation to consolidate the rule of law. This is important not only to secure respect for fundamental rights and the democratic process, but also to achieve a satisfactory degree of economic and social development. Moreover, it is obvious that the consolidation of the rule of law, with the consequent overcoming of dumb anomie, requires strengthening the independence, reliability, and efficiency of the judicial process.

To do this, Haiti must satisfy the guarantees which derive from the idea of due process of law. But in Haiti, due process is simply nonexistent.[64]

One way to attack these problems is through a radical change in the institutional structures of Haiti. The dominant constitutional tradition in the rich industrial countries, such as the United States, relies upon arrangements and practices tending (1) to use the fragmentation of power and the promotion of impasse as a safeguard of freedom and (2) to maintain political society at relatively low levels of political mobilization. But in the real conditions of a nation like Haiti, which is attempting to make the transition to democracy, structural reforms require at least two sets of institutional innovations.

First, the electoral characteristics of presidential regimes must merge, so that they create a periodic threat to oligarchic control of political power. For example, political organizing must be encouraged, and people must become more active in determining the conditions of their lives. There must be a facility for the rapid resolution of major political impasses through granting priority to programmatic legislation, liberal resort to plebiscites and referenda, and perhaps the vesting of power in all branches of government to provoke anticipated elections in the face of serious disagreements over the direction the country should take. Second, measures must be taken to heighten the level and broaden the scope of political mobilization in society, especially through strengthening of parties (districts and lists), public financing of campaigns, increased free access to television and radio, and the breakup of the broadcasting cartel.

In the organization of civil society, the prevailing legal tradition in the rich industrial democracies relinquishes the self-organization of civil society to private contract. But the integrity of economic and political institutions such as those I have described here requires a civil society that is both strongly organized and independent in this organization from governmental tutelage.

MICRO-POLITICAL CHANGE

Macro-political reform by itself, however, is simply insufficient to create the opportunities for democratic change. Micro-political reforms must also become an integral part of the process. Indeed, Haitian history is permeated by a dual social and politico-economic structure that stubbornly impedes any progress toward positive change.

Since its independence from France in 1804, Haiti has been divided between a small, but ruthless, ruling class and a vast poor majority.[65] Directly after the revolution, the Haitian elites attempted to restore the plantation economy that existed under French colonial rule. The former slaves, however, abhorred plantation labor and settled as small peasants on land bought or reconquered from the state or abandoned by large landowners.

The urban elites devised a dual strategy to counter the refusal by the peasants to return to a state of slavery and their yearning for freedom and liberty.[66] The first part of the strategy was economic. The elites turned the fiscal and marketing systems of the country into a mechanism that would allow them to siphon off the wealth produced by the peasants. As traders, politicians, and state employees, they simply lived off the peasants' labor. Taxes collected by the import-export bourgeoisie at the urban markets and customhouses—and paid by the peasants—provided the bulk of government revenues. In 1842, for example, more than 90 percent of government revenues were collected at the customhouses. In 1891, import and export duties accounted for more than 90 percent of state income.[67]

Coffee, Haiti's main agricultural export, was the favorite target of the elites and the centerpiece of Haiti's fiscal policy. The direct and hidden taxes imposed on the peasant coffee crop accounted for 60–90 percent of government revenues from the late 1800s to the first half of the twentieth century. Moreover, until the election of Aristide, charges on coffee amounted approximately to a 40 percent tax on personal income. But after almost two hundred years of independence, the government has yet to collect income taxes from most merchants, civil servants, or middle-class employees.[68]

The economic response of the elites posed serious obstacles to the creation of any form of democratic government. The elites made sure that they received their wealth even if it meant killing the nation. The state reproduced itself by living off the peasants and abusing them; the urban classes reproduced themselves by taking over the state and the peasantry.

These choices by the elites inevitably led to death and destruction and, of course, political instability.[69] To stabilize the political situation, the elites undertook a second strategy. This approach was to isolate the peasantry on its small mountain plots and thereby keep them away from politics. It was a brilliant but corrupt strategy. The very peasants who subsidized the state had no say whatsoever in how it was to be run. They were kept away from the political process "legally" and illegally through the manipulation of election laws and harsh repression. For example, before the twentieth century, it is doubtful that any elected politician ever received as many as one thousand legitimate votes.[70] Before the Duvalier dictatorship, many peasants could not even name the president. The peasants encountered the state mainly through the *presepté*, who collected their market taxes, and through the *chéf seksyon* (section chief), a member of the army who acted as the sole representative of the three branches of government in the deep countryside. It is clearly not an exaggeration to claim that the countryside was and remains a class colony of the urban elites.

The Haitian Creole language as well as the Haitian culture emphasizes the enormous rift between the elites and the peasantry in several complex and subtle ways.[71] The languages of Haiti and their uses suggest a variety of barriers.

For example, the word *leta* in Creole means both "the state" and "a bully." The urban people, in turn, refer to the rural peasants as *mounn andewó,* outsiders. There are other, more subtle language barriers. All Haitians speak Haitian Creole. Less than 8 percent of the population, however, speaks French comfortably. But this is not all. Only a tiny minority within the elites are truly bilingual in both French and Haitian Creole. Similarly, practices and beliefs associated with the major Haitian folk religion, Vodoun, are ubiquitous among the elites, despite their formal adherence to Christianity. Peasants see themselves as Roman Catholic Christians; they practice the annual cycle of Roman Catholic observances. But they also see themselves as "servants of the gods," members of the Vodoun religion.

Thus, the fundamental cultural division is not necessarily based on a difference in cultural repertoire. Rather, this division is based on the uses of these sometimes quite subtle differences to create a formidable social barrier. For example, more important than bilingualism per se is the number of times an elite child is told not to speak Creole. Moreover, the French language is used in schools and in the court systems and therefore obviously denies majority participation in those institution. In addition, the elites publicly associate Vodoun with evil, while consistently practicing aspects of it. Unfortunately, this is not the whole of the matter. Perhaps even more significant is the fact that successive governments have persecuted the "servants of the gods," often with zealous help from the Catholic Church.

Two features emerge from this sociohistorical sketch: the total rejection of the majority by the very groups that exert political and economic control, and the role of the state as the key mechanism of both rejection and control. Stated otherwise, the elites believed and continue to believe that their life-style is more important than the survival of the majority. This results in the use of the state to expropriate the economic output of the majority, and to simultaneously repress them. As Michel-Rolph Trouillot has so eloquently argued, the Haitian state is predatory; it has always operated against the nation it claims to represent.[72] Thus, class structure, not merely income, and historical tides, not simply the immediate past, are at the root of Haiti's modern crisis.[73]

The macro-politics of institutional change, therefore, remain inadequate to the aims of democratization and practical experimentalism unless complemented by a micro-politics that confronts the logic of habitual social interactions in Haiti. The typical elements of this logic are similar to those of many developing nations. There is a predominance of patron-client relations with their pervasive mingling, in the same associations and encounters of exchange, power, and sentimental allegiance. There is frequently an oscillation between rule formalism and personal favoritism, and each creates the opportunity and the need for the other. Moreover, there is a stark contrast between the treatment of *insiders* (anyone with whom, by virtue of the role you occupy, you have a preexisting relationship) and *outsiders* (everyone else), who are treated with the consequent shortage of impersonal respect and reliability.

A "transformative" politics that is capable of challenging and changing both the established arrangements of the economy and the polity and the intimate habits of sociability must appeal to each of the (at least) two parts of the Haitian nation that it wishes to unite. In this task, those who yearn for democracy must combine a strategic approach to the satisfaction of recognized material interests with the visionary invocation of a reordered society. In Haiti, a nation trapped in these impoverished visions, nothing is more important than to encourage the belief in the Haitian people that structural change is possible.

WHAT TO DO ABOUT MASSIVE HUMAN RIGHTS ABUSES

One way of beginning to enlarge the collective sense of the possible and to achieve some of the other suggested goals—making the rule of law an essential part of public and private life, changing the habits of social interaction, guaranteeing economic survival, and creating viable democratic institutions—is to address the question of how to deal with the massive human rights violations committed by the military dictatorship. These cases involve what Kant referred to as "radical evil"—offenses against humanity that are so widespread, persistent, and organized that normal moral assessments seem inadequate.

Formulating a policy to deal with this question depends to a great extent, of course, on the purposes of punishment and the justifications for democracy. Further complicating the problem is the fact that any government that attempts to make the transition from dictatorship to democracy must design a double human rights policy; one that deals simultaneously with the future and the past. As to the future, a number of laws may need to be passed to protect human rights and prevent massive violations. As to the past, a strategy must be devised that both punishes those responsible for these atrocities and heals the wounds caused by the commission of these acts. This may require an extensive investigation and a series of human rights trials.[74]

Any sensible starting point must focus on moral concerns.[75] Even if one rejects a retributive theory of punishment, it is difficult to draw any conclusion other than that those who have committed these atrocities deserve to be prosecuted and convicted under the law. This is necessary in order to inculcate in the collective conscience of the polity that no sector of society stands above the law and that under no circumstances may a human being be treated as a mere object, a means to a goal, no matter how important the goal. Stated otherwise, some degree of retroactive justice for massive human rights violations may help prevent their future occurrence by creating a positive system of values in that society. Indeed, the basic justification for government is the promotion of human rights. A government is simply illegitimate if its actions are not directed toward reaching this goal.

Nevertheless, when actual cases of human rights abuses are analyzed, it is clear that it is extremely difficult to punish people who have committed these acts without threatening the justificatory theory and birth of a democracy.[76] The problems of exacting justice for massive human rights violations involve complicated moral, legal, and political issues.[77]

One of the major moral problems concerns the diffusion of responsibility. Massive human rights violations simply cannot be committed without the consent, tacit or overt, of numerous people with widely different roles in the society. For example, are we to punish all of the numerous judges who failed to enforce the rule of law, journalists who failed to report on the atrocities, diplomats who concealed or attempted to justify the position of their government, and everyday citizens who decided to turn a blind eye to what was happening, refrained from telling others of these atrocities, or even justified the deeds? This leads to a view that if almost everyone had some complicity in these acts, everyone is guilty and thus no one is guilty.

This set of moral concerns translates into political and legal considerations that the democratic Haitian government—and its successor government, if and when it actually consolidates power in Haiti—must face in any attempt to take action against the military.[78] The conditions under which Aristide resumed office will, of course, determine in part the limits of the possible. Whether an amnesty will become a reality as part of the transition to democracy is a key unknown factor, as is the extent to which other measures of purge, investigation, or reparations will be possible.

Clearly it will be difficult to sustain prosecutions for the coup itself or for affronts against democracy. Punishing many of the perpetrators of these crimes may destroy the stability of an already tenuous democratic system. It may alienate entire social groups, keeping them from supporting the democratic system, and may cause resentment that severely harms the chances for a successful transition to democracy. The military and its paramilitary supporters, of course, may stage another coup to protect its leaders and rank-and-file soldiers from prosecution. Thus, an amnesty may be an absolute necessity for the very survival of the nascent democracy.

But what about the crimes that under international law cannot be subject to a blanket amnesty? The incorporation of international human rights treaties directly into Haitian law gives rise to an obligation on the government's part to take action against those who have assassinated, disappeared, tortured, and arbitrarily jailed thousands of Haitians. Complying with that obligation will require strong international and domestic support. But even assuming the best possible scenario, significant impediments remain to prosecutions or even to investigations of the abuses that were committed.

A key problem is defining the chain of responsibility for both criminal and civil purposes. Although the military has a clear-cut command structure, the relationship among the military, the police, and the "attachés" and other private goon squads is less clear for purposes of attributing both state and command responsibility. The lines of communication between the coup leaders and the attachés and rural section heads are ambiguous—the attachés and section chiefs are both adjuncts who receive orders and independent actors. Nonetheless, a plausible argument can be made that these individuals have over time become agents of the state, so that all their actions may be attributed to the state. In any case, even if these acts cannot be directly attributed to the state, the state is still responsible for not adequately investigating and prosecuting those responsible for the acts. A similar problem arises with respect to members of the economic elite who bankrolled and otherwise supported the coup, and who may have been involved in death squad activities. Should these individuals be held criminally or civilly liable for the results of their actions?

As can be seen from this preliminary sketch of the problems involved in dealing with massive human rights violations, the questions are not easy ones to answer. The transformation of Haitian society is fraught with many dangers. How the Haitians deal with these massive human rights crimes of the past is not the least of these dangers. The answers to these issues will help determine whether and to what extent Haiti will become a viable democracy.

CONCLUSION

There is no easy fix in the transition to democracy in Haiti. Economic, political, and social stability have not yet been achieved. The corporatist political and social structures have not yet been transformed to allow the less privileged majority to enjoy the basic necessities that ensure a life of dignity. Institutional structures, such as an independent judiciary, a representative congressional branch, and limitations on the executive power must be developed and stabilized. The rule of law—and thus, the basic guarantees of due process—have to be consolidated and become an accepted, basic requirement of social interaction. This is necessary not only to protect human rights and the democratic process, but also to reach a satisfactory level of economic and social development. Moreover, human rights trials are an important step in reaching these goals.

All of these problems and possible solutions cannot be successfully addressed, however, without a justificatory theory of democracy. Such a democratic vision requires a continuous order of mutually assured and encouraged autonomy in which political decisions are manifestly based on the judgment of members of that order who are free and equal persons. Moreover, the expression of self-governing capacities must operate both within the formal institutions of politics and in the affairs of daily life. The democratic order must satisfy the conditions of equal freedom and autonomy that define it. Without such a system, and thus, without the development of what Carlos Nino called a "moral consciousness"[79] in the citizens, nations striving to become constitutional democracies will inevitably be plunged back into the abyss of authoritarianism.

NOTES

Carlos Nino possessed the two major qualities of a public intellectual. First, as a public intellectual, he was actively engaged in public affairs. During the Alfonsín administration, he held a variety of political positions, including presidential adviser (1983–1989) and coordinator of the Council for the Consolidation of Democracy (1985–1989), and his influence is clearly visible in many of the political reforms implemented during Alfonsín's tenure in office. Nino also wrote extensively, both in scholarly journals and in lay publications, such as newspapers, on an entire range of public issues that consistently presented themselves for consideration over the course of his lifetime. He was extremely generous with his time and spent long hours in helping to educate and transform scores of young students into maturing scholars. Nino lived the principles he espoused. He believed passionately that the only way to resolve problems was through rational discussion.

Nino believed that rational discourse helps identify and eliminate errors from one's thinking and protects one from dogmatic views, and that such discourse is an essential element in the creation and protection of human rights and democracy. He therefore committed himself to the creation of an institution—the Centro de Estudios Institucionales (CEI)—that would provide the foundation for the development of rational discourse. This center has become a focal point for research on public issues, and for the training of young scholars and public figures. It has also evolved into an international meeting center for scholars from different legal cultures in Europe, Latin America, and the United States.

Nino also possessed the second major quality of a public intellectual: although actively engaged in public affairs, he owed his ultimate loyalty to the truth of ideas. His intellectual and political work is profound and prolific. He wrote approximately a dozen books and scores of articles. Moreover, he combined his writing with an almost inexhaustible passion for teaching. But the amount of his production is secondary to the significance of his work. Virtually every aspect of his teaching and writing was a search for truth. In his public, political work, he never deviated from this search.

I dedicate this essay to Carlos Nino.

1. Carlos Nino called this view of democracy a "pluralistic" view. For a thorough description and analysis of the variety of different conceptions of democracy, see Carlos S. Nino, *The Constitution of Deliberative Democracy* (New Haven: Yale University Press, 1996).

2. I call this family of justificatory theories the "moral" vision of democracy.

3. At least in theory, this is the role that political parties play.

4. This is, of course, a very brief and incomplete sketch of Carlos Nino's theory. While there are strong theoretical and practical challenges to his theory, I endorse it precisely because I believe that Nino's justifications for democracy afford nations undergoing the transition to democracy the best opportunity to reach that goal. If deliberative democracy is implemented properly, it should help create a moral consciousness in people that will stand as the strongest barrier against the enemies of human dignity. For an elaboration of theories of democracy, critiques of Nino's theory and development of the views I express in this essay, see Irwin P. Stotzky, *Silencing the Guns in Haiti: The Promise of Deliberative Democracy* (Chicago: University of Chicago Press, 1997).

5. The conception of a democratic order sketched out in this section of the essay is strongly influenced by the writings of John Rawls. See in particular J. Rawls, *A Theory of Justice* (Cambridge, Mass.: Harvard University Press, 1971); J. Rawls, "Kantian Constructivism in Moral Theory," 57 *J. of Phil.* 515–572 (1988). This is obviously a very brief description of the democratic order.

6. It is clear, therefore, that I agree with Nino on these points. *See* Carlos S. Nino, *Etica y Derechos Humanos* (Buenos Aires: Editorial Paidós, 1984); Carlos S. Nino, "Transition to Democracy, Corporatism and Constitutional Reform in Latin America," 44 *U. Miami L. Rev.* 129 (1989). See also Irwin P. Stotzky, "The Fragile Bloom of Democracy," 44 *U. Miami L. Rev.* 105 (1989). It is also clear, however, that a state must be restructured to some extent before it meets the demands of a dialogical community. This requires understanding the history and culture of the particular nation undergoing the transition, and an attempt to meet the basic material needs of its people.

7. How such changes should occur, of course, must be resolved through a process of collective deliberation. Allowing a small group of elites simply to reallocate and redistribute resources, without the validity of such a conclusion being reached through a process of collective deliberation, violates the principles of this democratic conception. Means and ends are integrally related to the validity of collective action.

8. Although Haiti enjoyed relative political stability under Jean-Pierre Boyer (1818–1843), his methods were certainly not always just. *See* David Nicholls, *From Dessalines to Du-*

valier: Race, Colour and National Independence in Haiti (Cambridge: Cambridge University Press, 1979), 67–82. See also Michel-Rolph Trouillot, *Haiti-State Against Nation: The Origins and Legacy of Duvalierism* (New York: Monthly Review Press, 1990), 47–50.

9. See, e.g., *Haiti-Today and Tomorrow: An Interdisciplinary Study* 255–256, Charles R. Foster and Albert Valdman, eds. (Lanham, Md.: University Press of America, 1984); Trouillot, *Haiti*, 100–104; Amy Wilentz, *The Rainy Season: Haiti Since Duvalier* (New York: Simon and Schuster 1989), 77; Jonathan Power, "Haiti Still Has a Chance to Survive," *Calgary Herald*, Nov. 1, 1993, A4. For a more detailed account of the American occupation of Haiti, see Hans Schmidt, *The United States Occupation of Haiti, 1915–1934* (New Brunswick, N.J.: Rutgers University Press, 1971).

Although the occupation of Haiti by the United States stabilized the currency and briefly reduced administrative corruption, the overall effect of the occupation severely damaged Haiti in a variety of ways. See Trouillot, *Haiti*, 102–108.

10. See George DeWan, "Reigns of Terror," *Newsday*, Oct. 26, 1993, 24; Reuters, "Haiti Coup Leader Sentenced To Life," *New York Times*, July 31, 1991, A5. See generally Bernard Diederich and Al Burt, *Papa Doc: Haiti and Its Dictator* (Mapplewood, N.J.: Waterfront Press, 1991); James Ferguson, *Papa Doc, Baby Doc: Haiti and the Duvaliers* (Oxford: Basil Blackwell, 1987), 30–59.

11. DeWan, "Reigns of Terror," 24 and 25 (estimating the number as up to 60,000, with millions more exiled). See also Ferguson, *Papa Doc, Baby Doc*, 57.

12. Trouillot, *Haiti*, 175–177, 213–214, 226.

13. On January 22, 1971, the official gazette, *Le Moniteur*, carried the amendments that were to be voted on in the national referendum. The amendments included one that lowered the age for the presidency from forty to eighteen. The ballot stated that Jean-Claude Duvalier had been chosen to succeed his father and listed two questions plus the answer: "Does this choice answer your aspirations? Do you ratify it? Answer: yes." The official count was 2,391,916 in favor and, of course, not a single vote opposed. See, e.g., Diederich and Burt, *Papa Doc*, 397.

14. Ferguson, *Papa Doc, Baby Doc*, 60–89. The popular will had been expressed in other ways prior to the first democratic elections in 1990. In 1984, for example, there were food riots in Gonaives, where the masses attacked the warehouses of nine charitable organizations. This was the first mass demonstration against the regime. The 1987 constitution was another expression of the popular will. (Interview with Cathy Maternowska, an anthropologist who lived in Haiti from 1985 to 1993, in Miami, Nov. 8, 1993; on file with author. Maternowska worked extensively with the poor of Haiti.)

15. Interview with Cathy Maternowska. At least five governments ruled the country until the election of Aristide. See, e.g., "Special Economic and Disaster Relief Assistance to Haiti: Note by the Secretary-General," 10, UN Doc. A/45/870/ADD.1 (1991) [hereinafter UN] (report on mission).

16. Steven Forester, "Haitian Asylum Advocacy: Questions to Ask Applicants and Notes on Interviewing and Representation," 10 *N.Y.L. Sch. J. Hum. Rts.* 351, 357 (1993).

17. See, e.g., Howard W. French, "Haitians Overwhelmingly Elect Populist Priest to the Presidency," *New York Times*, Dec. 18, 1990, A1; Lee Hockstader, "Haiti's Army Chiefs De-

fend Overthrow; OAS Delegation Holds Second Day of Talks," *Washington Post,* Oct. 6, 1991, A29.

18. See, e.g., Forester, "Haitian Asylum Advocacy," 359; Don A. Schanche, "Populist Priest Wins in Haiti, Is Backed by U.S.," *Los Angeles Times,* Dec. 18, 1990, A1; Human Rights Watch, *Human Rights Watch World Report 1992: Events of 1991* (New York: Human Rights Watch, 1992), 258–259.

    Aristide actually received even greater popular support. Approximately 400,000 votes in his favor had to be nullified because the ballots were so complex that many of the illiterate people marked the ballots incorrectly. These people were, of course, Aristide supporters. Interview with Cathy Maternowska.

19. See, e.g., Council of Freely-Elected Heads of Government, *The 1990 General Elections in Haiti* (Washington, D.C.: National Democratic Institute for International Affairs, 1991), 87, 92. Similarly, both the United Nations and the OAS took leading roles in post-coup efforts to restore democracy in Haiti. See Peter Hakim, "Saving Haiti from Itself: How a New OAS Effort Can Build Democracy," *Washington Post,* May 3, 1992, C1. See also Barbara Crossette, "Accord to Resume Constitutional Rule in Haiti Is Reported," *New York Times,* Nov. 16, 1991, 5.

20. For a useful account of the 1990 elections in Haiti, see Council of Freely-Elected Heads of Government, *1990 General Elections;* UN, "Special Economic and Disaster Relief Assistance to Haiti."

21. At least 70 percent of Haiti's population is illiterate and desperately poor. See, e.g., Howard W. French, "Haiti Premier's Installation Reflects Division of Rich and Poor," *New York Times,* June 21, 1992, 8; cf. "Haitian Vote, so Bloody Before, Is Peaceful," *St. Louis Post-Dispatch,* Dec. 17, 1990, A1 (citing the illiteracy rate as high as 80 percent).

22. Pamela Constable, "For the U.S. No Choice but Optimism After Haiti Vote," *Boston Globe,* Dec. 23, 1990, 4. See generally "Haitian Vote, so Bloody Before, Is Peaceful," A1.

23. Kenneth Roth, "Haiti: The Shadows of Terror," *New York Review of Books,* Mar. 26, 1992, 62–63 (pointing out that Raoul Cédras, whom Aristide selected to head the army, was credited with supervising the relatively peaceful December 1990 elections). This behavior directly contradicts claims made at that time by apologists for the military that the army was nothing more than a coalition of competing gangs and that the military hierarchy was unable to control the actions of its subordinates.

24. See, e.g., Howard W. French, "Troops Storming Palace, Capture Plotters and Free President," *New York Times,* Jan. 8, 1991, A1; "High Abstention in Second-Round Polls; at Stake Is Who Will be Aristide's Prime Minister," *Latin America Weekly Report,* Jan. 31, 1991, 10.

25. This reign of terror resulted in the deaths and tortures of thousands of innocent people. See, note 33 below. The coup itself resulted in the death of at least thirty people. See, e.g., "Haitian President Is Ousted; At Least Thirty Reported Killed as Army Troops Mutiny," *Chicago Tribune,* Oct. 1, 1991, 4.

26. Interview with Ira J. Kurzban, General Counsel for the Republic of Haiti in the United States, in Miami, Nov. 8, 1993.

27. Interview with Ira J. Kurzban. This was Aristide's inaugural address. *Haiti Progress,* a Cre-

ole-language daily newspaper in New York, published his address in full on February 1, 1991. A copy of the address cannot be obtained since the newspaper did not keep copies.

28. Interview with Ira J. Kurzban; Roth, "Haiti," 62.

29. Interview with Ira J. Kurzban; interview with Cathy Maternowska.

30. Aristide replaced section chiefs with unarmed "communal police agents" who were under the supervision of the local judiciary. This action was in line with the requirement of the 1987 constitution of putting police under civilian control and thereby separating police from control of the army. Americas Watch, *Silencing a People: The Destruction of Civil Society in Haiti* (New York: Human Rights Watch, 1993), 104.

31. Interview with Ira J. Kurzban; interview with Cathy Maternowska.

32. Roth, "Haiti," 62–63.

33. La Plate-Forme des Organismes Haïtiens de Défense des Droits Humains (the Platform of Haitian Organizations for the Defense of Human Rights) has documented 1,021 cases of extrajudicial executions from October 1991 to August 1992 and estimates that the number of cases could be as high as 3,000. Memorandum to the OAS Commission to Haiti, Aug. 17, 1992, at 3. Thousands more have been murdered since that time. Thousands were illegally arrested, detained, and tortured. A knowledgeable observer in Haiti estimates that between 200,000 and 400,000 people were also forced into hiding in Haiti. Interview with Cathy Maternowska.

34. See, e.g., "Haitian Troops Threaten Assembly," *St. Louis Post Dispatch,* Oct. 8, 1991, A1.

35. Douglas Jehl, "Clinton Addresses Nation on Threat to Invade Haiti: Tells Dictators to Get Out," *New York Times,* Sept. 16, 1994, A1; Christopher Marquis, "Clinton: 'Your Time Is Up,'" *Miami Herald,* Sept. 16, 1994, A1.

36. Douglas Jehl, "Holding Off, Clinton Sends Carter, Nunn, and Powell to Talk to Haitian Junta," *New York Times,* Sept. 17, 1994, A1; Christopher Marquis, "A Final U.S. Reach for Peace," *Miami Herald,* Sept. 17, 1994, A1.

37. "What They Signed," *Miami Herald,* Sept. 19, 1994, A8 (reproducing text of September 18 agreement). See Susan Benesch et al., "Back in the Brink," *Miami Herald,* Sept. 19, 1994, A1.

38. "What They Signed." In a speech to the United Nations on September 26, 1994, President Clinton announced that the United States would suspend all unilateral sanctions against Haiti "except those that affect the military leaders and their immediate supporters." See Christopher Marquis and Peter Slavin, "U.S. Lifts Haiti Sanctions," *Miami Herald,* Sept. 27, 1994, A18; "President's Words: Fight Between Hope and Fear," *New York Times,* Sept. 27, 1994, A6 (excerpts of speech).

   On September 29, 1994, the United Nations Security Council voted to terminate sanctions on the day after President Aristide returned to Haiti. S.C. Res. 944, U.N.SCOR, 3430th mtg., para. 4, U.N. Doc. S/RES 944 (1994).

39. Larry Rohter, "3,000 U.S. Troops Land Without Opposition and Take Over Ports and Airfields in Haiti," *New York Times,* Sept. 20, 1994, A1; Peter Slavin, et al., "Troops Enter Haiti Without Firing a Shot," *Miami Herald,* Sept. 20, 1994, A1.

40. See "Perry: Haiti Showing 'Significant Progress,'" *Miami Herald,* Oct. 9, 1994, A23.

41. "President Aristide Returns," *New York Times,* Oct. 16, 1994, §4, p. 14; Larry Rohter, "Aristide Can Speak But Can the U.S. Hear?" *New York Times,* Oct. 16, 1994, §4, p. 5.

42. John Kifner, "Aristide, in a Joyful Return, Urges Reconciliation in Haiti," *New York Times,* Oct. 16, 1994, 1.

43. There have certainly been improvements in every aspect of Haitian life since Aristide's return to power. For example, the army has essentially been dissolved; it has been purged and reduced from a force of approximately 7,500 to a fifty-person marching band, political assassinations have dramatically decreased, and serious attempts are being made to reform the judicial system. Nevertheless, the judicial system and security remain serious problems. For a detailed analysis of these issues, see Stotzky, *Silencing the Guns.*

44. For a thorough analysis of the plan, see Stotzky, *Silencing the Guns.*

45. Indeed, the question of whether certain Latin American and European nations remain in the transition toward democracy or have already completed the journey requires both empirical corroboration and conceptual clarification.

46. This is an estimate of various OAS and UN observers. Some observers claim that up to 10,000 people were murdered by the de facto regime. That figure, however, cannot be verified.

47. Crises of this magnitude would unavoidably lead to the destruction of any nascent democratic system. Yet the brutal dictatorship in Haiti appeared to grow stronger with each passing day. This clearly shows the force of the repression in Haiti and its intractable staying power.

48. The Haitian people began their armed struggle for independence in 1791, when Haitian slaves revolted against the French; they defeated Napoleon's army and achieved independence in 1804, after twelve years of bitter struggle.

49. During the de facto government's reign, between 1991 and 1994, the military took over some of the nation's economic monopolies which had traditionally been controlled by the economic elite. See, e.g., Howard W. French, "Power Means Brutality; Practice Makes Perfect," *New York Times,* Oct. 17, 1993, E1.

50. The concept of corporatism refers to two distinct situations. In the traditional sense, corporatism refers to the control exercised by the state over organizations and interest groups. The more technical meaning, usually used in the political arena, refers to the contrary phenomena: where these same organizations and interest groups acquire considerable influence and exert persistent pressure on state decision makers. See generally *Authoritarianism and Corporatism in Latin America*, James M. Malloy, ed. (Pittsburgh: University of Pittsburgh Press, 1977).

51. Most of the information about Haitian civil society is taken from an extensive interview with Cathy Maternowska, and from my own experiences in Haiti.

52. See, e.g., Alan Cowell, "Aristide Has Long Posed Problem for Vatican," *New York Times,* Oct. 28, 1993, at A4. But see "Friendship and Solidarity Visit by Aristide," *European Report,* Oct. 30, 1991, 5.

53. French, "Power Means Brutality," E1.

54. The Governors Island Agreement was one of several agreements entered into between the Aristide government and the de facto military regime to restore to power peacefully the democratically elected government of Haiti. See Agreement between President Jean-Bertrand Aristide and General Raul Cédras, July 3, 1993, reprinted in *The Situation of Democracy and Human Rights in Haiti: Report of the Secretary General,* A/47/975, S/

26063, 2–3 (July 12, 1993). The United States acted as a broker for the agreement. The de facto military regime violated every part of the agreement while Aristide meticulously complied with the agreement's terms.

55. For a comprehensive look at the role of the judiciary and the rule of law in the transition to democracy, see *Transition to Democracy in Latin America: The Role of the Judiciary*, Irwin P. Stotzky, ed. (Boulder: Westview Press, 1993).

56. See Lawyers Committee for Human Rights, "Paper Laws, Steel Bayonets: Breakdown of the Rule of Law in Haiti" (New York: Lawyers Committee for Human Rights, 1990), 1.

57. Haiti's court system is based on the Napoleonic Code that was in effect in France almost 200 years ago.

58. For example, Haiti ratified the American Convention on Human Rights on September 14, 1977, by a declaration signed by Jean-Claude Duvalier.

59. Texier, "Advisory Services in the Field of Human Rights," E/CN.4/1989/40 (Feb. 6, 1989), paras. 89 and 48.

60. Upon his return to power, President Aristide separated the police from army control.

61. President Aristide fired the section chiefs and replaced them with civilian officials. Yet the original section chiefs continue to maintain power in the rural areas.

62. Prison conditions, even though dramatically improved under the Aristide government, remain unacceptable.

63. Nino used the term "anomie" in describing a similar phenomenon in Argentina. See generally Carlos S. Nino, *Un País al Margen de la Ley* (Buenos Aires: Emece Editores, 1992).

64. The Aristide government has taken steps to deal with all of these issues. Results are, of course, uncertain. See Stotzky, *Silencing the Guns*.

65. For a thorough analysis of the sociocultural history of Haiti, see generally Trouillot, *Haiti*; Stotzky, *Silencing the Guns*.

66. This dual strategy was set up during the presidencies of Alexandre Pétition (1807–1818) and Jean-Pierre Boyer (1818–1843). See generally Trouillot, *Haiti*.

67. Trouillot, *Haiti*.

68. Trouillot, *Haiti*.

69. United States physician Jonathan Brown, who visited Haiti in the 1830's, wrote: "The country is saved from utter want and political dissolution solely through the spontaneous productiveness of its soil," Jonathan Brown, M.D., *The History and Present Condition of St. Domingo, II* (1837; rpt. London: Frank Cass, 1971).

70. Historians regard the legislative elections of 1870 in Port-au-Prince as one of the few legitimate electoral victories of nineteenth-century Haiti. Yet in 1870, less than one thousand Port-au-Prince residents had the right to vote.

71. For an intriguing discussion of Haitian culture see Léon Francois Hoffman, "Haitian Sensibility," in 10 *A History of Literature in the Caribbean: Hispanic and Francophone Regions* 368 (1994).

72. See Trouillot, *Haiti*; Michel-Rolph Trouillot, "L'Etat Prédateur; Nicaragua Aujourd'Hui," vols. 76–77 (1991), 25–27; Michel-Rolph Trouillot, "Etat et duvaliérisme par Michel-Ralph Trouillot" in *La République Haïtienne: Etat de Lieux et Perspectives*, Gérard Barthélemy and Christian Girault, eds. (Paris: Karthala, ADEC, 1993).

73. There also exists in Haiti a historical tension between the older "mulatto" elite and the

"black" middle class. This is, however, a very complicated issue. No aspect of Haitian history is more confusing than the physical appearance of its people. Haiti is said to be divided by color, but it is closer to the truth to say that there is a wide situational variability in consciousness of color and that for many people light skin is symbolically important. But this statement merely skims the surface of the issue. The skin color of people must be seen as part of a perceptual whole that goes beyond color. It includes hair type, nose type, lip type, eye color, ear size, amount of body and facial hair, and body type. The issue of color is even more complicated. It also includes such factors as the appearance of one's siblings and their in-laws. For men in particular, the color and appearance of one's wife and her family is extremely relevant. Even more important, it is not clear that color determined the emergence of a ruling class so much as did education, military record, and personal connections. Thus, while color is a significant cultural characteristic, neither at the birth of the nation nor today can it be used to define social groups. See Hoffman, "Haitian Sensibility."

74. For further discussion of how to address "radical evil," and justifications for trials or other forms of punishment, see essays in Part IV, this volume.

75. There are many moral issues involved in determining both whether to hold human rights trials and what the scope of the trials should be. There are, for example, moral problems associated with conceptual relativism and sincere convictions.

The problem of conceptual relativism raises the question of whether a state can legitimately carry on moral discourse outside its boundaries and thus subject people who do not share the assumptions of that discourse to courses of action based on its findings. This problem destroys any possibility of grounding public moral responsibility in consensus because even moral disagreement is foreclosed by conceptual divergence.

Sincere conviction poses problems for moral evaluations even if the society does not agree with the substantive content of the conviction. The mistaken character of the conviction has to be demonstrated. This problem raises questions about the foundations of human rights and about their scope and balance when several of them are in conflict.

For a discussion of these and other issues raised by human rights trials see Stotzky, *Silencing the Guns.*

76. See Jaime Malamud Goti, *Game Without End: State Terror and the Politics of Justice* (Norman: University of Oklahoma Press, 1996).

77. See Nino, *Radical Evil on Trial* (New Haven: Yale University Press, 1996).

78. There are, of course, other moral, political, and legal concerns that, while central to human rights trials in general, are less pressing in Haiti. For example, questions about the effect of international law, the jurisdictional power and type of tribunals that will try the offenders, and so forth are less difficult questions in Haiti than in other nations. See Stotzky, *Silencing the Guns.*

79. Carlos S. Nino, *The Ethics of Human Rights* (New York: Clarendon Press, 1991), 3.

Chapter 11 Power Under
State Terror

Jaime Malamud Goti

In this chapter I describe how political power may be manifested in societies subjected to long-term state terror. I lay out the thesis that state-
sponsored terrorism molds a peculiar kind of political power, one that
destroys social communication, warps our notion of authority, and
perpetuates the very terror under which it developed. Looking at the
years surrounding the 1976–1983 military regime in Argentina suggests that the eruption of state-sponsored violence represents merely
one facet of a more pervasive trend, more deeply characteristic of that
violent political culture. State terror in Argentina can be traced from
the early colonial period to civil wars of the 1800s to the conservative
administrations in the 1920s and 1930s through the first Perón regime.
With somewhat differing styles, intensity, and targets, the politics of
terror are still present today.[1] Understanding terror in this context requires an appeal to a range of interrelated concepts. The continued persistence of a world-view in which terror is an inherent feature of everyday life obviously affects all aspects of both society and individuals. In
order to get at the root of this societal malaise, we must look at new
examples and examine a variety of philosophical conceptions. Post-
dictatorial Argentina clearly illustrates this model of political power.[2]

In mid-June 1982, in the wake of Argentina's surrender to the British forces on the Falkland/Malvinas Islands,[3] de facto President General Fortunato Galtieri assembled the populace in the Plaza de Mayo, the square in front of the national government house in Buenos Aires. Although attendance was not as large as it had been at the rally to celebrate the April 2, 1982, invasion of the islands, the throng was large enough to fill the square and the adjacent streets. The Argentine polity at large expected an explanation of why and how the war had been lost. Deliberately inaccurate official reports about the progress of the military campaign had misled the population which, until a few days before the surrender, thought that Argentina's armed forces were achieving one glorious victory after another.

It seems clear today that Galtieri thought that he could manipulate the rally in order to create a groundswell of support for the military regime during this turbulent time. He was wrong. Most of those present in the square wanted to know how a war allegedly waged to defend Argentina's sovereignty had been lost so disastrously. Adding to the sense of injury and outrage was the government-sanctioned deception about the progress of the war.

The crowd grew angry when it became apparent that the president did not intend to offer an explanation but simply wanted to muster popular support. Tempers flared and the crowd began chanting anti-government slogans threatening to go on a rampage. In what seems a senseless display of violence, the gathering was disbanded by police with teargas grenades and a barrage of rubber bullets. At the cost of three dead and dozens of wounded, "order" was restored when the participants scattered through the city expressing their anger vociferously.

In addition to a general anti-government sentiment, all that the people at the rally shared was their perplexity about the war and its disastrous finale. While some argued that the military mismanaged the campaign, others thought that the conflict was untimely or that Argentine diplomacy had failed to prevent the U.S. from siding with the British. Very few claimed that the April invasion of the Falkland/Malvinas Islands by the Argentine armed forces had been unwarranted; and even fewer contended that it had been an altogether groundless military venture which cost the lives of hundreds of young conscripts.

The events at Plaza de Mayo were revealing of issues that went beyond the war itself. They were, in more ways than one, illustrative of the nature of the regime's power. The rally exposed the populace's extreme ignorance about the country's management in general. It also revealed that the officers in the regime had not expected the reaction that followed, as had other administrators aware of the populace's sentiments. It showed that the regime knew little if anything about the purposes that brought people to the square. This lack of understanding of political events led to what still seems in retrospect a pointless use of violence. The incident at the square was telling, finally, about the degree to which the meaning of events varied dramatically among the populace.

The violent aftermath of the rally exposes the nature of political power under an essentially terrorist regime and offers a model of power stemming from a polity's generalized confusion and disinformation. A failure of the basic communication links between the populace and the regime and the fragmentation of reality among the citizens themselves are the main circumstances that shape the exercise of power in a terrorist state.

The notion of political power is complex and elusive. It encompasses both the conscious will of rulers and the unconscious processes that shape our everyday life. It is both formal and informal: political power encompasses formal directives issued by individuals in certain roles and offices as well as persuasion and enticement by certain individuals acting behind the scenes.

Understanding post–dirty war events in Argentina illustrates the difficulty of linking social reality and the various ways in which political power manifests itself. Understanding Argentina's terrorist state in the 1970s requires the correlation of different conceptions of power usually considered irreconcilable. I will call these conceptions of power "articulating," "disarticulating," and "structural." Only an approach to power that combines these three conceptions can explain the failure to attain social concerted action.

"Articulating power" is political power in the most usual sense. This notion of power addresses the political issue of social cooperation.[4] The achievement of a common purpose requires that a government be able to induce individuals to perform specific voluntary actions by resorting to either threats or offers. Articulating power requires that specific goals be achieved by coordinating actions that require the participants' intent. These actions that demand coordination range from state security-related activities in which only few participate to regulating street traffic in which the entire community partakes. Articulating power does not really work in a terrorist state; it is disarticulating power that reigns.

Terror fragments society's beliefs. Perceived random brutality generates a most varied assortment of interpretations about the nature and purposes of lethal violence. A terrorist state is capricious; it keeps individuals guessing as to who will be the next direct target of violence and why. Owing to the confusion and disinformation it generates, state terrorism drives individuals to exercise restraint and splits the perception of reality among the members of a community.[5]

I call the ability to attain this effect "disarticulating power." Instead of organizing the citizenry to fulfill common goals, disarticulating power aims to prevent coordinated opposition. It does not operate by building coordination and consensus, but rather gains and retains political control over society by disarticulating that society. Ultimately to enhance cooperation, articulating power rests with the facilitating knowledge of a common social reality. Disarticulating power is at odds with the primordial state's goal of social coordination.

Argentine students recall their panic when they were routinely detained by military and anti-mutiny police units for identification and interrogation. Captors terrified them by lecturing them on the boundless liberty of army officers to torture and kill at will. Officers derived more than simple sadistic pleasure from this practice. They preempted any possible coordination between the detainees by effectively isolating every suspect. Each detainee built a different theory about their captors' pursuit and all were distressed by the danger of being associated with the rest of the "suspects." By these means the police also guaranteed the impotence of the detainees to protest their harsh treatment let alone escape. Deliberately or not, the military regime and its acolytes (and to a lesser extent the administration that preceded it) used terror as a general form of political power. They exercised the violence Simone Weil describes as the ability to turn persons into "corpses even before anybody or anything touches them."[6]

Although disarticulating power is characteristically dictatorial, all states may resort to it under pressing circumstances. Mostly at its benign expression and in face-to-face situations, most democratic systems use this power as a means of control. Limited to specific events, disarticulating power expressed as random, intense physical violence enables police forces to quell battles among street gangs and disperse out-of-control rioters. When the urgency of a particular situation makes nonviolent persuasion unfeasible, causing fear and confusion through arbitrary violence may sometimes be an acceptable remedy, even in rights-based democratic settings. Random baton blows and hydrant tactics enable comparatively small police forces to disband numerous throngs of angry rioters. In a democracy, however, these tactics are restricted to rare situations, and those who employ them are often subjected to severe penalties if they are not able to establish the futility of other means of control. In contrast with this extremely restricted use of disarticulating power, a terrorist state turns violence into a political style. Brutality becomes a general strategy to attain and retain control over the population. This tack strongly conditions "structural power."

Structural power is the way in which a particular society defines, ranks, and resolves its own conflicts. We usually refer to this phenomenon as ideological in a very broad sense. By ideology I do not necessarily refer to a set of articulated principles and values, but to a much simpler entity. Ideology is understood here as the beliefs and values that condition any kind of inquiry in a given society.[7] I use the word *ideology* to stress that state terror produces a limited set of basic principles and values upon which or through which all other experience is understood. Ideology encompasses the simple processes through which we understand the world. Those who believe that the world is full of enemies, for instance, will build their experiences differently from those who regard humans as basically friendly. These ways to define reality are, of course, unintentional; they are largely built into our basic system of belief (knowledge) as the way we "understand" the world around us.[8]

It is said that, until recently, in many isolated northern provinces of Argentina, Catholic clergy preached the value of being thankful for the small mercies the landowners were willing to disburse to the poor in return for their toil. Resistance was not only unfair, but immoral, sinful, and silly. In most cases, these sermons were not the result of a conscious effort to protect the landowners from the peasants' demands, but rather the consequence of the churchmen's unwitting and seemingly sincere desire to reaffirm and maintain social peace. Behind the priests' beliefs and their manipulation of the peasants' minds in getting them to acquiesce to the status quo lie the different degrees by which certain individuals or groups advance their interests in a particular society. Structural power consists of certain individuals or groups obtaining satisfaction from other people's (convenient) understanding of social facts and their notions of right and wrong, correct and incorrect, and convenient and inconvenient. The common denominator among those who endure oppression is their conviction of having no better options although these options are actually available. The exploitation of prostitutes in developing countries, for instance, is often the consequence of misinformation about the possible availability of less humiliating means of sustenance for young women. Taking advantage of popular misinformation, misinterpretation of events, and the beliefs that go with them are the structural power of political tyranny.

The experience of power thus conceived is to be found in the system of meaning and values that we call culture.[9] The Catholic church hierarchy "recognized," either consciously or unconsciously, that its survival depended on the landowners' financial contributions to the church and balanced its needs and those of the peasants, landowners, and ultimately, those of society at large in a delicate equilibrium. Sincere or not, from this perspective power adopts an essential role in configuring people's conceptions of reality in a culture of terror.

To the detriment of individual autonomy, articulating power plays a minimal role. In allowing room for the exercise of choice, only articulating power is compatible with the "democratic," autonomous individual. Unlike articulating power, disarticulating power is incompatible with the standard notion of free will. The threat of torture and assassination eliminates choice, first because our ignorance about the rules by which violence is administered drives us to build our own personified understanding of the political setting. Second, prospects of suffering torture and assassination activate our urge for survival and thus eliminate the existence of choice according with our standard notion of free will.[10] Unlike articulating power, which generates a desired intent in those on whom power is exercised, disarticulating power rests on the idea that only those who exercise the violence qualify as free human agents. Terrified individuals cannot possibly be considered autonomous agents; they are instruments of those who have the force.[11] Viktor Frankl describes the spirits of the victims of the Holocaust as feeling that they are in the hands of fate and that it is better to abandon themselves to fate's "decisions."[12] Structural power is incompatible with autonomy in a more subtle way: it operates as a surreptitious limit to understanding our own "actual" options and our ability to accomplish our ends.

In *On Violence,* Hannah Arendt defines power as the capacity to elicit compliance from a second person.[13] For Arendt political power includes the second person's (the addressee) performing a particular action out of compliance with the first person's (the addresser's) threats. For this version of Arendt's work, power is grounded not only in the addresser's credible threats or offers but also in his or her moral standing.[14] Beyond the specific intent of addressers and addressees, the goal of political power, Arendt explains, is to achieve a concerted action for a collective purpose.[15] Accordingly, power ought not to be confused with violence. Violence is a one-sided process. When violence is present, the volition of the addressee is rendered meaningless because the addressee is reduced entirely to an object of the emitter's agency. According to this conception, power is a complex collective process that cannot be located solely in the addresser or the addressee, but rather in the relationship between the two. Even if the addressee's choices are extremely limited by the beliefs that terror implants in people, it is a form or process of interaction between individuals or groups.[16] Although articulating power cannot exist without the capacity to resort effectively to violence in Arendt's conception, it is essentially a relational category whereby certain individuals or groups are in a position to deliberately induce other people to undertake (intentionally) particular actions or achieve certain states of affairs.[17] Thus, the conflated version of articulating power and authority as Arendt presents it in *On Violence* does not allow room for power under a terrorist state.[18]

More recent writers have established a sharp distinction between power and authority. They couch the concept of authority in the idea of respect for the will of some person or group. A person (addressee) complies with the injunctions of another person or group (addresser) because he or she finds that doing so is morally compelling.[19] An agent does not obey an authority to obtain a benefit or avert harm, but rather from the belief in the moral correctness of complying. The moral property attached to the concept of authority renders the promised benefits or threatened evils irrelevant. A morally motivated agent (addressee) is indifferent to the personal benefits or harms that the action may entail.

Unlike authority, power induces individuals to obey because compliance is advantageous to the addressee. Essential to power relations is the avoidance of certain evils, like punishment, or the attainment of promised advantages. Yet, as we shall see, authority and articulating power not only overlap in many ways but also define each other. Threats and offers lie at the core of the notion of articulating power,[20] yet threats and offers become more or less effective when the addresser is in a position of prestige and his or her will is germane to the interests and values of the doer.

The nature of the exercise of articulating political power is collective in two relevant ways. First, the exercise of power depends on the community's values and beliefs to the extent that these values and beliefs encourage, accept, or reject the exercise of power. Societies in which unbounded individualism is highly regarded will be more reluctant to accept the idea of fostering cooperative schemes through coercion than will those more supportive of collective endeavors.

Like authority, power implies the existence of values and beliefs shared between those who issue orders, the addressers, and those who obey them, the addressees. Power is based on the generation of incentives to perform or not perform certain actions.[21] Control over addressees demands an understanding of their behavior, their forces, their responses, their strengths and weaknesses.[22] To be able to exercise power, a person must know that his or her threats and offers are meaningful to the addressee. A ruler who is ignorant of the citizens' values cannot coordinate effective civic actions.[23] First, to make threats and offers effective, the addresser must know that they are meaningful to the addressee. A ruler who is ignorant of the citizens' values cannot coordinate effective civic actions.[24] The addressee may consider, for instance, that achieving a particular goal exacts too high a cost. He may decide that a loss of face is too drastic a consequence of carrying out a "nonsensical" directive. He may consider that dignity is too valuable to jeopardize in exchange for being spared from a particular evil the addresser has threatened to impose upon him if he doesn't perform the action the addresser desires.

The exercise of power also depends on the acceptance of the values behind a legal directive and the willingness of the parties involved to implement effectively the legal threats and offers. Threats of punishment will not work if they predictably are not to be imposed by a community that perceives the action to be acceptable. If there is no consensus as to both the definition of a harmful act and the justification of the law punishing that act, then the law will not be enforced and the entire exercise is meaningless.[25]

Threats and offers are effective insofar as they cover a limited number of actions. The drive to broaden control over the population by vaguely identifying punishable actions weakens rather than strengthens articulating power. Indeed, the vaguer the definition of the transgression, the less people will know what they are expected to do or not to do. Perceived as random violence by the populace, terrorist activities inevitably generate confusion. Thus, the ignorance among Argentines as to what they were expected to do or refrain from doing brought about fear and confusion, hence neutralizing articulating power and effective democratic action.

Since articulating power is, by definition, exercised for the benefit of the community by those in political office and official roles, general respect for and recognition of such offices and roles become essential for effective governance.[26] Penalties imposed by a person or body that the community considers representative of its interests will have a more dissuasive effect than those enacted by persons or institutions considered to act independently of the community's will. Like the general acceptance of positive rules this is a case where, for practical purposes, articulating power and authority concur.

The exercise of articulating power requires more than just minimal precision of communication. To achieve social coordination by inducing certain actions presupposes a fluent exchange of information between the government and the citizens, as well as among the citizens themselves. To achieve their purposes those in power require cooperative schemes based on groups and individuals easily and consistently exchanging messages to make their contributions fit common endeavors. Essential to the exercise of power thus conceived is the existence of a common normative reality. In the execution of standard practices individuals are expected to coordinate their actions by observing common practices governed by generally acknowledged rules: activities such as driving cars would be impossible if they were not carried out on the basis of common assumptions, in this case that the rest of the drivers will conform to an identical set of rules and practices.[27]

Terror makes these coordinated practices unattainable. In broad terms, political disengagement and fear of participating in group activities isolate individuals and, as some authors have mentioned, competition and self-help take the place of assistance and cooperation.[28] State terrorism hampers coordination and frustrates the exercise of articulating power. It seems only too obvious to point out that when terror reigns all communication becomes substantially impaired. Anguish drives citizens to select information (whimsically) to build their reality on individually "chosen" bits and pieces of social events, and the resulting variety of beliefs about a particular topic makes meaningful communication unfeasible. The vast diversity of perceptions—with no consistent possibility or means of confirmation—generates a communication gap between individuals and between sectors of society. Under a terrorist state, the gap between individuals results not just from different perceptions of reality but also from a conscious reluctance to communicate.[29] With very few exceptions do we feel safe enough to expose ourselves to others when ominous and vague threats haunt us. We become chronically afraid that, by being overheard or carelessly quoted, our opinions will reach those who are continually watching.

In Buenos Aires, everybody "knew" that their telephones were bugged and their conversations monitored. Although the state regime must have had some capacity to eavesdrop on suspects, such supervision would have required thousands of communications and intelligence experts to tap half the telephones whose owners were certain to be under surveillance. In the face of "certainty" of having their telephones tapped, large sections of the middle class "communicated" only in a contrived coded language which increased confusion and anxiety even further. This coded language consisted of utterances that evoked certain persons or situations. We expected our associations to be matched by our interlocutor. This improvised system led, of course, to perplexing misunderstandings. Thus, terror created an insurmountable barrier to the exchange of even the most ordinary messages.

Terror also posed a comparable obstacle to the necessary communication between state and citizens. Communication between the government and the citizenry is by definition impeded when individuals have no idea about what acts, utterances, or gestures other than sheer and visible obeisance may turn them into enemies of the regime. For the majority, official secrecy and the randomness of state-sponsored violence left little room for safety. The policy of terror not only splits citizens' perceptions of reality but persistently inculcates a sense of worthlessness among them. Individuals have no rights. They are constantly reminded that respect does not exist, only force does.

In a world of secrecy and arbitrariness even subaltern state officials are inevitably thrown into confusion. Frequently not privy to their superiors' whims, lower-level security personnel find themselves confronting a world of danger and hostility. Often targets themselves of the left-wing insurgency until the midseventies, police personnel in Argentina knew little about the meaning of the violence and even less about the overall strategy they were to implement.

Despite being direct participants in the repression campaign, police officers were nevertheless ignorant of the design behind the dirty war. It was for them a disorienting experience. Reluctant to give up a façade of control over the situation, low- and middle-rank police officers became extremely hostile to the population at large. They too found themselves uninformed and confused. The little room a terrorist state has for articulating power is largely confined to those contexts in which proximity allows for the effectiveness of direct and specific orders. Take for instance a military patrol signaling drivers to take a detour. Beyond these direct orders, the effect of terror transforms power into the ability to destroy connections among citizens, thwarting any possible coordinated opposition. The whole notion of power as an intentional process is largely narrowed down to disarticulating power, to "the ability to talk and not to listen."[30] This renewed need to resort to force and the thousands of persons tortured and made to disappear instilled the (implicit and explicit) notion that, in Argentina, suffering was an inevitable fact of life. As perceived by the population at large, the inevitability of pain provides the explanation for the acquired practice of blaming the victims of state brutality: the form of structural power stemming from a terrorist state.

Blame plays an important role in the everyday life of a rights-based community. Scholars in the liberal tradition often claim that when some individuals break the rules of this society and cause harm to others, outrage for these deeds is converted into blame. By blaming the transgressors, liberals maintain, we foster a sense of moral responsibility both in the perpetrator and among members of society at large. Blaming also strengthens solidarity among individuals.[31] As a vehicle of control, blame conveys moral disapproval for harmful actions and converts this disapproval into indignation. By blaming those who infringe our rights we are issuing a message to society at large that such actions ought not to be repeated, while providing reasons for the wrongdoer to realize that he or she has trampled our values.[32] This ideal form of blame is actually entrenched in our moral practices and beliefs in two ways: first, by denouncing those who break society's rules; second, by convincing those who have wronged others that they deserve our condemnation. Thus, while based on past events, blame is also forward looking in that it creates an incentive for fostering respect for social values and practices.[33] For the liberal version, blame bolsters the authority of legal rules and practices. This notion of blame, however, is only a moral ideal.

Attaching lofty moral overtones to blame assumes that we can squarely distinguish certain actions as bringing about harmful consequences. This process of identifying those morally responsible for harming others is inherently the case for those judged "guilty" of transgressions of criminal law. Based on the dual logic of "guilty" and "innocent," criminal legislation purports to provide clear parameters to establish which actions are relevant in bringing about certain harms. Beyond the realm of the criminal legal practice, however, the issue of moral responsibility is, by and large, subject to disagreement, negotiation, and constant change. In the 1940s and 1950s few people in the United States would have blamed the automobile manufacturers for the accidents suffered by those driving their cars. The locus of blame fell generally on the driver's possible negligence, as did our blaming the swimmers for the diseases they contracted in waters contaminated by industrial waste.[34] While retaining its claim to moral authoritativeness, the practice of blame has shifted over time, as did our notions of causation and moral responsibility. Beyond the practice of the criminal law, "one-factor" explanations that posit the blame on a single party are usually the consequence of oversimplifying events.[35] As a general principle, the more we reflect on the origins of suffering, the more we conceive of it as the outcome of a complex set of circumstances rather than the effect of a single cause. In defining reality as consisting of only "friends" and "enemies," the authoritarian mind is prone to this kind of one-factor oversimplification.

The process of this changing and often concurrent understanding of the causes of harm and the resulting shifts of blame does not detract from our original assumption that, as currently practiced, blame has strong moral overtones. It expresses moral disapproval and indignation and seeks to transform the future behavior of those who belong to the class of the individuals we blame.

The Argentine terrorist state drastically modified the connections between blame, morality, and the transgression of accepted rules and values. Silencing our outrage at brutality becomes a structural feature of society because conscious indignation against state violence becomes both too painful and too dangerous. People live in constant fear that their condemnation will become known and thus draw the violence upon themselves. Moreover, the sense of inevitability of suffering strips the practice of blaming of its mission of inhibiting future harmful actions. Blame ceases to be a morally based mechanism of social control. As a consequence, Argentine society developed the habit of blaming the victims of repression. The system of terror had, to use Barrington Moore's words, "expropriated" the citizens' moral outrage.[36] In consequence, people shifted the focus of their anguish from the perpetrators to the victims.

In October 1982 an upper-middle-class businessman named Marcelo Dupont was, like many others in the 1970s, abducted and found murdered in an empty lot in downtown Buenos Aires with physical signs of having been brutally tortured. The general assumption was, and still is, that Dupont had been murdered in retaliation for his brother's efforts to investigate the murder of diplomat Elena Holmberg. At the time of her assassination, Holmberg was serving as a military regime's representative official in Paris, and the general conjecture was that she had learned about covert transactions in Europe between the regime and the Montoneros, a left-wing insurgent Peronista group.[37] A few days after the discovery of Dupont's corpse bearing signs of torture, I mentioned the issue to a colleague I ran into at the courthouse. His reply was simple and very familiar in Argentina: "¿quien lo manda meterse?" (who asked him to interfere). He meant, of course, that by sticking his nose where he should not have, Gregorio Dupont had brought about his brother's assassination. The victim's brother, in a sense a victim himself, must have been responsible for the assassination.

This seemingly strange practice of displacing blame onto the sufferer is impeccably described in the prologue of *Nunca Mas*:

> In the Argentine society, the idea of un-protection became increasingly entrenched, the dark fear that anybody, no matter how innocent, could fall victim to that infinite witch hunt. Some were absorbed by overwhelming fear, while others were controlled by the conscious or unconscious proclivity to justify horror: "It must be something s/he must have done," was the whisper, as wanting to favor inscrutable Gods, looking at the children or parents of the disappeared as if they were pest-ridden. These sentiments were vacillating, because it was known that so many had been swallowed up by that bottomless abyss without being guilty of anything; because the struggle

against the "subversive," with the drift that characterizes the hunting of witches and the possessed, had turned into a dementedly generalized repression; because the epithet "subversive" had such a vast and unpredictable reach.[38]

In a state based on terror, blame serves several psychic functions that have little to do with the standard moral sentiments I have described. Blame constitutes a way to distance ourselves from those who suffer.[39] By "establishing" that the victim did something worthy of chastisement, and we did not, we diminish our fear that we will be the next to suffer. We are not exactly like them; after all, they belong to a social category different from our own. We also feel less impotent before injustice. By blaming the victim we attempt to safeguard ourselves. Additionally, in attaching blame to the victim's actions we suppress our own responsibility for the occurrence. But in a state of systematic brutality blame has yet another effect that, one could say, places us as close to the torturers and the assassins as our conscience will allow. By censoring the victim we convey a subtle message, perhaps imperceptible to ourselves, that we do not oppose the repressor's actions, either because we simply take death and suffering as a given or because we approve of the terrorist tactics. By blaming the tortured and the disappeared we place ourselves beyond any suspicion that we empathize with the victim.

State-sponsored violence generates extreme uncertainty and confusion.[40] The commonly perceived inevitability of harm and the mechanism of directing our reproach toward the suffering, with the unconscious expectation that "something will improve," become outstanding features of structural power in a state of terror. This aberrant use of blame had an extremely negative impact on society's moral standards. Transformed into the expression of anguish, blaming the victim also became the language of our self-interest, waiving a possible claim to impartiality as moral authoritativeness demands. Consequently, in a roundabout way, by giving up this moral authority to suppress violence, society learned to condone this violence. The answer to the suppression of the individuals' moral worth and dignity was to acknowledge that people, in fact, had no rights.

Thus conceived, blame fed into the rulers' assumption that the world was a gigantic conspiracy. Only those who sympathized with the subversive would condemn the regime or, worse, lobby foreign and international human rights organizations.

To summarize, in a terrorist state power adopts peculiar forms. Devoid of authority, officials in such a state find that the absence of adequate communication channels makes the exercise of articulating power extremely limited at best. This deficiency in the capacity to coordinate actions is replaced by the further use of disarticulating power and an increased reliance on (and an implicit justification of) random violence.

The dramatic increase in the use of disarticulating power alters society's beliefs and practices, thereby re-molding structural power. One of the consequences of this change consists of detaching the practice of blame from its usual moral connotations. Instead of focusing on those who bring about pain, we focus blame on the victim as a mechanism to minimally control future events and avoid (or at least reduce) our anguish: we think of the victims as members of a community separate from ours.

Events since the early 1990s in Argentina seem to indicate that the practice of state-controlled terror still translates into the habit of blaming the victim. There are numerous examples of this phenomenon,[41] but few are illustrative as the incidents that unfolded at the "Rural Expo 1993" Exposicion Rural 1993. This annual affair is the showcase for the largest and most powerful ranchowners association in Argentina. On August 14, 1993, violence erupted as an organized gang assailed spectators who jeered at President Carlos Menem after his inaugural speech to protest against his administration's economic policies. Oblivious to the heavy police presence in the area, the gang went on to attack protesters outside the compound. Journalists covering the events were also the victims of the violence, and some of their cameras destroyed.

With violence reminiscent of the military dictatorship's dirty war techniques, the area seemed to have become a "free zone" (zona liberada) where mobsters enjoyed an immunity similar to that of the anti-subversive hit-squads in the 1970s. Not a single assailant was arrested in spite of the abundant witnesses and security personnel deployed in the exposition's area given the presence of the president and members of his cabinet.[42] Conjectures about where the attackers had come from varied considerably. For some, the brow-beaters had been recruited at a soccer club whose president, a man called Barrionuevo, belongs in Menem's closest circle. Others presumed that, like other bands operating in the Buenos Aires area, the gang had been hired by Menem's supporters at the Mercado Central (Central Market). Other researchers believe that some members of these gangs had operated among the army's gangs (patotas) and task forces that performed abductions and assassinations during the military dictatorship.[43] After publishing a note in *Pagina 12*[44] explaining how bullies were recruited at the Mercado Central, a journalist named Hernan Lopez Echague was attacked on August 19. A week later he suffered a second and almost fatal assault. He was taken to the nearest hospital by a beneficent taxi driver who found him lying unconscious in the street. In what clearly seems a deterrent to reporters' intrusiveness, a second reporter had his face slashed with a switch blade. President Menem and Eduardo Duhalde, his former vice president and now the governor of Buenos Aires province, did not reveal the slightest alarm. They non-chalantly attributed the violence to passing partisan political passions that, like the cold weather, would soon wither away.[45]

To nearly everybody's amazement, government officials remained undisturbed by the episode at the Rural Exposition. Secretary of Agriculture Felipe Sola candidly explained to the press that the attacks "were caused" by those who had attended the inauguration "to insult the President."[46] In reference to the beating of journalists, President Menem's former ambassador to Honduras, Alberto Brito Lima, who had witnessed the incident, disclosed a similar view. The violence, Brito stated, was a "logical reaction to the press' unfair reports."[47] For those familiar with recent Argentine history, Brito's statements did not come as a surprise: Brito had been an eager participant in the hunt for left-wing "subversives" in the pre-military 1973–1976 elected regime.[48] Thus, his assessment that "there was something they must have done to bring the beating upon themselves" was indeed Brito's foreseeable reaction.

Information surfaced that old extreme right-wing Peronista militants were also present at the exposition. Experienced brow-beater Jorge Cesarsky had also attended the Rural's inauguration. Cesarsky had a reputation as the underling of ultra-right-wing Peronista Lieutenant Colonel Jorge Osinde, who allegedly commanded the killings and torturing of hundreds of young left-wing militants near the Ezeiza airport when Perón returned from Spain in 1973.[49] An admirer of Jose Primo de Rivera,[50] Generalissimo Franco's fascistic ideologue in the 1930s, Cesarsky bluntly justified the aggression.[51] With the same words with which Perón dispatched the left-wing activists to their fate in 1973, Cesarsky explained that those who had suffered the violence at the exposition were "infiltrators."[52] He added that the "real aggressors" were those who suffered the blows: the "subversive of the 1970s."[53] The pervasive appeal to violence that Argentina's society exhibits at different levels exposes the degree of the country's authoritarian contempt for individual rights, which may surprise many who observed the support of the 1985 human rights trials.

In spite of the widespread support that individual rights groups enjoyed in the early and mid-1980s, especially in 1985 during the trials of military officers, it seems that individual rights have lost their appeal in the Argentina of the 1990s. Except for a very small group of political and human rights activists, and a similarly small number of students, basic rights are unimportant for the population at large. Indeed, the populace seems well adapted to violence. Other cases that point to the population's readiness to tolerate torture explain the hypothesis that, in Argentina, blaming the victim is still an ideological response to the practice of terror.

Thus, there seem to be some indicators against the usual assumption that articulating, disarticulating, and structural power stem from incompatible conceptions of social reality and that it is futile to contrast "intentional," conscious ways of exercising articulating and disarticulating power to unconscious, ideological manifestations of power. It seems that the nature and breadth of articulating power conditions the extent of disarticulating power and the extent and nature of structural power as well. This interpretation, and the shape of structural power in particular, point to the regeneration of violence and to the perpetuation of terror.

NOTES

1. See Carlos S. Nino, *Un Pais al Margen de la Ley: Estudio de la Anomia como Componente del Subdesarrollo Argentino* (A Country Beyond the Law: Anomie as a Component of Argentinean Underdevelopment) (Buenos Aires: Emece Editores, 1992). In this book Nino deals with Argentina's anomie, a problem in a society whose members permanently disregard express rules of conduct.
2. Between 1976 and 1983, Argentina was ruled by a terrorist military regime. Under the de facto control of four juntas, military personnel made extensive use of torture and assassination in the name of saving the country from internal "subversion."
3. I use both names of the islands to quell two kinds of critiques: first, that of being impervious to reality, and second of deserting the Argentinean traditional claim to the archipelago. I thus acknowledge the legal fact (one shared by almost the entire world) and attempt to avert being considered callous, disloyal or both. Calling them "Falklands" is realistic; calling them "Malvinas" averts friction with my compatriots.
4. Richard Flathman, *The Practice of Political Authority: Authority and the Authoritative* (Chicago: University of Chicago Press, 1980), 128.
5. See, for instance, Patricia Weiss Fagen, "Repression and State Security" in *Fear at the Edge: State Terror and Resistance in Latin America,* ed. Juan Corradi, Patricia Weiss Fagen, and Manuel Antonio Garreton (Berkeley: University of California Press, 1992), 39–71.
6. Simone Weil, "The Iliad: Or the Poem of Force," *A Pendle Hill Pamphlet,* Wallingford, Pa., trans. Mary McCarthy, no. 91 (1956).
7. See for instance, Bryan Magee, *Popper* (London: Fontana and Collins, 1973).
8. I claim that this ideology is the basis upon which we define reality, thus rendering learning about this reality as a confirmation of our predictions rather than a "discovery."
9. See Carolyn Nordstrom and JoAnn Martin, "The Culture of Conflict: Field Reality and Theory," in *The Paths of Domination, Resistance and Terror,* ed. Carolyn Nordstrom and JoAnn Martin (Berkeley: University of California Press, 1992), 6.

10. One can assimilate the option of suffering excruciating pain to that of the moral notion of duress.

11. Simone Weil, "The Iliad: Or the Poem of Force."

12. See Viktor E. Frankl, *El hombre en busca de sentido,* Herder, Spanish trans. by Giorki, 15th ed. (Barcelona, 1993), 62.

13. Hannah Arendt, *On Violence* (San Diego: Harvest HBJ, 1969).

14. Arendt, *On Violence,* 43 and 46.

15. Although Arendt conflates the notion of authority with one of power, she acknowledges that only authority lies on the "unquestioned recognition" of a particular person or an office (Arendt, *On Violence,* 45.)

16. Arendt, *On Violence,* p. 37.

17. Arendt, *On Violence,* p. 37.

18. This distinction is acknowledged by Hannah Arendt in other works, for example, *Between Past and Future: Eight Exercises in Political Thought* (Auckland: Penguin Books, 122).

19. See Joseph Raz, *The Morality of Freedom* (Oxford: Clarendon Press, 1988), ch. 1.; Richard E. Flathman, *The Practice of Political Authority: Authority and the Authoritative* (Chicago: University of Chicago Press, 1980), ch. 7.

20. See Michael Taylor, *Community, Anarchy and Liberty* (London: Cambridge University Press, 1982), 10. To the concepts of threat and offers Taylor adds the concept of a "throffer." A combination of punishment and reward, a throffer consists of O obtaining a benefit if he does X, and a punishment if he does not do X.

21. See Taylor, *Community, Anarchy and Liberty,* 13.

22. see David Garland, *Punishment and Modern Society: A Study in Social Theory* (Chicago: University of Chicago Press, 1990), 138–139.

23. Garland, *Punishment and Modern Society,* 149.

24. Garland, *Punishment and Modern Society,* 149.

25. See Thomas E. Wartemberg, *The Forms of Power: From Domination to Transformation* (Philadelphia: Temple University Press, 1990), ch. 7.

26. Flathman, *The Practice of Political Authority,* 150.

27. See, for instance, Jean Piaget, *Les operations et la vie sociale,* Publications des Sciences Economiques et Sociales de L'université de Genève (Geneva: Georg, 1945).

28. Juan Corradi, "The Culture of Fear in Civil Society," in *From Military Rule to Liberal Democracy in Argentina,* ed. Monica Peralta-Ramos and Carlos H. Waisman (Boulder, Colo.: Westview Press, 1987), 113–131.

29. See Patricia Weiss Fagen, "Repression and State Security," in *Fear at the Edge: State Terror and Resistance in Latin America* (Berkeley: University of California Press, 1992), 39–71.

30. See Karl W. Deutsch, *The Nerves of Government: Models of Political Communication and Control* (New York: Free Press, 1966), 111.

31. See Garland, *Punishment and Modern Society,* ch. 3.

32. For instance, R. A. Duff, *Trials and Punishment* (Cambridge: Cambridge University Press, 1991), 47.

33. See Marion Smiley, *Moral Responsibility and the Boundaries of Community: Power and Accountability from a Moral Point of View* (Chicago: University of Chicago Press, 1992), 177.

34. See Smiley, *Moral Responsibility and the Boundaries of Community*, 167.

35. Paul Watzlawick, *Change: Principles of Problem Formation and Problem Resolution* (New York: W. W. Norton, 1974), 45.

36. See Barrington Moore, Jr., *Injustice: The Social Basis of Obedience and Revolt* (New York: M. E. Sharpe, 1978), 500.

37. See Martin Edwin Andersen, *Dossier Secreto: Argentina's Desaparecidos and the Myth of the "Dirty War"* (Boulder, Colo.: Westview Press, 1993). According to Andersen, the abduction and assassination of Marcelo Dupont was carried out by Army Intelligence Battalion 601 personnel in an effort to discredit Naval Service Commander Emilio Massera. What made Massera the top suspect was the fact that Marcelo Dupont's brother Gregorio was investigating the assassination of diplomat Helena Holmberg, allegedly slain by Massera's thugs.

38. Prologue, *Nunca Mas: Informe de la Comision Nacional Sobre la Desaparicion de Personas*, 14th. ed. (Buenos Aires: Editorial Universitaria de Buenos Aires, 1986), 9.

39. Judith Shklar goes one step further to claim that blame itself lies with those who are empowered. Blaming others for an injustice differs from mere fatalities in that, in the case of the second, the victim is devoid of control over the situation to consider the event as a simple accident, an inevitable mishap. See Judith N. Shklar, *The Faces of Injustice* (New Haven: Yale University Press, 1990).

40. Moore, *Injustice,* 458.

41. Argentine acceptance of torture in the 1990s is revealed not solely by reports of brutal police procedures. A large portion of the citizenry accepts the inhumane treatment of suspects when such treatment is allegedly employed to protect the security and property of "decent citizens from a growing street criminality." For example, a crowd staged a demonstration in the suburbs of Buenos Aires in support of police officer Luis Patti after his indictment for torturing prisoners under investigation (*Pagina 12* [Buenos Aires newspaper], Sept. 14, 1990). When the court arrested Patti for torturing two detainees, the community at large stood up in defense of the police officer. For instance, the forensic experts that examined him declared on Patti's behalf that some detainees would harm themselves—"even with electrified wires"—in order to cast blame on their captors. A Buenos Aires journal reports that the country's public opinion was split between those who considered Patti a torturer and those who considered him a defender of security. The Oct. 19, 1990, issue of the Buenos Aires journal *Ambit Financier* reports that in districts where he had served, Patti's reputation for brutality earned him the blessings of a vast sector of the population. Turned into a public figure, the policeman became a frequent guest at social events, including a television show where he danced the tango before millions of spectators. Patti declared that he "not only makes people dance but also dances himself." (In Argentine jargon to "dance" means to suffer inflicted pain.) He made this statement when asked to dance on a popular television show (Channel 9, Silvio Soldan's show in Buenos Aires)). Argentina's former vice president, Eduardo Duhalde, pointed out that Patti was a "model for policemen." (*See Buenos Aires Herald,* Aug. 8, 1991. See also *Pagina 12*, Sept. 14, 1991.) Furthermore, Patti's reputation induced Argentine President Menem to choose him for a special assignment, namely to investigate a case of rape and murder of

a young woman, Maria Soledad Morales, in the northern province of Catamarca (ibid.) The case had become the focus of public attention throughout the country because of the personalities implicated in Morales's death. Among them were high police personnel, members of Catamarca's governor's inner circle, and a national congressman, Guillermo Luque (see *Pagina 12*, Sept. 9, 1991.) An overwhelming majority of distant Catamarca's population enthusiastically welcomed Patti's arrival. Patti became elected major in the May 1995 local elections.

The case of Horacio Santos is another example of the inclination to approve brutality. A respected engineer from Buenos Aires, Horacio Santos killed two young men for having stolen his car stereo. The victim of previous minor, nonviolent assaults on his property, Santos engaged in a frantic car chase that ended in the death of both robbers at the hands of their pursuer. Santos literally executed the thieves by shooting them in the head at point-blank range once they had stepped out of their car and offered to return the stolen stereo. Journalists, politicians, and a vast sector of the Buenos Aires public opinion declared that Santos had done the right thing. Like Patti's case, Santos's incited heated arguments. His supporters, however, were astonishingly numerous. Well-known television journalists justified the killing, stating that they would have acted in the same way had they been in Santos's shoes. When queried by television journalists, Santos's neighbors praised his action as a contribution to cleansing the vicinity of potential thieves. Lawyer Antonio Troccoli, President Alfonsín's Minister of the Interior, stopped short of applauding Santos by blaming the occurrence on the state's inability to curb street crime. If ordinary citizens are forced to bear arms from want of security in the streets, Troccoli reasoned, unsavory episodes like that of Santos's are likely to occur.

Argentina's renewed contempt for human rights has had international repercussions. Current violations of human rights in Argentina were brought to the attention of the Spanish public when a Spanish police officer was convicted of torture after the tribunal rebuffed his claim that he had acted under his superiors' directives. A journalist commenting on the case wrote that it was unfortunate that the officer had performed torture in Spain instead of Argentina, the "kingdom of impunity." (See Juan Carlos Martinez, *Pagina 12*, Oct. 30, 1990.)

An illustrative analysis of police abuses is reflected in Paul G. Chevigny, "Police Deadly Force as Social Control: Jamaica, Argentina, and Brazil," 1 *Crim. L. R.* 389 (1990). See also Americas Watch and Centro de Studios Legales y Sociales, *Police Violence in Argentina: Torture and Police Killings in Buenos Aires* (Report) (1991).

42. See Buenos Aires newspaper *Pagina 12*, Aug. 14 and 15, 1993; *La Nacion*, Aug. 19, 1993, 7.
43. See Laura Termine et al., "Las jaulas abiertas," *Noticias* (magazine), Sept. 5, 1993, 72.
44. See *Pagina 12*, Aug. 22, 1993.
45. See James Neilson, "La lucha es cruel," *Noticias*, Sept. 12, 1993, 76.
46. Televised news on Aug. 16, 1993.
47. *Pagina 12*, Aug. 18, 1993.
48. See Eugenio Mendez, *Confesiones de un Montonero: La otra cara de la historia*, 3rd ed. (Buenos Aires: Sudamericana-Planeta, 1986), 81.

49. For example, Joseph A. Page, *Peron: A Biography* (New York: Random House, 1983), 462.

50. Many right-wing Peronistas had adopted the image of Primo de Rivera as their hero. See Leonardo Senkman, "The Right and Civilian Regimes, 1955–1976," in *The Argentine Right: Its History and Intellectual Origins, 1910 to the Present,* ed. Sandra McGee Deutsch and Ronald H. Dolkart (Wilmington, Del.: Scholarly Resource, 1984), 131.

51. See *Pagina 12,* Aug. 18, 1993.

52. See *Pagina 12,* Aug. 18, 1993.

53. See *Pagina 12,* Aug. 18, 1993, 2.

Chapter 12 Deliberation, Disagreement, and Voting

Jeremy Waldron

The opening pages of Carlos Nino's *Constitution of Deliberative Democracy* are dominated by a contrast between the *pluralist* model of democratic decision-making and his own favored *deliberative* conception.[1] The prime virtue of deliberative democracy, according to Nino, was its capacity "to *transform* people's interests and preferences" through the mechanism of collective deliberation.[2] The method of deliberative dialogue and majority decision-making has, he said, "a greater tendency to impartial solutions than any other method of reaching decisions which affect the group, such as that provided by the reflection of an isolated individual."[3] In a democracy, everyone is entitled to a hearing. In a democracy organized around the idea of deliberation, the advancement of one's interests must be accompanied by an account of their importance which might conceivably appeal to others (i.e., by something approaching a justification). And in a deliberative democracy where decisions are taken by majority voting, everyone has an interest in maximizing the number of others who end up supporting the view that he or she is putting forward. These three characteristics of deliberative democracy make it, in Nino's words, "more probable that democratic decisions in the intersubjective moral sphere [decisions that affect more than one person] will be correct than those adopted by other methods."[4] They give deliberative democracy what Nino calls an "epistemic edge" over its more familiar pluralist rival.

Read carelessly, the fact that Nino used the word *pluralism* for the model of democracy that he rejected might suggest, by way of contrast, a necessary connection between impartiality and *singularity* in the context of deliberative democracy. It might suggest something along the following lines.

The partial interests to which pluralism panders are many and various: my interests are not the same as yours, her interests are not the same as his, theirs are not the same as ours, and so on. Impartiality by contrast is singular: there are many partial interests but only one *im*partial solution. Thus what deliberation can offer us is not just impartiality but consensus. Inasmuch as we are each oriented toward an impartial solution, we are each oriented toward the same solution; and this sense of common orientation guides us in our deliberation with one another. Or to put it the other way round: any lingering plurality of views, any lingering dissensus, is a sure sign that some partial interests have not yet been completely transformed into impartial ones.

Of course, we should know better than this. The term *pluralism* refers only to the multiplicity of interests in society, and to a theory of democracy that proposes to handle such interests on their own terms and not to try to transform them into something else. It is not intended to suggest that monism is a distinguishing feature of opposing conceptions. The contrast is rather between theories that take individual *interests* as the appropriate currency of politics, and theories that take individual *views or opinions about the common good* as the appropriate currency of politics. That contrast says nothing about whether we can expect there to be only one impartial view about the common good or many such views abroad in society, both inside and outside the arenas of deliberation. In other words, plurality or pluralism—in the sense of the existence of a diversity of well-reasoned and reasonable positions—may be as much a feature of a deliberative conception as of those interest-based approaches to democracy that we are more used to characterizing as "pluralist."

The link that Nino set up between deliberative democracy and voting is particularly interesting in this regard. Deliberative democracy and majority voting can easily be made to seem odd bed-fellows. Deliberation, we are told, characteristically aims at consensus; yet it is only under circumstances of *dis*sensus— an unresolved diversity of opinion or position—that anything like voting is called for. As a last resort, maybe, when deliberation seems unable to take us any further, we may need simply to count heads and see which of the competing positions has the greater support. But there is something embarrassing about voting in a deliberative context—or at least that is the impression we are given—and those committed to deliberation will often go to extraordinary lengths to avoid it.

Voting seems like an admission of failure, for it shows that a discussion based on the merits has failed to resolve the issue. Voting shifts us from the qualitative consideration of substance to the sheer quantitative business of seeing which proposition enjoys the support of the greatest number. When those who write about deliberation turn their attention to voting, the sense of distaste is almost palpable: the sneer-quotes which Ronald Dworkin puts around the phrase "the crude statistical view of democracy" is a fine example, as though a commitment to majoritarianism were a blind and meaningless faith in numbers, and as such an affront to the view that our decisions should be made for reasons.[5]

The two issues—the relation between deliberation and voting and the relation between deliberation and plurality—are of course connected. We sense that there is something arbitrary about making decisions on a statistical basis. We are aware, however, that there may be nothing else to do but vote if deliberation has left us with an unredeemed plurality of opinions in a situation where a single course of action is called for. Reasoning backward, it seems that the stubborn persistence of a plurality of opinions is incompatible with deliberative democracy after all. For if it were not, the idea of resolving a matter finally by voting would not seem such a gigantic affront to our sense of what deliberation involves.

I would like somehow to break up the rigidity of this logic by turning the argument in the other direction. I think we should start from a sense that there is likely to be a diversity of impartial opinions about justice or the good, and that consensus is not ordinarily to be expected on the subject matter of politics. We should take that as our premise, and then work toward the conclusion that therefore there cannot be this repugnance between deliberation and majority voting. I want in other words to call for the development of a theory of democracy that makes voting the natural culmination of deliberation, rather than an indication that deliberation has been in some sense inadequate. We need a theory of deliberation that dovetails with voting, not a theory of deliberation that is embarrassed by it.

Is Nino's conception such a theory? In a way, yes, and in a way, no. The prospect that, at the end of the discussion, there will be a vote and that the social decision will be taken by majority rule, is, on Nino's account, an important element in the transformation of partial expressions of individual preferences into opinions that are somewhat more impartial. I favor the policy choice that offers more money for myself, but I quickly recognize that this consideration by itself is not an instant passport to political success, and that I will have to develop arguments for the policy I favor that offer something to the other voters whose support will be needed if this choice is to prevail. The need for majority support is what makes me take the interests of others into account in the proposals that I make. That was the essence of Nino's argument.

In fact, of course, there is no guarantee that the exigencies of majority voting will have this effect of making the substance of particular proposals more impartial. They may have instead the effect of encouraging rather simple logrolling: you support my self-interested proposal and I will support yours. The political positions themselves remain untransformed. That, many think, is the condition of legislative politics in the United States.

But even if Nino's model had the effect that he anticipates, it is not quite the conception I am looking for or that I think we need. If you think of a deliberative process from start to finish as a black box, with inputs (the participants' initial positions) and outputs (the participants' final positions), then Nino's model postulates partial expressions of interest as the inputs and impartial positions (or in the ideal case, maybe just the one "correct" impartial position) as outputs, with majoritarianism playing an important role in the transformation that takes place in between. It is less easy to see what role the majoritarian process is supposed to play if we postulate instead that the various inputs are already impartial positions or opinions concerning the common good.

I do not mean that deliberation has no further transformative effect if voter's positions are already impartial. Clearly it can have a useful and salutary effect. People can pick up on one another's errors of reasoning, remind one another of things they may have overlooked, pool their experience and information, enrich one another's insights, and so on. In these and other ways, the deliberative process can take certain given inputs—people's initial impartial positions—and transform them into different—one hopes richer, more nuanced, better informed—positions than they were to begin with. It is less clear what role the specifically majoritarian aspect of deliberative democracy plays in this transformation. For the deliberative transformation from impartial inputs to better impartial outputs, it is clear why deliberation matters but it is not clear why it matters that the deliberation be conducted with a view to eventual voting in the event that disagreement persists. (I say "not clear why it matters," not as a coy philosopher's way of saying that it does not matter, but as a way of calling for a theory of deliberation which would show why it does.)

It is something of an embarrassment for political philosophy that we have not developed a convincing theory or array of theories to justify the practice of majority voting among people who disagree about what the common good requires. It is an embarrassment to have to admit—for example, to one's students—that the strongest argument we have for majority rule—a utilitarian argument—assumes that voters are *not* voting impartially but are instead voting their own self-interest. So even the best argument we have is not very good.

That argument goes as follows. If people vote their own preferences, there may be some rough equivalence between the formal outcome of a majority process and the substantive recommendations of a utilitarian political morality. As long as votes represent the prospect of individual satisfactions, then the utilitarian principle favors the policy that attracts the largest number of votes. But the equivalence between the principle of utility and majority voting is both rough and very precarious. To take but three obvious problems, the equivalence presupposes: that the class of voters comprises all those whose interests are deemed relevant by the principle of utility; that they are accurate judges of the probability that a given policy will give them what they individually want; and that the political equality accorded to their votes corresponds to an actual equality in the intensity of their preferences. Not only that, but the argument also presupposes that the principle of utility provides the criterion of substantive correctness on all issues of politics, whereas most of us believe that it provides an appropriate criterion for some cases and not for others.[6]

So there are problems enough with the utilitarian defense of majority rule. Anyway, the logic of this argument gets absolutely no grip at all if we take individuals to be voting not their own interests or preferences, but their view of what the common good requires. There may be some point to maximizing the satisfaction of preferences if votes represent preferences, but no utilitarian ever argued that it was good in itself to maximize the number of individual *opinions* about the common good which are followed in the policies we select.[7] We need to look elsewhere for a theory of majority rule in this circumstance; and it is not clear where, exactly, we should turn.

I say that this is an embarrassing predicament for political philosophy in part because we continue to hold out to one another, as citizens, the norm or the ideal that each person's political views should reflect some conception of justice and the common good. We hold this, I believe, as a resilient ideal. The fact that there is disagreement about justice and the common good, and that a vote is going to have to be taken, is not regarded in normative political theory as a reason (or a license) for citizens to abandon their impartial views and revert to voting their self-interested preferences. We therefore ought to have a theory that explains why it is reasonable to require people to submit to majority decision not just their self-interest, but their most impartial, their most earnest, their most high-minded convictions about what justice or the common good requires.

Someone may object that, in the United States at least, this is *not* what our political morality requires. It may require us to submit our impartial views about policy choice to majority decision, but it does not require us to submit our principled moral convictions about justice or rights to the majority process. Quite the contrary, according to this objection: we reserve a special way—a nonmajority or countermajoritarian way—of making decisions on the matters that citizens regard as having the greatest significance for justice and rights. Issues of principle affecting justice or rights are (or can be) decided by the courts; they are regarded as too important to be left to the tender mercies of the majoritarian process. It is thus emphatically not the case, according to this objection, that we have to develop a theory explaining why majority rule is an appropriate or reasonable principle to use on matters of such importance.

I believe this objection to be wrong-headed; and the reason it is wrong-headed is quite telling in the context of my concerns.

Is it in fact our practice to abandon the principle of majority rule when an issue is shifted from popular or representative decision-making to the courts? The answer is clearly no. The principle of majority rule remains as the fundamental basis for settling disagreement about the merits of an issue among the members of a given court. In the Supreme Court of the United States, for example, decisions are taken by voting; and five votes prevail over four, whatever the merits of the individual decisions. (How could it be otherwise? Given that the justices may disagree about the merits, and that they are the final appeal on the matter, what can they do except vote?) The difference, when an issue is shifted from legislature to court or from referendum to court, is a difference of constituency, not a difference of decision method. We stick with the principle of majority rule; only now it is applied to a decision-making body of nine individuals, rather than a body of hundreds (in the case of a legislature) or millions (in the case of a popular initiative). Certainly our practice of referring certain matters to the courts for final decision reflects a distrust of democratic decision-making. But it is a distrust of persons: we don't trust ordinary voters or their representatives on these matters; we prefer the judges. It is not a distrust of the majority principle, for that is a principle we continue to deploy.

I suggest that we should take this as our clue for the development of a more general theory that reconciles voting and deliberation. For there is surely no doubt that the Supreme Court is a deliberative body, and it does not cease to be so when its members disagree with one another, even though their disagreement means that, at the end of their deliberation, the matter before them has to be determined by a vote. This, I say, we should regard as our clue—for it shows that in principle there is nothing incompatible between deliberation, disagreement, and voting. If the combination makes sense in the courtroom, then maybe it also makes sense at the level of a more general theory of deliberative democracy.

What is it about a tribunal like the U.S. Supreme Court that makes voting among the justices a desirable, or necessary, or at least unavoidable feature of its practice? What analogies can we draw between the position of this august body and the circumstances under which men and women generally might come together to deliberate on issues of justice or policy?

1. The first and most obvious point is that the Court comprises several individuals, not just one. We think it inappropriate, for whatever reason, that the final appeal on matters of constitutional importance should be to one person, a sort of judicial or constitutional monarch.

It is interesting that this view is taken for granted, but seldom defended in political or constitutional theory.[8] The contrary view, the case for vesting final authority in one person rather than a group of persons, is stated by Thomas Hobbes: "a Monarch cannot disagree with himselfe, out of envy, or interest; but an Assembly may; and that to such a height, as may produce a Civill Warre."[9] In making his case for a *supreme* court at the national level, Publius in *Federalist XXII* sounded a Hobbesian warning about a plurality of courts: "If there is in each State a court of final jurisdiction, there may be as many different final determinations on the same point as there are courts. . . . To avoid the confusion which would unavoidably result from the contradictory decisions of a number of independent judicatories, all nations have found it necessary to establish one court paramount to the rest." He did notice that the problem arose within courts, not just between them: "There are endless diversities in the opinions of men. We often see not only different courts but *the judges of the same court* differing from each other."[10] But he did not pursue the point. As I say, the matter is rarely addressed explicitly. We just think it obvious that a supreme court should be, in Publius's words, "a distinct body of magistrates," not a single judge.[11] It is as though we have an instinctive preference for the anti-Hobbesian position articulated by Hannah Arendt when she wrote in *The Human Condition* that "sovereignty, the ideal of uncompromising self-sufficiency and mastership, is contradictory to the very idea of plurality. No man can be sovereign because not one man, but men, inhabit the earth."[12]

2. The second feature of the Court's position that is relevant to this discussion is associated with plurality, but logically distinct from it. In theory, one could have a tribunal comprising several individuals who thought alike on all important issues. In practice we expect that reasonable persons, even the wise and learned members of a judicial tribunal, will often disagree on the sort of issues that come before the court. Plurality foreshadows diversity and controversy. The idea of *reasonable* disagreement has recently been elaborated by John Rawls in his account of why the diversity of ethical, religious, and philosophical views must be regarded as a permanent feature of modern society. In *Political Liberalism,* Rawls asks: "Why does not our conscientious attempt to reason with one another lead to reasonable agreement? It seems to do so in natural science, at least in the long run." Rawls uses the phrase "the burdens of judgement" as a way of articulating his answer to this question. The "burdens of judgement" are "the many hazards involved in the correct (and conscientious) exercise of our powers of reason and judgment in the ordinary course of political life."[13] For example, he says that, on any plausible account, human life engages multiple values and it is natural that people will disagree about how to balance or prioritize them. Also, on any plausible account, people's respective positions, perspectives and experiences in life will give them different bases from which to make these delicate judgments. These differences of experience and position combine with the evident complexity of the issues being addressed, meaning that reasonable persons may disagree not openly about what the world is like but about the relevance and weight to be accorded the various facts and insights that they have at their disposal. Together factors like these make disagreement in good faith not only possible but predictable. "Different conceptions of the world can reasonably be elaborated from different standpoints and diversity arises in part from our distinct perspectives. It is unrealistic . . . to suppose that all our differences are rooted solely in ignorance and perversity, or else in the rivalries for power, status, or economic gain." Thus, Rawls concludes, "many of our most important judgments are made under conditions where it is not to be expected that conscientious persons with full powers of reason, even after free discussion, will arrive at the same conclusion."[14]

In *Political Liberalism* the burdens of judgment are used primarily to characterize disagreements about the good, or more broadly, disagreements in comprehensive philosophical conceptions. Evidently, though, the idea can be used to characterize political disagreement as well, including disagreements about rights and justice.[15] The circumstances under which people make judgments about issues like affirmative action, the legalization of abortion, the limits of free speech, the limits of the market, the proper extent of welfare provision, and the role of personal desert in economic justice are exactly those in which we would expect, given Rawls's account of the burdens of judgment, that reasonable persons would differ. As in the case of religious, ethical, or philosophical disagreement, we do not need to invoke bad faith, ignorance, or self-interest as an explanation. The difficulty of the issues is itself sufficient to explain why reasonable people disagree.

Elsewhere I have argued that the prospect of reasonable disagreement *about justice* poses grave problems for Rawls's account of public reason in a well-ordered society.[16] Here it is enough to apply the burdens of judgment to the situation of judges on a court attempting to wrestle with complex questions of justice and right (not to mention the interpretation of a constitutional text): given the nature of the issues they are addressing, it is not reasonably to be expected that nine justices will come up with nine identical opinions.

3. The third feature that characterizes the Supreme Court is one that might be thought to mitigate disagreement, and tilt the institution more toward consensus. We know that the justices come from different backgrounds with different political views, instincts, and ideologies. But they are not just asked for their views on various issues. Arguments are put to them; and their response to those arguments is supposed to be a long and reasoned opinion, not just a vote "Yea" or "Nay." Thus they deliberate about their decision, not only each in his or her own office with his or her own clerks, but also informally and formally with the other justices, and through various practices in our legal system indirectly with all the justices who have gone before on any issue that has anything important in common with the one they are currently addressing.

These highly structured norms and practices of deliberation make the Court in some ways a paradigm of deliberative politics. Indeed Rawls entitles one section "The Supreme Court as Exemplar of Public Reason."[17] This does not mean that Rawls or any one else envisages a whole people acting in the way the members of the Court behave: deliberative democracy, because it involves millions of citizens not just nine, and an open-ended range of issues, must of course be structured differently. Regarding the Court as paradigmatic in this regard is instructive, nevertheless. The fact is that disagreements among the justices survive their best efforts at deliberation. If this highly rarified and formalized process of deliberation on issues that are carefully defined (not to mention related systematically to a document—the Constitution—whose authority is beyond question) does not yield consensus, then it is quite implausible to suppose that deliberation among the citizens at large—however serious—could be expected to yield consensus.

Or if this argument for some reason does not convince, think of the academic profession arguing our way through these issues. We have nothing to do but deliberate, and virtually no incentive—except perhaps intellectual vanity and the exigencies of academic patronage—to make ourselves impervious to reasons and arguments put forward by others. The result is that there is perhaps greater disagreement—certainly more elaborate disagreement—among us than there is among those whose positions and decisions really count, where there really would be incentives to treat reasoning and discussion as just a sham.

I am not saying that deliberation in the Court or among philosophers or in the deliberative democratic polity that we are imagining would have no impact on a decision. It would. It can be expected to enrich people's positions, and it will sometimes reduce disagreement by ensuring that all have access to the same insights and the same information. Even so, we are perfectly familiar with the way in which deliberation can also enrich and elaborate disagreement, can heighten and exacerbate it. I often hear colleagues say at faculty meetings, "I came into this meeting with some mild misgivings about the proposal; but now that I have heard what has been said in its defense, I am utterly and adamantly opposed." This is not always bloody-mindedness. The point, or certainly the effect of deliberation, is often to make explicit the bases of disagreement,[18] and give everyone a reasonably clear picture of what is at stake. The idea that we should think of deliberation as a way of smoothing over our differences to prepare the path to consensus is a terrible distortion: that is the trade of facilitators, mediators, and therapists, and it has nothing in common with politics where values and principles are sometimes robustly at stake.

4. I compared the Supreme Court earlier, in its deliberative aspect, to academics' work in seminars, journals, and conferences. There is of course a crucial difference, the fourth point I want to raise. Whatever their differences and disagreements, the justices are required to come up with a decision—which can count as the decision of the court—on each issue that comes before them. They cannot just agree to differ or to pursue the matter another time. In this sense, their situation is, as ours is not, *political.* For all that they disagree, and for all

that their disagreement is substantively irresolvable, they face a deadline (of sorts) and they must give an authoritative ruling to the parties who come before them.[19]

This fact distinguishes all political bodies—and *a fortiori* all deliberative political bodies—from academic institutions, debating organizations, and the like. (Or rather it distinguishes the political aspect from the nonpolitical aspect of all organizations.)

We can adapt another Rawlsian concept here. Rawls talks about "the circumstances of justice"—the factual aspects of the human condition, such as moderate scarcity and the limited altruism of individuals, which make justice as a virtue and a practice both possible and necessary.[20] (Similarly, the existence of danger, and the human experiences of both fear and resolution, are the circumstances of courage.)[21] We may say, along similar lines, that the felt need among the members of a certain group for a common policy or decision or course of action on some matter, even in the face of disagreement about what that policy, decision, or action should be, are the *circumstances of politics*. Like scarcity and limited altruism in the case of justice, the circumstances of politics are a coupled pair: disagreement would not matter if people did not prefer a common decision; and the need for a common decision would not give rise to politics as we know it if there was not at least the potential for disagreement about what the common decision should be.

This topic—the circumstances of politics—deserves much greater attention in political and legal philosophy than it has received. It is, I believe, the foundation of many of the distinctively political virtues, and it is of course indispensable for an understanding of procedural decision-rules and the concomitant ideas of authority and obligation.[22] In political philosophy we have been far too busy elaborating our own substantive views on justice, rights, and so on to devote much attention to the way in which a polity should approach irresolvable disagreements about justice and rights.

It is because the Supreme Court faces the circumstances of politics that it must take its decisions by voting. Some decision must be reached as between, say, the submission of the appellant and that of the respondent. Moreover, if the members of the Court disagree about the merits of the issue, the invocation of a substantive decision-rule such as "Let right(s) prevail" or "Let the party with justice on its side prevail" will not do. There is no alternative in these circumstances to settling the matter by a procedure which in its terms makes no reference at all to the points on which the decision-makers disagree.

5. This leads to a fifth and very important point about the situation of the Supreme Court. Suppose that the members of the Court disagree on the merits of some decision in front of them, and because a decision is called for, they take a vote. Now there are clearly discernible majority and minority positions, and someone may think it obvious that the majority position should stand as the decision of the *court*. Suppose, however, that a naive young justice opposes this or at least questions it. He or she may say:

> We should not present the majority decision as the Court's decision simply on the ground that there are more justices in favor of it than against it, or more justices in favor of it than in favor of any alternative. That is an outrageously statistical approach to the exercise of the court's authority. This court is supposed to stand for justice (or rights, or the Constitution). So, at most, what we should say is that the majority position stands as the decision of the Court, provided it is *not unjust,* or provided it *respects people's rights,* or provided it is *a proper interpretation of the Constitution.* If on the other hand, the majority decision is unjust or disrespectful of rights or the Constitution, then it should not stand, because justice, rights, and the Constitution are supposed to trump purely procedural or statistical considerations of majority rule.

It would not take long for the more senior justices to point out the defects in this proposal. The provisos that the young justice has proposed are exactly the matters on which the Court disagrees. What is more, the Court is the final appeal on these matters—there is no further Super-Supreme Court to adjudicate the question of whether the proposed provisos are satisfied. And even if there were such a Super-Supreme Court, exactly the same problem would recur in regard to deliberation and disagreement among its members. Justice, rights, and the Constitution cannot trump the majority position, then, because justice, rights, and the Constitution, and their bearing on the case at hand, are exactly the things that the majority and the minority disagree about. At the very least, it would be incumbent on the young justice to stipulate *which view* should be taken as the correct view about justice, rights, and the Constitution for the purposes of his or her proposal. And of course that stipulation would itself be controversial; indeed, it would reproduce exactly the controversy that the Court was called upon to determine in the first place.

So the feature of the Court's position that I want to emphasize under this fifth heading is the non-existence of any "Archimedean point" from which the justice, morality, or constitutionality of a given decision can be assessed. Or rather there are too many such points. Each of the contestant parties, or each of the disagreeing justices, will present his or her view, earnestly held and fiercely defended, as *the* appropriate perspective from which to assess the propriety of the decision being proposed. There is thus no conception from which proposed decisions by the Court can be assessed which is not also one of the contestant views that the Court is being called upon to decide between.

My moral realist friends bristle at this. They will accuse me of moral subjectivism or emotivism or relativism (actually, I am an emotivist, but the distinction is irrelevant for this argument). They will say, "What about objective values—true justice or the truth about rights? Don't those provide a perspective, an Archimedean point, from which the objective truth or correctness of a majority decision can be assessed?" And of course they are right about that. Each justice will scrutinize his or her own position and that of the others in terms of objective values; only, they are likely to disagree about that, too. As long as these vaunted objective values fail to disclose themselves to us, in our consciences or from the skies, in ways that leave no room for further disagreement about their character, all we have on earth are opinions or beliefs about objective values. We have nothing beyond this as a basis for calling some views about values and rights true and others false. Of course, the moral realists will insist stubbornly that there really is, still, a fact of the matter out there. And maybe they are right. But it is surprising how little help this purely existential confidence is in dealing with our decision-problems.[23]

The Supreme Court is a good forum to use in making this point, precisely because it has become in our system the institution of final appeal. But the point applies to democratic decision-making generally. We say things like "The majority should prevail provided it doesn't trample on minority rights," but we often forget that what the majority and minority characteristically disagree about (and why the issue has had to come to a vote) is whether the minority actually *have* the rights that are in question. Some think they do and some don't. (Think of the abortion debate, for example.) Maybe when people say that the majority should prevail provided it doesn't trample on minority rights, they are referring implicitly to the Supreme Court as a separate deliberative body that can address the issue of rights that this raises. In which case, what they are implying is not that the majority decision should be second-guessed by a substantive standard, but rather that one majority decision should be second-guessed by another.[24]

The account I have given of the U.S. Supreme Court as a body that takes its decisions by majority voting is no substitute for the general theory of democracy that I said we need: a theory that not only reconciles deliberation with disagreement and voting, but also makes voting seem the natural upshot of deliberative democratic decision-making, rather than something that indicates the inadequacy or unsatisfactoriness of the deliberation that takes place. But the example or analogy of the Court should be a sign that such a theory is neither impossible nor undesirable. We should think of deliberation with a view to voting, and voting in a way that looks back to what took place in deliberation, as a unified exercise of political (or judicial) virtue, rather than an unsatisfactory compromise between disparate models of democracy.

The other thing that I have not done is provide any argument for the specific principle of majority rule in the sort of circumstances in which the Supreme Court, like other deliberative political bodies, finds itself. I will hide behind the standard excuse: there is no room to attempt that here. I want to conclude, however, by indicating two points in addition to the five above—again about the Supreme Court's situation—that are relevant to this project. Those points are the authority and, so far as authority is concerned, the equality of the justices.

6. We say that the Court itself is an authority, but it is also true that each of the nine members of the Court for the time being is an authority, at least for the purpose of determining what the Court's position ought to be. The fact that Justice Clarence Thomas, for example, is in favor of a decision for the appellant in some particular case is not irrelevant to what the court's decision should be in that case. On the contrary, it should count in favor of the appellant and indeed prevail, unless some other justice holds the opposite view.

This proposition sounds innocuous, even trivial—but its effect is to rule out certain procedures that would otherwise be available to generate a decision in circumstances of disagreement among the justices. We could, for example, toss a coin when the justices disagree. But such a procedure would be objectionable precisely because it did not take the fact that at least one justice was in favor of a given decision as a reason for going with that decision rather than the alternative. Coin-tossing treats the justices' opinions as uninteresting (except perhaps to establish the background of disagreement necessary to invoke the coin-tossing procedure). It does not accord even the conditional authority I described at the end of the previous paragraph to any justice's opinion.

7. Like John Locke, when I say that the justices are equal, "I cannot be supposed to understand all sorts of Equality: Age or Virtue may give Men a just Precedency: Excellency of Parts and Merit may place others above the Common Level."[25] The members of the Court are ranked by seniority, and the public

commonly ranks them by their virtue, learning, and effectiveness, not to mention their politics. They have an order of precedence in their dealings with one another and so on. But in the authority accorded to their opinions—at least as far as the case at hand is concerned—the rule is that they are equal. Particularly when they disagree, the fact that the Chief Justice or a senior justice takes one side or the other makes no difference to the weight accorded to his vote.

This may not be the case in their deliberations. No doubt the arguments and opinions of some justices are taken more seriously and others less so. But to the extent that deliberation is conducted with a view to voting, winning support for one's position from the least wise or most junior judge counts for as much, finally, as winning the support of the greatest jurist among them.

This equality of voting does have the sort of connection with deliberation that I am looking for. Because each member's vote counts equally, deliberation under circumstances of equality is respectful of its audience in a way that deliberation under circumstances of inequality might not be. If the more senior judges had two votes or if their votes counted triple, someone arguing a position in the justices' discussions might be inclined to pay greater attention to their questions and objections than to those whose vote counted for merely one.

There are all sorts of complications here with order of speaking, swing votes, and so on, which are played out in spades when we move to the level of the whole polity as a deliberative body. Still, there may be something to the idea that equality of individual authority gives character to deliberation that it might otherwise lack. We began with Carlos Nino's theory of the deliberative transformation of individual interests in a democracy; and I think it is true there too that it is deliberation in *circumstances of final equality of decisional authority*, not deliberation by itself, that does the transformative work.

That is as far as I have got. I am not in a position to prove (I am not even sure what it takes to prove) that these two propositions—individual authority and individual equality—are by themselves sufficient to require the choice of majority rule as the only appropriate procedural principle. But I suspect that something along these lines is the case. After all, what other procedural principle respects these two constraints?[26]

In any case, I offer this incomplete set of arguments and considerations as a respectful supplement to Nino's work on the transformative relation between deliberation and voting, confident, as I said, that a theory of democracy cannot flourish without an account of what to do—and why—when deliberation fails to resolve or eliminate disagreement. And because we cannot do without such a theory, the best model of democracy will be one that integrates or dovetails its account of deliberation with its account of voting and majority rule, along the lines I have sketched out.

NOTES

1. Carlos Nino, *The Constitution of Deliberative Democracy* (New Haven: Yale University Press, 1996).

2. Nino, *The Constitution of Deliberative Democracy,* 1 (my emphasis).

3. Nino, *Establishing Deliberative Democracy,* 2.

4. Nino, *Establishing Deliberative Democracy,* 2.

5. See Ronald Dworkin, *A Bill of Rights for Britain* (London: Chatto and Windus, 1990), 36.

6. This is an important consideration for evaluating Nino's hypothesis. Nino assumes—quite rightly—that a voter's ultimate decision should be based on some sense of the just impact of the policy she favors on all citizens, not just herself. In the jargon of public choice, her vote ought to reflect her commitment to some social welfare function, not merely her own personal utility. Nino speculates that the existence of a majoritarian procedure encourages this. But it may encourage voters to employ the *wrong* social welfare function—for example, an aggregative utilitarian one, rather than one that is more sensitive to, say, equality or rights.

7. This needs to be stated a little more carefully, taking into account Dworkin's argument about the difference between personal and external preferences. See Ronald Dworkin, "Rights as Trumps," in Jeremy Waldron, ed., *Theories of Rights* (Oxford: Oxford University Press, 1984).

8. I am grateful to Martin Shapiro for confirming my impression that this is the case.

9. Thomas Hobbes, *Leviathan,* ed. Richard Tuck (Cambridge: Cambridge University Press, 1991), ch. 19, p. 132. Hobbes acknowledged, however, that this "one thing alone I confess in this whole book not to be demonstrated but only probably stated."

10. James Madison, Alexander Hamilton, and John Jay, *The Federalist Papers,* ed. Isaac Kramnick (Harmondsworth: Penguin Books, 1987), 182 (my emphasis).

11. Madison, Hamilton, and Jay, *The Federalist Papers,* LXXXI, p. 451.

12. Hannah Arendt, *The Human Condition* (Chicago: University of Chicago Press, 1958), 236.

13. John Rawls, *Political Liberalism* (New York: Columbia University Press, 1993), 55, 56.

14. Rawls, *Political Liberalism,* 58.

15. Thus Rawls says, *Political Liberalism,* 56, that the burdens of judgment affect not only our estimation of the place that various ends and values have in our own way of life, but also our assessment of the claims others might make against us.

16. Jeremy Waldron, "Disagreements About Justice," *Pacific Philosophical Quarterly* (1995), 372–387.

17. Rawls, *Political Liberalism,* 231–240. Note also Rawls's comment: "the idea of public reason does not mean that the judges agree with one another, any more than citizens do" (237).

18. But compare Cass Sunstein, *Legal Reasoning and Political Conflict* (New York: Oxford University Press, 1996), chapter 2.

19. I am not referring here to the practice of producing a single written *opinion* that is to count

as the opinion of the Court. That practice is quite contingent, and is not followed, for example, by the House of Lords in England (where even those in the majority on a particular decision may produce separate opinions, often advancing quite different and contrary reasons.

20. Rawls, *Theory of Justice,* 126–130. The classic account of the circumstances of justice is that given by David Hume in *A Treatise of Human Nature,* ed. L. A. Selby-Bigge (Oxford: Clarendon Press, 1888), book III, part II, section ii, pp. 493–495, and especially in *An Enquiry Concerning the Principles of Morals,* in David Hume, *Enquiries,* ed. L. A. Selby-Bigge (Oxford: Clarendon Press, 1902), section III, part I, pp. 183–192.

21. Cf. Michael Sandel, *Liberalism and the Limits of Justice* (Cambridge: Cambridge University Press, 1982), 35.

22. I have discussed the idea briefly in "A Right-Based Critique of Bills of Rights," *Oxford Journal of Legal Studies,* 13 (1993), 31–35, in "Freeman's Defense of Judicial Review, *Law and Philosophy,* 13 (1994), 34–35, and in "The Circumstances of Integrity," *Legal Theory,* 3 (1997), 1–22. See also Jeremy Waldron, *Law and Disagreement* (Oxford: Clarendon Press, 1998), chapters 9, 10, and 12. I believe the discussion in chapter 6 of Jean Hampton's book, *Hobbes and the Social Contract Tradition* (Cambridge: Cambridge University Press, 1986), is highly relevant here, illuminating the game-theoretic structure of what I have called the circumstances of politics. See also, Waldron, *Law and Disagreement,* chapter 8.

23. I have elaborated this argument in "The Irrelevance of Moral Objectivity," in Robert George, ed., *Natural Law Theory: Contemporary Essays* (Oxford: Oxford University Press, 1992), esp. 176–184.

24. Or rather, they are implying that one majority process engaging potentially all of the millions of citizens affected by the issue should be reviewed and overruled by a majority process engaging only nine of them. And though I do not want to argue the point here, that proposal loses a lot of its plausibility once we recognize that, apart from the paraphernalia of legalism, the positions held by justices on the Supreme Court are not markedly different in substance, tone, and quality from positions held by citizens in the streets, on the hustings, and in the legislatures.

25. John Locke, *Two Treatises of Government,* ed. Peter Laslett (Cambridge: Cambridge University Press, 1988), II, sect. 54, p. 304. See also the discussion in Jeremy Waldron, *The Dignity of Legislation* (forthcoming, Cambridge University Press, 1999), chapter 6.

26. See the discussion in Bruce Ackerman, *Social Justice in the Liberal State* (New Haven: Yale University Press, 1980), 283ff. See also Waldron, *Law and Disagreement,* 113–116.

Chapter 13 Deliberative Democracy and Majority Rule: Reply to Waldron

Amy Gutmann

One of Carlos Nino's central concerns was to defend a kind of democracy that was more deliberative than conventional theories of democracy recommend or perhaps even admit. Jeremy Waldron, by contrast, moves us away from any concern about the quality of political deliberation in democracy to focus on the value, first, of voting, and second, of majoritarianism in democracy. Waldron argues that voting is essential to provide deliberative democracy with the transformative effect on opinion it seeks. Voting is the decision-making moment of deliberation. But Waldron apparently does not think that the transformative effect of deliberation bears any positive relation to the aim of our reaching more rather than less justifiable policies by deliberating. He declares himself (in a parenthesis) an emotivist. Even without the declaration, however, it is clear enough that his defense of majority rule as *the distinctively democratic act* rests on the claim that there is generally no justifiable policy in politics except one that conforms to majority will, or at least one that is recommended by majority rule.

In these necessarily brief comments, I show that identifying majority rule as the core principle of democracy, while commonplace, is ultimately indefensible on the grounds that Waldron offers. Waldron offers among the strongest arguments to date for considering majority rule the moral core of democracy. His defense of democracy as essentially constituted by majority rule (and its preconditions) does not work. In making the case against conceiving of democracy as essentially majority rule, I also show that conceiving of democracy as a deliberative ideal (where deliberation includes but also goes beyond the act of voting) is more defensible, morally and intellectually.

My critique of democracy as majority rule both builds upon and supports the defense of deliberative democracy that Dennis Thompson and I offer in *Democracy and Disagreement*.[1] The arguments that support a deliberative conception over an essentially majoritarian conception of democracy are not abstract or inconsequential; they have important implications for democratic practice as well as democratic theory. Democracy in the United States today suffers from a deliberative deficit, but not from too little majority rule. The increasing reliance on referenda in California, for example, is not something that democrats should applaud if we understand democracy as a moral ideal, and not merely a modus vivendi (which any number of quite different political procedures might be).

Waldron's claim that voting is an essential value of democracy is nonetheless correct. The claim is all the more important because many discussions of democratic deliberation ignore, downplay, or sometimes even deny that the simple act of voting is an essential part of democratic deliberation. I therefore start with this significant point of agreement. Voting is essential to the ideal of deliberative democracy. Why? Not for the reasons based on moral skepticism that Waldron offers. Voting is essential because (1) people reasonably disagree during and after deliberating on political issues, (2) people's reasonable disagreements ought to be respected, and (3) one way of respecting those disagreements—and respecting people as political equals—is to count all their views in the final voting.

A critic might ask, suppose some people regularly have the right views in advance of deliberations, why go through the rigmarole of deliberation and voting? The answer is because we typically do not know who these people are in advance of deliberation. Even if we did, once unaccountable political power were conferred on those people they would be far less likely to have the right views (because absolute power corrupts, and does so quite quickly).

On this account, deliberation dovetails with voting for a very different reason than the skeptical one, which would ultimately undermine the value of voting. We need not be skeptics about there being right answers to political questions or our being able to achieve reasoned agreement on the right answer to think that deliberation should issue in voting. (Indeed, were we skeptics, we would have less reason to value voting.) Jury deliberation aims for reasoned agreement, and often even arrives at a justifiable conclusion. Voting focuses the mind on the need to decide. Deliberation without voting loses a large part of its point.

Now suppose that one wants to go one step further and argue that deliberation should dovetail not just with voting but also with majority rule because majoritarianism is distinctively democratic. Can this argument for the distinctively democratic nature of majority rule succeed? Begin by considering the case of juries in the United States, which have long been thought to be a distinctively democratic institution, reflecting the civic respect that a democracy accords each and every (law-abiding, adult) individual. Juries in criminal trials reach verdicts not by majority rule but rather by a rule of unanimity. Why is this rule not undemocratic? It helps protect people who are accused of crimes against guilty verdicts for which there remain reasonable doubts.

Perhaps unanimity is not the best voting rule even for juries in criminal trials. Certainly the jury procedure is imperfect. (So is almost every political procedure.) But is the jury procedure any less *democratic* for being non-majoritarian? Each juror, selected by lottery rather than by majoritarian vote, is treated as a person capable of reasoning and arriving at a well-reasoned decision, but (unlike in the more commonly cited cases of public decision-making) one reasonable person's dissent is taken to be sufficient to block a guilty verdict. Why? Because the aim of jury deliberation in the United States is to find people guilty only if they are guilty beyond a reasonable doubt. By the democratic standard of equality of individual authority, jury deliberation that culminates with a unanimity voting rule is democratic, assuming that the rules for selecting jurors do not violate the assumption of individual equality and the procedures do not violate the deliberative ideal of decision-making.

Someone might argue that juries should not be considered political decision-makers. We may therefore expect more agreement among jurors than among those elected and appointed public officials who make and interpret (rather than enforce) our laws. According to this argument, majority rule is uniquely appropriate to deliberation in law and politics whereas unanimity is appropriate to jury deliberation. In response to this argument, we might recall that juries were once constituted to interpret the law as well as to enforce it, so the dichotomy between juries and legislative bodies for the purposes of validating distinctive voting rules should strike us as suspect simply on historical grounds.

But the major, morally relevant difference between juries and legislative bodies remains today even after the evolution of juries away from their quasi-legislative functions. It is not well captured by saying that juries are not political decision-makers, while legislatures are. Rather, we have reason to give special protection to preserving the status quo in the case of jury deliberation as we do not in the case of most legislation. The status quo leaves the defendant free from punishment by the state. There is no similarly strong reason to privilege the status quo in most other political deliberations. To give a minority veto power is morally more dangerous in the legislative arena than it is in criminal trials, but it is not therefore less democratic.

In all these forums, people's basic interests and well-being are at stake. The likelihood of achieving justifiable agreement differs depending on what the issue is and who the deliberators are. But it does not follow that disagreement is reasonable on all political issues, as a general deference to majority rule suggests. Almost everyone can recognize the difference between the quality of arguments that one can propose in opposition to punishing rape versus punishing unpopular political speech, or in favor of restricting the right of women to vote or the right of women to an abortion on demand, or in favor of instituting a poll tax or a districting plan that underrepresents African-Americans relative to their proportion in the population.

Deliberation in each of these cases has justifiable agreement as its primary aim. Should we be skeptics about the aim of justifiable agreement because justifiable agreement is more often than not impossible in politics? Consider Waldron's statement that "there is likely to be a diversity of impartial opinions about justice or the good, and [therefore] consensus is not ordinarily to be expected on the subject matter of politics." It is importantly ambiguous between two distinct claims, a strong claim and a weak claim about the value of dissensus on matters of justice. The strong claim is that conflicting positions on matters of justice are equally reasonable and justified. Waldron relies on this strong claim to recommend majority rule, but he says nothing to defend the strong claim, and it is hard to see what would justify this claim. Waldron's skepticism about knowing the truth undercuts his claim that in truth there exists a plurality of conflicting justifiable positions on all or most political matters.

The weaker claim is that, regardless of whether there is a singular justified position on every matter of justice, we should expect reasonable disagreement over a plurality of conflicting positions on many matters of justice. I would add to the imperfection of our moral understanding our collective inability to discern who among *us* has the best understanding and the best moral character to be entrusted to decide controversial issues on behalf of others. Suppose this weaker claim is correct. It does not establish Waldron's conclusion that dissensus should be resolved by majority rule because majority rule is distinctively democratic.

In defending this conclusion, Waldron understandably wants to dispel a notion that he attributes to deliberative democrats and liberal constitutionalists alike. The notion is that a commitment to majoritarianism reflects "a blind and meaningless faith in numbers," or a "crude statistical view of democracy." Can this worry be dispelled?

To answer this question, we need to consider positive reasons why we should identify democracy with a commitment to majoritarianism. Waldron tentatively proposes that the procedural principle of majority rule uniquely respects the equal political authority of every individual. Were this the case, then the relationship between democracy and majority rule would be far from mysterious. We might simply say that democracy is the form of government that respects the equal political authority of every individual first by counting every vote as one, and second by moving in the direction of the larger number of votes.

The problem with this argument is that there are other ways of respecting the equal political authority of every individual. I have already indicated that the unanimity rule in jury deliberation respects this idea as well as if not better than would majority rule, given the political purpose of jury deliberations. But suppose we set aside the case of juries and use legislatures and courts—including the Supreme Court—as Waldron's own argument suggests, to test Waldron's identification of majority rule with democracy. What about the claim that majority rule is *the distinctively democratic* principle for voting for representatives, within legislatures, for constitutional amendments, and among Supreme Court justices? In some of these cases, in some political contexts, plurality rule, proportional representation, or even supermajority rule might offer a greater likelihood of achieving just results and still treat citizens as political equals.

Suppose proportional representation lessens the likelihood of perpetuating racial discrimination in a state with a racist majority. To oppose proportional representation on grounds that there is something uniquely and essentially democratic about simple majority rule is to subordinate a defensible political morality that treats people as equals, both in and out of politics, to an indefensible faith in the moral authority of the majority in politics.

We misleadingly speak of "*the* majority principle" when we imply that the same principle, or the same justificatory grounds, justifies majority rule in the Supreme Court, majority rule in juries, majority rule in determining legislative representation, and majority rule in amending the constitution, even though the context and content of these practices and their political purposes are very different. Why think that democracy requires the principle of letting the majority of members of a deliberative political body rule? Majority rule, taken out of a political context, without consideration of the substantive purpose of a political practice, is a numerical version of might makes right. All individuals, regardless of whether they are willing or able to deliberate, are deemed equally powerful, and 50 percent plus one of a group are deemed sufficiently powerful to move the entire body whatever way they please.

Why is it not necessarily democratic or morally defensible to move the political body in the direction of the majority? In the United States, as in many other countries, when the moral merits of voters' views are held constant, some voters consistently have a far greater chance of constituting the majority than others, because of the preferences of the majority, their distinctively different interests, or both. Majority rule loses its moral appeal when there are discrete and insular minorities whose equally meritorious political views are consistently less likely to prevail than those of a relatively cohesive majority. In such a context, majoritarianism works unjustly to disadvantage already disadvantaged minorities, and there is nothing distinctively democratic about defending majority rule despite its systematically unjust results *if* there are procedural alternatives that would more equally protect the basic interests of minorities *and* allow their voices to be more equally represented in decision-making bodies.

A second feature of most political contexts that undermines the egalitarian claim of majoritarianism is the built-in incentive for majorities under a pure majoritarian system to violate the institutional conditions of democracy (such as freedom of political speech) and the vital interests of individuals (such as religious freedom for minorities) because majorities can better secure their hold on political power by subordinating the vital personal and political interests of minorities to their own interests. Nonmajoritarian decision-making rules may better protect both the conditions of democracy and the vital interests of individuals. (Majorities can even recognize this, and agree to bind themselves into the future, when they will be tempted to violate minority rights. But majorities also change over time, and it is not a necessary condition of justifying nonmajoritarianism that every majority consent to the non-majoritarian protection of the conditions of democracy. In practice, this would undermine the very purpose of the protection.)

When a non-majoritarian decision-making process protects the conditions of democracy, on what grounds could a majoritarian claim that the process is undemocratic? Unjust? The majoritarian would have to show that non-majoritarian decision-making did not protect the conditions of democracy better than majoritarian decision-making. Disagreement on what constitutes those conditions does not by itself tell in favor of majority rule. If disagreement alone tells us enough to defer to majority rule, then the disagreement that still exists in this society about whether African-Americans, Jews, atheists, and homosexuals should have basic civil and political rights (as basic as freedom of religion and of political speech and the rights to privacy and to vote and hold political office) would by itself constitute an argument in favor of majority rule resolving this disagreement. There is no good argument for this position. Majority rule typically comes into its own, morally speaking, only when it turns out to be the best way of either expressing the equal political status of citizens or of securing at least provisionally justifiable outcomes, or both.

Things may be different, and more favorable to majority rule, if we limit our consideration, as Waldron sometimes seems implicitly to be doing, to political disagreements that are genuinely hard to resolve on the basis of the moral reasoning, empirical evidence, and the most plausible assumptions and methods of inquiry that are publicly available to us. Perhaps in this more limited realm of disagreement, a case may be made for a presumption in favor of majority rule after due deliberation. But Waldron, like other majoritarians, does not make this case, nor does he limit his argument for majority rule to this more limited realm of genuinely reasonable disagreement. Even in this limited realm, there is more to be said for making democratic processes more deliberative than there is to be said for ensuring majority rule rather than some other egalitarian decision-making rule.

Majoritarians have not offered us a strong, morally presumptive, or prima facie, reason to reject, on grounds of either democracy or justice, proportional representation in districts with cohesive racist majorities, supermajoritarian amendment procedures for basically-just constitutions, and unanimity rules for juries in criminal trials. What is compelling in Waldron's case is the claim that deliberative democracy should dovetail with voting. This claim is an important part of what deliberative democrats need to emphasize about the meaning of deliberation and its relationship to decision-making. Deliberation in democracy should not be confused with intellectual discussion in a senior common room. Deliberation is more accurately understood as the give and take of public argument with the aim of making an action-guiding decision that can be justified to the people bound by it.

Discussion, even heated debate about political matters, is not by itself deliberation. Academics typically discuss. They do not deliberate, because they rarely argue with the aim of making an action-guiding decision. Academic arguments rarely have a decision-making point. That's what it means for an argument to be "academic." Deliberation by contrast to academic discussion aims to justify actual decisions to the people who are bound by them. It often fails to do so, but so does every political process often fail in this sense. If a non-majoritarian decision-making rule is more likely to produce justifiable decisions, or likely to produce more justifiable decisions, than the available alternatives, and if that rule is consistent with the civic equality of individuals, then there is good reason for democrats not to insist on majority rule.

In short, there is no reason for deliberative democrats (or any democrats dedicated to morally defending democracy) to be embarrassed by the idea that majority rule is not what democracy or the defense of human rights is mainly about.

NOTE

1. Amy Gutmann and Dennis Thompson, *Democracy and Disagreement* (Cambridge, Mass.: Harvard University Press, 1996).

Chapter 14 The Epistemic
Theory of Democracy Revisited

Carlos F. Rosenkrantz

Irwin Stotzky writes about the virtues of a conception of democracy in a way that draws approvingly upon the work of Carlos Nino. To counterbalance Stotzky's contribution to this volume, I offer here a critique of Nino's philosophy. This is so not only because arguments and counterarguments better pave the way toward truth, but also because Carlos Nino would have preferred to be antagonized rather than praised. Carlos always welcomed criticisms. Those who met him know the reason: criticisms were his Archimedean points for new and better defenses of his always deep and interesting ideas.

I want to summarize the justification of the democratic system that Nino had in mind. This is not an easy task since his ideas were rather complex. However, I am confident that the following five points summarize the essential characteristics of what he labeled the "epistemic justification of democracy."

First, Carlos Nino was very concerned with the failure of contemporary political theory to offer a coherent and appealing reason that explains and justifies our preference for democracy over other kinds of political systems. He thought the failure was due in part to the fact that we usually resist the idea that the democratic system has intrinsic moral value. Indeed, we are reluctant to see any connection between what a majority decides and what is morally right. The most we are willing to say is that the democratic system has instrumental value, meaning that the democratic system usually yields better results vis-à-vis all other forms of government.

Nino thought that this was wrong. His most basic and general conviction was that the democratic system has a value that is not instrumental of nor reducible to nor dependent on the value of anything else. He thought, unlike most of us, that there is a connection between what a majority decides and what is morally right,[1] which is not merely instrumental. His "epistemic justification of democracy" was precisely an attempt to correlate in an intrinsic way the democratic system with what is morally true—that is, to establish a principled connection between majority rule and moral reasons or moral value.

Second, he thought that this connection was epistemic. For Nino, the fact that a majority makes a particular decision is a reason to believe that what the majority decides is morally right.[2] Nino thought that the reason to believe that a democratic decision is morally right was very difficult to contest. His idea was that we are subject to epistemic restrictions that make it very unlikely that any one of us would have a more reliable means of ascertaining moral truth than the democratic process. Thus, the reason to trust a democratic decision was always more compelling than the reason to trust individual judgment.

Third, Nino differed from utilitarians in believing that the right was not an aggregative social function of our individual interests. In his view the right could not be reduced in such a way. If we identified the right with what satisfies an aggregative social function, the right would be unable to meet its basic aspiration of recognizing and preserving our existence as separate beings from one another. In light of this aspiration, and central to his concept of the right, Nino thought that every theory that conceives the right as the sole product of interest aggregation must be wrong.[3]

Fourth, despite point three, for Nino the right was not completely disassociated from our interests. In his view, morality could not be utterly formal. It had to be connected, one way or another, with what is good for each of us. It thus has to be connected with our interests.

Fifth, Nino thought that the connection between what is right and our interests was not direct, as utilitarians claim. On the contrary, in his view the connection between the right and our interests is mediated by those principles of harmonization that not only pay attention to the interests of each one of us, but also try to make those interests compatible with everyone else's.

These five points uniquely define Nino's philosophy. They depict his convictions about the right, his convictions about the connection between the right and the good, and finally, his convictions about the connection between the right and majority rule. Further, these five points differentiate and distinguish Nino's epistemic justification of democracy from other epistemic theories.

Indeed, for Nino the epistemic significance of a majority vote does not stem from the fact that a majority vote indicates that more, rather than fewer interests are satisfied. This version of the epistemic theory could be defended by utilitarians—that is, by those who think that the right is identified with what satisfies an aggregative social function of our interests. According to utilitarians, more votes in favor of a particular decision means that more interests are presumably satisfied (assuming that each one of us is the best judge of our own interests), and if the right is an aggregative social function of our interests, the more likely that what the majority votes for is morally right. Nino would not accept this version of the epistemic significance of democratic theory. It violates his convictions about the right, as described in point three above.

But Nino's epistemic justification of democracy was also different from the one recently offered by Susan Hurley. For Hurley the epistemic significance of the democratic system derives from the fact that the democratic system preserves the conditions of autonomous public deliberation, and in so doing gives us more reasons to believe that the decisions adopted according to the democratic system are morally right or true.[4] This epistemic theory contradicts the fourth and fifth points referred to above, insofar as it does not relate the epistemic significance of the democratic system to the existence of a connection between the right and the satisfaction of our interests.

Carlos Nino rejected these two versions of epistemic theory and held that the principle of harmonization of interests adopted by a majority is more probably right than a principle of harmonization of interests adopted by a minority. This is so if only because the principle of harmonization of interests chosen by a majority is more likely to pay attention to everyone's interests than any principle that does not get a majority vote. Even though the explanation for this assertion is included in the description of the five points referred to above, I will say a few more words to avoid any misunderstanding.

Nino resisted the idea that more votes in favor of a decision only shows that more interests are satisfied. Indeed, if more votes only showed that more interests were satisfied, the only appealing version of the epistemic significance of the democratic system would be the one offered by utilitarians. Indeed, this version, as distinct from Nino's, connects the right with the satisfaction of interests considered in the aggregate.

His rejection of the utilitarian version relied upon the conception of democratic deliberation. Nino thought that, by definition, democratic deliberation provides the best principle for harmonizing interests. In other words, in a democracy we do not discuss first and foremost our interests. Democratic deliberation does not directly tell us much about our interests. It reveals our interests but only as they are contained in our judgments about the best way to make our interests compatible with everyone else's. Consequently, more votes cannot be plain evidence that more interests are satisfied.

What democratic deliberation meant for Nino was that more votes counted as evidence that more people thought that a particular principle of harmonization of interests was right. Accepting this, if a given principle was adopted by a majority, we have more reason to believe that this principle is in fact right than if the principle in question were chosen by a minority.

Confronted with the question of why more votes in favor of a principle of harmonization of interests makes it more probably right than an alternative principle, Nino would have said that, assuming that each one of us is the best judge of his own interests, more votes showed that the principle in question satisfied more interests and, given point four above concerning the relationship of the right with our interests, the more interests that were satisfied the more probable that the principle in question was right.

Incidentally, let me say that Nino's epistemic justification of democracy helps us to explain why Jeremy Waldron's attempt, and for that matter John Rawls's attempt, to compare the appeal of majority voting in the demos to majority voting in a court are doomed to fail.[5]

We could agree that at the level of a court, majority voting is justified as the system that better preserves the conditions of autonomous deliberation. But if Nino's epistemic justification of democracy is right, the justification of majority voting in the court has nothing to do with the justification of majority voting in the demos. In the demos, as opposed to in the court, majority rule is justified as the system that makes it more probable that the principle of harmonization of interests voted by a majority is right.

The difference of the justification of majority voting in the court and majority voting in the demos that Nino's view suggests is, I think, evidence that both domains are structurally different and that they cannot be conceived, as Waldron and Rawls do, as a continuation of one another.

The core distinction between the demos and the court is that while in the demos we are supposed to talk about and discuss our interests, even though in the form of what is the best way to harmonize our interests with everyone else's, at the court every discussion of interest is, or should be, absolutely forbidden.

I will now turn to a discussion of objections to Nino's views. The first criticism I want to mention is the one that Irwin P. Stotzky raises: the "realities of political life."

For those who criticize Nino based on "the realities of political life," what is wrong with the epistemic justification of democracy is that it tells us that we have reason to believe that a democratic decision is justified or has epistemic moral value even in those cases in which we know that the democratic decision in question is not justifiable. This is the concern of Martin Farrell, for example, who asks the following question: how could we say that the democratic procedure has epistemic value when some democratic decisions are unjustifiable, without any margin of doubt?[6]

Even though this criticism is superficially appealing, it can be convincingly addressed, as Stotzky does, by showing that when the democratic system yields unjustified results, it is because the requirements that give the democratic system epistemic significance have not been satisfied. For example, one of those requirements is that the ballot be preceded by a well-informed process of deliberation. Without deliberation a majoritarian vote has no epistemic value. Without deliberation there is no guarantee that citizens know what they are voting about, and therefore no guarantee that the way in which they vote makes it more probable that everyone's interests are satisfied or, more accurately, no reason to believe that they choose the best principle of harmonization of interests.

But a democratic decision not preceded by the fulfillment of those requirements that give a democratic system epistemic significance does not present a problem for Nino's theory. Nino can meet the objection of the "realities of political life" without contradicting any of the essential points of his epistemic theory. In those instances in which the democratic system does not give us reason to believe that the decision reached is more probably right, Nino can respond that this result is due not to any weakness in the epistemic justification of democracy but to the fact that its requirements were not met.

A real world objector may persevere and argue that Nino's theory, though not false, is useless. Given the demanding requirements for an epistemically significant democratic decision, it is impossible to use the epistemic justification of democracy as a standard for evaluating existing democratic systems.

Indeed, most of the existing democratic systems do not come close to satisfying the requirements for the epistemic justification of democracy. For instance, none provide the proper conditions for deliberation that Nino required. The real world objector would point to the fact that in these instances the epistemic justification of democracy would have nothing to say, other than that the democratic system does not confer any epistemic value on the decisions of the majority. But we want a theory of democracy, a real world objector would insist, to tell us when and why a democratic system is to be preferred to other systems, for example, a despotic or countermajoritarian one. If the epistemic justification of democracy does not help in this search, we would be better off without it.

This criticism was effectively addressed by Nino. He thought that his theory could afford to be demanding, and to be silent in many circumstances. His idea was that "democracy" is a regulatory concept, and as such it does not aspire to make sense of, or describe, the real world, or to provide us with standards to evaluate every instance of something that looks like a democratic regime. On the contrary, in his view, the concept of democracy should only serve to define an ideal that points us toward the direction in which the world should change.[7] That is all we should expect from a theory of democracy.[8] In short, Nino asserted that the claim that the epistemic justification of democracy neither serves to evaluate every situation nor to compare every democratic system with different regimes is not a powerful critique.

One may reply that Nino's answer to this objection shows that his conception of democracy is utopian in the pejorative sense of the word. That is, his answer assumes that we are different from what we are or may become, or that we have institutions different from the ones we could have or could create.[9] Although I have criticized Nino's theory of democracy precisely because of its utopian flavor,[10] the essential points of his theory could be presented in a way that is not utopian—that is, in a way that we are equipped intellectually to understand and psychologically to pursue.

Indeed, Nino could argue that the epistemic theory of democracy is suited for common people like us. His theory does not require a radical transformation of our nature, but only that we commit ourselves to a collective discussion of the question of the principle that better serves the interests of us all, and then that we cast our votes based upon our best understanding of the best answer to this question.

But there is one commonsense objection to Nino's theory that I find very powerful. It asserts that there is something inappropriate with the epistemic justification of democracy to the extent that it cannot justify institutions, or modes in which our institutions function, that we believe without doubt are justifiable. In other words, Nino's problem is not that his theory is useless or utopian but rather that his theory cannot make sense of what we find perfectly sensible according to our considered judgments. The problem with the epistemic justification of democracy is that it does not explain everything that stands in need of explanation. (Why Nino's theory cannot make sense of what we find perfectly sensible or justifiable is something I cannot develop here. I suspect, however, that it is a consequence of his starting point; that is, his understanding that the subject matter of political philosophy is ideal practices and not the idealized forms of the practices we in fact have.)

I will use the constitution as an example of an institution of which the epistemic theory of democracy cannot justify or make sense. We know that constitutional democracies are perfectly justifiable. Furthermore, we know that constitutional democracies meet requirements of objective justification that monistic democracies cannot meet.[11] If a theory of democracy cannot make sense of a constitution, it must be, at least to that extent, an inappropriate or incomplete theory. This is precisely the weakness that I find in Nino's theory.

First, to avoid any misunderstanding, let me characterize what I understand by a constitution. A constitution is neither a text nor a compact of norms, but a practice of interpretation of a text which establishes the general structure of government and the rights and liberties of citizens. In addition, it does so in a normative or authoritative way. In other words, the constitution specifies how government is to operate and determines what rights citizens have. A constitution aspires to be the last word on these two questions.

Second, I want to state clearly what I understand by a justification for the constitution. Since what defines a constitution as such is its aspiration to be the last word on political issues, I assume that a justification for the constitution is a narrative that tells us why the constitution is binding, why we have to honor and respect its norms, and why we have to refrain from those actions that may contradict what those norms require from us. We leave the constitution unjustified if we fail to provide this narrative.

Let me discuss the most popular explanations for the binding force of the constitution to see first, whether they are consistent with the epistemic justification of democracy and, second, whether they are good explanations of the constitution. If we could find a theory that meets both requirements, Nino's philosophy could be defended from the charge I am putting forward against it.

To start with, one may say, as Nino did in his early work on the connection between reasons and norms,[12] that the constitution is morally binding because it embodies self-enhancing restrictions—that is, restrictions that improve the functioning of the majority rule.[13]

If the constitution were just a body of self-enhancing democratic restrictions, the epistemic theory of democracy might provide a justification for it. Indeed, self-enhancing democratic restrictions, by definition, are justified by the same kind of reasons by which one justifies that which is enhanced. Therefore, if democracy is justified by epistemic reasons, the constitution, as a self-enhancing restriction that furthers democracy, may be justified by epistemic reasons as well.

At first sight this justification of the constitution seems to work. It tells us something that may convince us to act as directed by the constitutional text. However, this is a good justification for the binding force of an ideal constitution, but not for the constitution we in fact have. The reason, simply enough, is that our constitutions are loaded with restrictions that cannot be understood as self-enhancing, but that have a completely different rationale. To cite just one example, consider the clause of the Argentine constitution of 1853 which requires the president to be Catholic. This clause does not help the democratic system. It is totally disconnected with what is required by a democracy to function efficiently. To the extent that our constitutions have clauses similar to the Argentinean Catholic clause, the justification of the constitution as a self-enhancing democratic restriction cannot work. Therefore, supporters of the epistemic justification of democracy need to explore different terrains. They cannot maintain that democracy is justified because a democratic process gives us reasons to believe that a democratic decision is morally right and that the constitution, as a self-enhancing democratic restriction, is justified in a similar way.

A second justification of the constitution that seems to support the epistemic theory of democracy is the one that claims that the binding force of the constitution derives from the fact that a democratic system needs constitutional restrictions to work or function. This idea has been supported by many constitutional lawyers in Argentina and the United States. While this second justification for the binding force of the Constitution is similar to the first one, it should not be confused with it. Here, unlike the previous explanation, constitutional restrictions are not justified as leverages that enhance the epistemic value of the democratic system, but as mechanisms that permit the democratic system to function.

This second explanation stems from the conviction that the democratic system cannot work in its purest form. Therefore, restrictions on the democratic system are always needed. Being that this is so, the constitution is better conceived of as a self-sustaining restriction on the democratic system rather than as a self-enhancing restriction.

This second explanation cannot make sense of the binding force of a real constitution, either. This second explanation enjoys some superiority over the first insofar as it acknowledges that the constitution may entail restrictions that limit democratic procedures, and is not merely self-enhancing as the first explanation claims. However, this second explanation cannot make sense of the practical importance of those constitutional restrictions that are not preconditions of a democratic rule.

In every constitution there are many restrictions that are not needed for the democratic system to work or function. The previously mentioned Catholic clause of the 1853 Argentine constitution is a good example. The requirement that the president be Catholic is not only not self-enhancing, but also not self-sustaining. This being the case, this second attempt to provide a narrative for the binding force of the Constitution that is consistent with the epistemic justification of democracy should be put to rest.

A third justification for the constitution is a variation of the previous one. One could argue that the constitution is a founding element of a normative practice that makes democracy possible. The idea behind this explanation is that democracy is a complex social invention that could not have evolved as it has (and presumably could not have existed) unless we acted pursuant to the constitution. Part of Nino's work went in this direction.[14] I would characterize Bruce Ackerman as one of the supporters of this view.[15]

The difference between this explanation for the role of the constitution and the previous one is the following: while the previous explanation assumes that the democratic system is not possible without certain limitations, and that these limitations justify the existence of a constitution, this third explanation assumes that the democracy we happen to have is not possible without certain limitations, and that it is the continuation of this democracy which explains the existence or binding force of the constitution.

This third explanation has some advantages over the previous ones insofar as it can explain the binding force of all those constitutional restrictions that give our current democracy the features it presently has. It can explain even those restrictions that are not self-enhancing, or that are not needed for the functioning of the democratic system.

However, in my view this third explanation leaves the constitution unexplained. According to this explanation the binding force of the constitution is dependent on the binding force of the democracy we happen to have. Because of its dependent nature, this explanation does not provide us with a reason to honor the constitution just because it is our constitution.

Let me offer an example. Suppose you are a judge and you have to adjudicate a case in which freedom of speech is at stake. It is your view that the case should be decided in a way that restricts the speech of a few to enhance the speech of the many. Your constitution has a very restricted conception of freedom of speech that does not allow the suppression of the speech of the few to enhance the speech of the many. Suppose as well that you have such great persuasive power that you could present your opinion as a new interpretation of the constitutional text, and that many constitutional lawyers would feel comfortable with your opinion, regardless of whether you are in fact interpreting the constitution or changing the constitutional requirement altogether. Finally, suppose that by restricting the speech of the few to enhance the speech of the many you improve the democracy you happen to have.

In a case like this, the third explanation of the constitution would recommend that you ignore the constitution. It would tell you that you should use the constitution as a smoke screen for your favorite opinion without really taking into consideration what the constitution demands.

Indeed, the third explanation tells you that you have reasons to honor the constitution only if you have reasons to honor, maintain, and perpetuate the democracy you happen to have. Conversely, it tells you that if you have no reason to preserve the democracy you happen to have, because there is an attainable and better democracy, you have no reason to honor your constitution.

But an explanation of the constitution that renders it irrelevant in such a way, that subordinates it to other standards—for example, the best attainable democracy—cannot be a plausible explanation of the binding force of the constitution. To explain the constitution we need to provide a narrative that presents it as the last word on the two questions of how government should operate and what rights its citizens should have. This explanation does not do so.

The preceding comments suggest, I hope, that the epistemic justification of democracy is problematic. I considered three justifications of the constitution and its binding force that are congenial with the epistemic justification of democracy. The first two failed to justify our constitutions. If anything, they justified ideal constitutions different in kind from the ones we have. The third justification of the constitution was also lacking. It subordinated the question of the binding force of the Constitution to the value of the democracy we happen to have, and by so doing it left the constitution unexplained. Though I have tried hard I cannot imagine any other way of providing a narrative which, consistent with the epistemic justification of democracy, tells us why we have to honor the constitution as the last word on issues of political organization and the rights of individuals.

However, nothing that I have said should lead us to question the assertion that a principle of harmonization of interests chosen by a majority of a community (after a collective discussion of what is the best way to satisfy the interests of each one of us) is more probably right than a principle chosen by the minority of such a community. This assertion may be true, and if so, Carlos Nino should be credited with it. Rather, what I have tried to say in the preceding discussion is that the epistemic justification of democracy cannot explain everything that stands in need of explanation. This is a particularly acute problem since what is left unexplained is something—the Constitution—that we find sensible or justifiable beyond all doubt.

My contribution here undermines many of the ideas that Carlos Nino deeply believed in. Indeed, he thought that the epistemic justification of democracy was far-reaching and able to solve all the questions concerning a justified form of government. He was convinced that his theory was the yardstick by which to evaluate the way we conduct our common affairs. But if I am right, and the epistemic justification of democracy cannot explain the constitution by itself or by any other theory that derives or is consistent with it, Nino's ambitious project cannot succeed.

If I am right, in order to render our political world intelligible we would need to supplement with new theories the conviction that more votes in favor of a particular decision makes it more likely that that decision is morally right. We would have to offer other theories that explain why and when a restriction to the democratic system is justified. The problem for Nino's view is that when we do so we will soon discover that these new theories in many cases contradict what the epistemic justification of democracy has to say about a particular system or about the moral value of a particular democratic decision. This would make it impossible to maintain that the epistemic justification is the yardstick Nino claimed it was. In such cases Nino's theory will have to cohabit, and sometimes defer to, other theories of justified government.

NOTES

1. See Carlos Nino, *The Ethics of Human Rights* (New York: Clarendon Press, 1991), 245–255.
2. See Carlos Nino, *El Constructivismo Etico* (Madrid: Centro de Estudios Constitucionales, 1991).

3. See Nino, *Ethics of Human Rights,* 148–161.

4. See Susan Hurley, *Natural Reasons, Personality and Polity* (New York: Oxford University Press, 1989), chap. 15.

5. See John Rawls, *Political Liberalism* (New York: Columbia University Press, 1993), 231ff.

6. See Martin Farrell, "En búsqueda de la voluntad de Dios," *Análisis Filosófico,* Buenos Aires, vol. 1988.

7. See, Carlos Nino, "La democracia epistémica puesta a prueba: Respuesta a Rosenkrantz y Ródenas," *DOXA* 10 (1991), Alicante, Spain.

8. Giovanni Sartori has argued the same point in a strikingly similar way. See *The Theory of Democracy Revisited* (Chatham, N.J.: Chatham House, 1987), 58–85.

9. For a lucid description of the problem of utopianism see Thomas Nagel, *Equality and Partiality* (New York: Oxford University Press, 1991), 22ff.

10. See Carlos Rosenkrantz, "La democracia: Una crítica a su jutificación epistémica," *DOXA,* 10 (1991), Alicante, Spain.

11. For an explanation of a monistic theory of democracy, see Bruce Ackerman, *We the People: Foundations* (Cambridge: Harvard University Press, 1991), and Bruce Ackerman and Carlos Rosenkrantz, "Tres Concepciones de la Democracia Constitucional," 29 Cuadernos y Debates, Centro de Estudios Constitucionales, Madrid (1991).

12. See Carlos Nino, *La Validez del Derecho* (Buenos Aires: Ed. Astrea, 1986).

13. One of the contributors to this volume has also defended this view. See Stephen Holmes, "Precommitment and the Paradox of Democracy," in J. Elster and R. Slagstad, ed., *Constitutionalism and Democracy* (New York: Cambridge University Press), 195–241.

14. See Carlos Nino, "La Constitución como convención," *Revista del Centro de Estudios Constitucionales,* 6 (1990), Madrid, and Nino, *The Constitution of Deliberative Democracy* (New Haven: Yale University Press, 1996).

15. See Bruce Ackerman, "Rooted Cosmopolitanism," *Ethics,* 104, no. 3 (April 1994), 516.

Chapter 15 Democracy and Philosophy: A Reply to Stotzky and Waldron

Paul W. Kahn

Reading Carlos Nino's *Constitution of Deliberative Democracy*, I could not help but be impressed with the deeply personal character of the inquiry Nino was pursuing. He was, as Irwin P. Stotzky has said, a public intellectual. As long as I knew him, he always seemed to be doing two things: pursuing ideas as an intellectual committed to unconstrained theoretical inquiry, and participating in Argentine politics as that state sought to construct a democratic political life. At the heart of his work on deliberative democracy is a single question: Can a moral philosopher be a democrat? He was determined to think through the relationship between these two aspects of his life: theory and practice.

Practically, we are likely to take the answer to this question for granted. Moral philosophers seem to flourish under democratic conditions. Censorship is not conducive to theoretical inquiry, especially moral inquiry. But when we answer the question in this way, we are assuming Plato's attitude toward democracy: its virtue lies in the multiplicity of life-styles that it permits. Philosophers are less likely to be bothered in a democratic regime. This, however, is only a negative answer to the question. Philosophers benefit from democracy, but only in the same way that anyone with an unconventional life-style may benefit from democratic freedoms. The connection between democracy and philosophy remains external and contingent.

To someone as deeply concerned with philosophical inquiry as Carlos Nino, the question of democracy was both more serious and more difficult. For him, the question was not just that of the practical conditions under which moral philosophy could be pursued. He answered that question when he went to England during the years of rule by the Argentine military. The more difficult issue was to understand the point of contact between moral theory and political order. The richer the substance of one's moral theory—that is, the more one is willing to argue for the truth of moral propositions—the more likely it is that one will find oneself outside of the political order, judging its authoritative commands from the perspective of moral truth. The moral philosopher seems already deeply committed to an adversarial relationship to the authority of the state— any state at all, including a democratic state. The authority of the state stands outside of the moral claim of rights.

Democracy, on this view, may be the best we can do practically, but like every other political order, it is to be viewed with considerable skepticism. Philosophers begin their education with a reflection on Socrates' execution by a democratic Athens. This image of the philosopher standing against the state never really leaves their minds. Truth opposes power, democratic or otherwise. Standing for moral truth can be a dangerous proposition, even in a democracy.

So we must take seriously Carlos Nino's claim that he offers "a theory of the value of democracy which radically differs from most" others.[1] For his end was to align democracy with truth and thus overcome the philosopher's skepticism about power and political authority. To the question of whether the moral philosopher could be a democrat, Nino answered that the philosopher could not be anything but a democrat. This was not because democracy promised to leave the philosopher alone, but because democracy properly carried out *was* the philosophical inquiry.

This is what he meant by an epistemic justification of democracy. He claimed that in a properly structured democracy, there is "a greater tendency to impartial solutions than any other method of reaching decisions which affect the group . . . [including] reflection of an isolated individual." "Impartiality" is, for him, the "mark of validity" of proposed solutions to moral difficulties. This claim is really quite startling for a moral philosopher. He proposed that regardless of the certainty with which I reach a moral conclusion—regardless of my belief in the validity of the arguments I deploy—the conclusion reached by a properly organized democratic state is more likely to be correct. The place for conscientious objection disappears because the conscientious philosopher has better grounds to doubt the truth as it appears to him than the authoritative command of a democratic state.

Now this is, in my view, a crazy claim. Nevertheless, to do justice to Nino we must recognize just how radical a claim it is. His justification of the state's authority does not simply align the state with morally correct outcomes; it makes of the state a deliberative community that satisfies the conditions of moral inquiry. He takes the Socratic model of a dialogical community and projects it onto the operations of a modern nation-state.

To achieve this epistemic ground for political authority requires the reworking of virtually every aspect of the present community's organization. Nino's proposals, at least during the transitional stage, would make of him the most radical philosopher-king imaginable. The revolutionary character of this project is driven by his vision of the gap between contemporary democracies and the realization of a deliberative community of inquiry. His proposals cover the shape and character of citizen participation, the role of political parties, the nature of representation, the political responsibilities of the media, the geographical and temporal shape of the community, and the character of institutional authority within a democratic government. In short, they cover everything.

If his answer to the question of whether a moral philosopher can be a democrat is not just yes, but a necessary yes, we can nevertheless say that the state of which the moral philosopher is a citizen shares with Plato's *Republic* another trait: it exists only in the mind of the philosopher. The radical and revolutionary character of Nino's answer can be rephrased as follows: The philosopher can be a democrat, but only if the state is completely restructured to meet the conditions of philosophical inquiry. Philosophy—if taken seriously—is a hard political taskmaster.

I said that Nino's political vision is crazy because I believe it to be essentially an anti-political proposal. By reconstructing politics on the model of philosophical discourse, he eliminates from politics everything that makes it a distinct sphere of meaningful activity. His state exists in the ideal only, because it has no relationship to its own past. History has no role in the construction of citizen identity in this state. But history is the domain of meaning that defines what it is to be a member of the state. Similarly, political discourse as we experience it is rhetorical, not deliberative. Nino has about as much tolerance for rhetoric as Socrates. For both, rhetoricians corrupt the possibility of realizing moral truth within the state. But we will never get to the heart of our own political identities without reflecting upon the way in which political rhetoric moves us to make commitments and endure sacrifice. Finally, I cannot help but feel that Nino's state would be a rather unexciting place. It is stripped of the challenges that come from a political project that defines the self against other communities, and that seeks achievement within history.

These are some of the topics that contributed to my endless arguments with Carlos Nino. I do not want to pursue them here, even though they go to the heart of what we want, and what we can demand, of the political order. Instead, I want to turn briefly to the essays in this volume by Irwin P. Stotzky and Jeremy Waldron. These chapters make a positive contribution to evaluating Nino's thought by illustrating the distance of his ideal from the real. Nevertheless, in doing so they tame the revolutionary character of his thought. We are in danger of seeing him as just another political philosopher.

Stotzky reminds us that the transition to democracy is not a problem of abstract theory but a problem of transforming existing institutions and established habits of political life. Nino's epistemic concerns seem hardly to get off the ground when we face the realities of poverty and power in Haiti. What would it take to create a deliberative community in a political culture in which there is no expectation of fair treatment from government? What are the implicit assumptions about the character of civil society upon which Nino's new political order would rest?

I am reminded of Hannah Arendt's claim that the social question, whenever it arises, inevitably derails the revolutionary political agenda. The social question is precisely the question of economic redistribution from the elite wealthy minority to the impoverished masses. Democracy will find no fertile ground as long as it fails to feed the people. This is not just a warning about Haiti, but the lesson we may be relearning in Eastern Europe as well. Feeding the masses may, in the first instance, be a question best addressed by managerial experts, deployed under a scheme of foreign intervention.

Just as Stotzky reminds us that the politics of an impartial, discursive morality may begin only after the needs of the body have been met, he also reminds us that a community is formed by its past well before the philosopher arrives on the scene. At various points, he tells us that the Haitians do not share the political and moral vision that we usually take for granted. Their political values center on status and connections; they admire force, not deliberation and impartiality; theirs is a political culture of illegality, not the rule of law. This is not a community in which an epistemic conception of democracy is likely to make much of an impression.

We do not need an epistemic defense of democracy to see that the Haitian economic order must be restructured and to see the need for stabilization under the rule of law. If poverty is great enough and abuse of human rights extreme enough, then intervention may be justified. Stotzky is arguing for intervention and transformation on the familiar grounds of our ordinary political values. Economic redistribution to the poor and the rule of law are the conventional elements of our discourse about transition. Both contribute to the virtues of stability in a political order. Stability is the end of a policy of intervention.

Faced with the difficulties of transition of an impoverished, undeveloped country, Stotzky imagines a reorganization that would achieve a more just distribution of resources and a more just use of the power of the state. Nothing he says, however, would suggest that at the end of that transition, a convincing argument could be made that the moral philosopher must be a democrat. Economics and law are both beside the point in Nino's argument for a morally supportable political order. Indeed, the rule of law cuts against his argument for an ongoing moral discourse. Nino's rejection of this line of inquiry is made clear when he states: "The stability of a political system . . . should not be achieved at any cost."[2] But in the real world, stability may matter more than other values. Or, at least, the value of a political order cannot easily be separated from its stability.

Stotzky shows us that too close a concern with the actual political situation in any community, with the possibilities of actual political transformation, tends to tame the radical political thinker. Revolutionary vision will be obscured by the possible. Attention to the social question will lead us away from the question of political revolution. The prophetic voice of the philosopher is drowned out by the conventional framework of ordinary politics.

Jeremy Waldron shows us the opposite threat to revolutionary political thought, which arises from changing the focus of political theory. Waldron never reaches the question that Nino put at the center of his inquiry: can a philosopher be a democrat? Instead, Waldron's quite different theoretical question is, what is the best theoretical explanation of our existing democratic institutions?

He is "embarrassed" by the absence from political theory of an explanation of the central role we assign to voting in our institutional arrangements. If voting can be explained only on utilitarian grounds, then we would have to give up the defense of democracy on deliberative grounds. This he is not willing to do. Deliberation and voting must therefore be linked in theory, if we are to justify our existing arrangements.

This inquiry leads Waldron to a closer examination of the U.S. Supreme

Court as an example of deliberation within a political structure of majoritarianism. Decision by a majority is thought to be consistent with argument and deliberation on the Supreme Court. Accordingly, an explanation of the Court's operations may provide the grounds for a theory linking deliberative discourse and voting in larger political arenas.

Waldron has some very interesting things to say about the irreducible character of disagreement within political debate. Disagreement, not unanimity, describes political discourse. More talk will only produce more disagreement. If this is so, then the need for a political decision-making mechanism in the face of disagreement is not merely a consequence of the fact that political necessities never allow enough time for the deliberation to run its course and reach a unanimous outcome. If disagreement is an essential element of political discourse, then we need a decision-making mechanism that operates in the face of that disagreement. Waldron finds his defense of majority rule just here.

Waldron, however, has hardly elaborated Nino's epistemic defense of democracy by this line of inquiry. Rather, he has abandoned it. Nino's claim was that, properly structured, a democratic discourse moves toward true moral propositions. For Waldron, there is no single moral truth toward which discourse is moving. The problem of political theory is to justify decisions under conditions in which no one can appeal to truth. Nino, however, sought an argument for supporting democratic government that would link it to truth, not disagreement.

I do not want to decide between Waldron and Nino on the availability of moral truth in political discourse. I want rather to point to the shift in project that Waldron represents. For him, the problem is to justify the institutions and procedures we have. He does not ask, for example, whether a Supreme Court that operates under a rule that grants authority to a majority should simply be abandoned as inconsistent with the grounds upon which a moral philosopher can attach himself to the state. Nino's project, however, was radical in just this way. He wanted to retrace the Platonic ideal of "building the city in speech." Philosophy and politics are to be one and the same. Waldron wants to find the philosophical ground of our existing political practices. That does not preclude change, but it misses the revolutionary character of Nino's project.

Despite my many disagreements with Carlos Nino, he remains for me a model of the philosopher in politics. He struggled to work with the possible, but also to remain true to the ideals of theory. Most important, he did not confuse these two projects. Philosophers have no excuse not to engage the world they find themselves thrown into. The range of the possible cannot be ignored by an exclusive focus on the ideal. Nevertheless, we should not let the possible corrupt the work of theory. The philosopher either is a revolutionary figure or has abandoned the philosophical project. Carlos Nino's work on deliberative democracy was an insistence that truth must be the judge of power.

NOTES

1. Carlos Nino, *The Constitution of Deliberative Democracy* (New Haven: Yale University Press, 1996), 143.
2. Nino, *The Constitution of Deliberative Democracy*, 160.

Part Five **Confronting Radical Evil**

Chapter 16 Punishment

and the Rule of Law

T. M. Scanlon

This essay will consider how some central issues that Carlos Nino discussed in his writings on the philosophical theory of punishment are relevant to the difficult empirical and political problem of building a legal order that preserves the rule of law and provides remedies for victims of past human rights abuses. Carlos Nino was remarkable in combining philosophical scholarship with important and courageous contributions to this difficult political problem. My first contact with him came when he submitted his article "A Consensual Theory of Punishment" to the journal *Philosophy and Public Affairs,* of which I was then an associate editor. This article attempts to provide a justification for criminal penalties that avoids retributivism but also explains why a system of penalties cannot be justified solely on the basis of its deterrent effects. It was, for me, an exciting paper to read. I very much agreed with the main line of Nino's theory, although I thought that there were certain rather subtle ways in which it went astray. We had a brief but stimulating correspondence about these issues. In retrospect it is striking—indeed, to someone like me who has spent his adult life in the sheltered academy it is truly amazing—that the seemingly academic issues discussed in Nino's article, including the rather subtle point on which we disagreed, turned out later to be of very considerable practical importance.

Philosophical reflection on the problem of punishment has focused on two general questions: the justification for punishment and the limits on its legitimate application. Theoretical reflection of this kind bears on the practical problems we are discussing in at least four ways:

1. It bears on the grounds and interpretation of the prohibition against retroactive punishment.
2. It bears more generally on the state of mind required in an offender as a precondition of legal guilt.
3. It bears on the permissibility of selective punishment. Nino stated, for example, in his response to Diane Orentlicher in the *Yale Law Journal* that only a retributivist theory of punishment requires punishing *all* of those believed guilty of a given offense.[1] All other views, he argued, leave open the possibility that even where punishment is merited, it may be omitted for other reasons, including reasons of political necessity.
4. Finally, theoretical reflection on the problem of punishment bears on the interpretation and legitimacy of the demands of victims for legal response to the wrongs done them.

Let me begin my consideration of philosophical theories by distinguishing four moral ideas that are often cited in arguments about punishment. We will need to bear in mind the degree to which each of them figures in a rationale for having a *system* of punishment or in a rationale for carrying out punishment in an individual case.

The first idea is *retribution*. I will identify retributivism as an account of the rationale for legal punishment, with the view that, first, it is a good thing morally that those who have committed certain moral wrongs should themselves suffer some loss as a result and, second, that bringing about this coincidence between welfare and desert is a central part of the justification for legal institutions of punishment. On such a view there are good moral reasons to bring about losses to those who are guilty of wrongdoing, and the force of these reasons is sufficient to justify not only the suffering of the guilty parties but also the costs to others involved in bringing this about. Both the guilt in question here and the reason for repaying it with loss are to be understood in an extrainstitutional (that is to say a moral, not a legal) sense. So understood, retributivism is to be distinguished from the view that because the institution of the criminal law is justified on other grounds, there is reason that those who are *legally* guilty should suffer the penalties that are *legally* prescribed.

Nino was firm in rejecting retributivism as a justification for punishment, and in this he was in agreement with the majority of contemporary philosophical and legal thought. The reason for this widespread rejection is not skepticism about the ideas of moral guilt or moral justification but one or both of two further ideas. The first is rejection of the notion of moral desert, at least in the form of the thesis that it is a good thing, morally, that those who are guilty of moral wrongs should suffer. The second is the idea that even if this thesis is accepted it is not a proper basis for the justification of a political institution. An institutional practice of depriving some citizens of their rights and inflicting other losses on them cannot be justified simply on the ground that this brings their fate more nearly in line with moral desert. I myself accept both of these ideas, and therefore agree with Nino in rejecting retributivism.[2] The central thesis of retributivism struck both of us as, in Herbert Hart's words, "a mysterious piece of moral alchemy, in which the two evils of moral wickedness and suffering are transmuted into good."[3]

But something *like* retributivism is not so easy to avoid. In the Argentine context, retributivism was appealing to many because it seemed to support what they thought of as the correct answers to the four questions I listed: it explained why retroactive punishment was justified; it identified what it was about the torturers and kidnappers that called for punishment: the evil of their actions; it provided a basis for insisting that all such criminals must be punished; and it thereby accounted for the legitimacy of the demands of the victims' families for a response to what had been done to them and their loved ones.

The main alternative to retributivism as a rationale for punishment has, of course, been *deterrence*. This is in the first instance a rationale for having a *system* of punishment, and it provides a rationale for punishing in individual cases only indirectly: punishment should be carried out in an individual case because that is required by an institution that is (in light of its deterrence effects and perhaps other considerations) justified.[4] Thus, while punishment is addressed to a past crime, its rationale is addressed to future possible crimes which, one hopes, may not occur. So, in cases of the kind we are concerned with in this volume, the deterrence account appeals to the need, first, for a general practice of punishing human rights offenders even if their actions were allowed by the legal and political order in place at the time they were committed, and then, second, to the justifiability of punishment in particular cases as something that must be required by any such system.

This future orientation makes pure deterrence theory seem deficient from the perspective of another moral idea, which I will call *affirmation* of the victims' sense of having been wronged. This idea is not often discussed in philosophical theories of punishment, but nonetheless plays an important part in our thinking about the subject.[5] It is, I am afraid, a rather vague idea. I will try to clarify it as I go along, but part of my point is simply to call attention to the importance of examining the various ways in which this idea might be understood and incorporated into a larger theory of punishment.

This importance is particularly clear in the Argentine case, in which one crucial political element was the pressure of victims' groups such as the Madres de la Plaza de Mayo, who demanded retribution. In fact, as Carlos Nino points out in *Radical Evil on Trial,* insistence on a retributivist view of punishment was something that the Madres and the members of the juntas had in common, although they of course used it to draw opposite conclusions.[6] The Madres argued that everyone who took part in the dirty war was guilty and therefore must be punished; the generals maintained that none of them should be punished, since what they had done was morally justified. This agreement between opposites is not surprising. Both are drawn to retributivism because each is looking for a standard safely beyond law: in the case of the generals, in order to argue that whatever the law may be now, their acts were *morally* justifiable and hence unpunishable; in the case of the Madres, in order to argue that whatever the law may have been *then,* these acts were morally evil and hence deserve punishment. This common strategy suggests that in its emphasis on an extralegal standard, the rationale of retributive theory is in some tension with the idea of the rule of law.

Despite this tension, if retributivism is the only theory of punishment that adequately incorporates the idea of affirmation, this may seem to count in favor of its claim to moral adequacy. Even more likely, this will give retributivism real political force, especially in a dramatic context like that of Argentina in the 1980s but also in the somewhat cooler debates about crime in the United States.

So it is worth asking whether demands like those of the Madres de la Plaza de Mayo might be recognized as legitimate (but in a more tractable form) outside of a retributive theory. This illustrates a more general suggestion that philosophical theory can contribute to actual politics by helping to distinguish various ways in which popular demands can be understood.

Another intuition that is sometimes cited as supporting retributivism is the widespread sense that there is something seriously amiss when those who have committed terrible crimes are allowed to go on living as normal citizens as if nothing had happened. In the Argentine case, for example, many expressed outrage that the officers who had ordered and carried out the kidnaping, torture, and murder of thousands of citizens should be allowed to go on living as respected members of Argentine society. I share this intuition, but I do not believe that what it supports is properly called retributivism. It is important that terrible wrongs be recognized by an appropriate response, and the victims of such wrongs are demeaned when the victimizers are treated as respected citizens with no mention of their crimes. But what makes it appropriate to recognize these wrongs is not that this involves suffering or loss on the part of the wrongdoers. It is rather that the absence of such recognition reflects indifference on the part of society toward the wrongs and those who suffered them. What is crucial is recognition, not suffering. Ideally, of course, one wants the perpetrators themselves to acknowledge these wrongs and express contrition for them. This will be painful, but it is not the pain that makes it desirable.

Like retribution, affirmation is an aim that responds to the past and is addressed in the first instance to each particular case. But it also provides a reason for having a system in which particular claims to be wronged can be recognized and given a form in which they can be publicly expressed and responded to.[7] Having such a system is also relevant to the aim of deterrence, understood in a general sense of discouraging future crime, rather than the narrower sense of doing this by threatening retaliation.[8] People whose sense of being wronged is not recognized and affirmed by the law have less respect for and less investment in it. Lack of affirmation, then, supports what Nino calls anomie, the cynical lack of respect for law which he identified as a main problem of Argentine society. The right response to the demand for affirmation may undermine this dangerous tendency, thereby building the rule of law. As Nino emphasized in his writings on deliberative democracy, the public character of the proceedings within a trial, and the public discussion surrounding it, can play a crucial positive role of this kind. One can hope that occasions like the dramatic trials of the members of the juntas in the Federal Court of Buenos Aires will lead to greater public commitment to the rule of law. Surely they are one of our best hopes.

I have mentioned affirmation as a value and suggested that it is something citizens may reasonably demand of a system of law. It does not seem likely that a system of law that fails, in general, to respond to such demands is likely to survive. I am not suggesting, however, that victims have a right that those who have wronged them be punished. A defensible legal order must, in general, define and defend citizens' rights, but this does not require that every offender be punished. In the case of the crimes of the dirty war, for example, prosecution of those in decision-making positions, and those who went beyond orders to commit private wrongs (i.e., those in Alfonsín's first two categories)[9] could be held to represent adequate recognition of every sufferer's wrong, even though not every wrongdoer was called to account. There is also the possibility, which I will not be able to explore here, that legitimate demands for affirmation of wrongs may be met through means other than punishment—for example, through some form of public authoritative recognition and declaration.[10]

Finally, let me mention a fourth value, or category of values, which I will label *fairness*. Considerations of fairness do not provide a justification for having a system of criminal punishment, but constitute a class of reasons for insisting that this system be of a certain kind. In principle, fairness might provide a reason for insisting on punishment in a particular case insofar as refraining from punishment is seen as unfair or arbitrary, in view of the fact that others were punished for similar crimes.

In this respect, fairness may seem to be allied with retributivism, and perhaps even to presuppose some form of it. It may seem to presuppose retributivism insofar as the idea of fairness appealed to is that punishment should go equally to those who are equally *deserving* of it. But this need not be retributivist in the hard sense I am discussing, since fairness need not appeal to a pre-institutional sense of moral desert as the relevant standard. Still, fairness may seem allied with retributivism in the answer it implies to my third question, about the permissibility of punishing some offenders but not others, for political reasons.

Carlos Nino believed that selective punishment could be defended as a political necessity. As I have mentioned, he said that only a retributivist theory of punishment would require punishing *all* of those believed guilty of a given offense. All other views, he argued, leave open the possibility that even where punishment is merited, it may be omitted for other reasons, such as political necessity. Against this, it might be claimed that considerations of fairness, which need not have a retributivist basis, at least *normally* speak against selective punishment. There is room for argument, however, that unequal punishment for reasons of political necessity would not be unfair (even though differential penalties for political reasons of other sorts would be). I will not pursue this argument here. My point is just that this is another case where a consideration whose moral significance might seem to rest on (and hence to support) retributivism can in fact be explained on other grounds.

I have suggested in passing that one important step in building respect for the rule of law lies in ensuring that people have the right sense of what they can demand from a legal system and that they see the legal order as valuable because it provides these benefits. Looking at the various possible rationales for punishment from this point of view, we can ask what answers they suggest to the question, what can citizens reasonably demand from a system of criminal law?

I have suggested that it is not appropriate for them to demand retribution. What they can demand of a system of law is:

1. That it be effective in deterring private wrongdoers.
2. That it affirm their rights and provide a hearing for their sense of having been wronged.
3. That it be fair.
4. That it be safe.

The creation of a coercive apparatus of punishment to enforce the criminal law is the creation of a potentially dangerous instrument of force and violence. Even though this may be necessary as a protection against private wrong, law-abiding citizens can reasonably demand assurance that it will not attack them as well.

This question of safety brings me to the second side of the philosophical theory of punishment: from the justification for punishment to the limits on its application. The safety just mentioned was that of law-abiding citizens, but the theoretical question is why the safety of law-breakers should be any less important. Why is it permissible to inflict losses on those who break the law, in order to deter future crime, when it is not permissible to "use" others in this way? The aim of deterrence itself provides no answer, since sweeping a wider net that inflicts losses on guilty and innocent alike may have an even greater deterrent effect, and may be claimed to make everyone safer in the end. Justifications of this kind were actually offered for the "dirty war against subversion," and they are a chilling reminder that this argument is not just a stale academic warhorse. This point was particularly important for the Alfonsín administration: because one of the things they most wanted to overcome was the crude expediency of the juntas' justification of their policies, they needed a principled basis for deciding who could be punished for the crimes of that period. Merely to appeal to the importance of deterring such acts in future would just be more expediency.

Retributivists have an answer to this question: it is all right to punish law-breakers insofar as they are morally guilty and hence deserve to suffer. And retributivists might go on to add that the problem I am now addressing is just the natural result of replacing retribution, the proper moral aim of punishment, with the mere expediency of deterrence.

Nonetheless, Nino and many others (myself included) reject retributivism, so we need some other answer. Nino's answer is provided by his consensual theory of punishment. According to this theory, those who commit crimes thereby consent to the normative consequences of their actions. This consent provides the crucial element in "licensing" punishment, even though it does not justify or require it. I want to examine this theory in more detail.

Following Herbert Hart, Nino pointed out that there is a wide range of cases, not restricted to punishment, in which acts implying consent have a licensing effect—that is, they make permissible other actions to which there would otherwise be serious objections.[11] He mentions in particular two such cases. The first is that of legal contracts, in which the consent implied by entering into a contract licenses the state in enforcing it, thereby depriving the party of a liberty he or she would have otherwise enjoyed. The second example is the assumption of risk in tort cases, in which the fact that a person voluntarily undertook some risky behavior licenses the denial of a remedy when injury results. In order for an act to "imply consent" in a way that has this licensing effect, Nino says, an act must be voluntary and the agent must know what the legal consequences of his or her action are—know, for example, that he or she is giving up certain legal claims or immunities.[12]

The idea of consent (or of an action implying consent) fits the case of contract much better than it does cases of assumption of risk. The condition of knowledge that Nino mentions seems out of place in the latter context: surely a person need not be aware of tort law in order to "assume a risk" in a legally significant way. Even in the case of contracts, the requirement that an agent know the legal consequences of his or her act may seem too strong when understood literally. But it does seem that a party to a contract must intend, and hence believe, that he or she is laying down some legal right (whether or not he or she must know exactly what that right is). This makes it appropriate to speak of consent. In the case of assumed risk, however, it is a stretch to speak even of implied consent to a *legal* consequence. In both cases we may say that some right is laid down, or some possible future claim estopped, but in saying this are we merely reiterating the *legal* consequence or saying something more?

If these examples are to point toward an answer to the question that puzzled us in the case of punishment, rather than merely being further examples which raise that same question, they must suggest some explanation of why defensible legal institutions must take a particular form—why they must, for example, make the loss of certain legal immunities dependent on actions that imply consent (or something like it). To provide this explanation we need to appeal to some extra-institutional value, like the extra-institutional idea of desert on which retributivism is founded. To what value should we appeal?

One possibility is the idea that, *morally speaking,* consent has a licensing effect. This may be what Nino had in mind. He wrote, "Another way of describing the situation is to say that the consent to certain *legal* normative consequences involves *moral* normative consequences. The individual who, for instance, consents to undertake some legal obligation is, in principle, morally obligated to do the act which is the object of that obligation."[13] What is appealed to here is not an idea of desert, but a deontological idea about how people's actions affect what they are (morally) entitled to, hence what they can (morally speaking) demand of their legal institutions. But insofar as this idea involves a full-bodied notion of consent it is, as I have said, more clearly applicable to the case of contracts than to torts or punishment.

An alternative would be to appeal not to deontological ideas of consent and entitlement but rather to the value that people reasonably place on having certain forms of control over what happens to them. Because we have reason to value these forms of control, they are factors that must be taken into account in assessing legal institutions. Such factors play somewhat different roles in the two cases Nino mentions.

In the case of contracts, the value of control figures both positively and negatively. Positively, it is a central aim of the law of contracts to give effect to the wills of the parties. In order to do this, it must make the legal normative consequences of an act dependent on the beliefs and intentions of the agent. Negatively, this dependence greatly weakens the case of a person who complains about the enforcement of a contract knowingly and voluntarily undertaken: if he or she wished not to be bound, he or she could simply have refrained from consenting. In offering this way out, the law gives us a crucial form of protection against unwanted obligations.

The law of torts has a different aim: compensating people for loss and injury. The positive part of the case just made thus has no application in the case of torts, but an analogue of the negative part still applies. The law of torts is supposed to protect us against injury and loss, but there are limits to the protection we can demand. By having the opportunity to avoid loss simply by avoiding behavior that can be seen to be very risky, we already have an important form of protection against that loss. Indeed, it can be argued that this is as much protection as can reasonably be asked.

This account explains why Nino's strong requirement of knowledge of the legal normative consequences of one's action makes more sense in the case of contracts than in that of assumed risk. In the first case, creating legal normative consequences that reflect the parties' intentions is a central aim of the law. (This was the "positive" appeal to the value of control.) So knowledge, or something like it, has a natural relevance.[14] Where only the negative value of control is at issue, however, an agent's state of mind is less relevant. Since the question is whether the person had the protection provided by an opportunity to avoid the loss, what is relevant is not what the person knew about the normative consequences of his or her act but what he or she could have known, by exercising a reasonable level of care, about its likely consequences, and about the availability of alternative courses of action.

With all this as background, then, let me turn to the case of punishment. In Nino's view, the consent-implying character of a criminal's act licenses punishment but does not justify it. That is to say, the inclusion in a system of law of the requirement that punishment can be inflicted only on those who have voluntarily (and perhaps knowingly) violated it is a necessary but not sufficient condition for that system's being morally justifiable, and the occurrence of a consent-implying act is a necessary but not necessarily sufficient condition for punishment to be justifiably applied in a particular case. The idea of consent thus fills the "gap" discussed above in the justification of punishment. The fuller account of that justification is summarized by Nino as follows:

> If the punishment is attached to a justifiable obligation, if the authorities involved are legitimate, if the punishment deprives the individual of goods he can alienate, and if it is a necessary and effective means of protecting the community against greater harms, then the fact that the individual has freely consented to make himself liable to that punishment (by performing a voluntary act with the knowledge that the relinquishment of his immunity is a necessary consequence of it) provides a prima facie moral justification for exercising the correlative legal power of punishing him.
>
> The principle of distribution, which that moral justification presupposes, is the same as that which justifies the distribution of advantages and burdens ensuing from contracts and the distribution achieved in the law of torts when the burdens that follow from a tort are placed on the consenting injured party. This justification of course presupposes that several conditions have been satisfied. First, the person punished must have been capable of preventing the act to which the liability is attached (this excludes the rare case of punishing an innocent person that pure social protection might allow). Second, the individual must have performed the act with knowledge of its relevant factual properties. Third, he must have known that the undertaking of a liability to suffer punishment was a necessary consequence of such an act. This ob-

viously implies that one must have knowledge of the law, and it also proscribes the imposition of retroactive criminal laws.[15]

There is much in this account that I agree with. In particular, the idea of using something *like* consent to fill the logical gap left by the removal of desert is very appealing. I want, however, to raise two related questions. The first is whether the knowledge requirement entailed by Nino's notion of consent is too strong. The second is whether the underlying moral idea, which explains, among other things, the permissibility of retroactive criminal laws, is best understood in terms of consent or in some other way.

The question of knowledge is well raised by the problems faced by successor governments in punishing human rights violations under prior regimes. A coup d'état, we may suppose, is a heady affair. Might not those who carry it out be convinced by the rhetoric of their own decrees and believe that previous law had been swept away, giving them full legal power to do what they thought necessary to put the society in order? If they did believe this, and hence did not *know* that their acts had the normative consequence of leaving them legally liable to punishment, would this provide a defense against later charges?

I am not in a position to say what the facts were in this regard in the cases of the members of the Argentine juntas. They sounded as if they were convinced that what they did was *morally* justifiable. Perhaps they also thought it was legally permitted; perhaps not. Perhaps they simply did not give much thought to matters of legality, at least not until the end when thoughts about what the next government might do led them to enact the "self-amnesty" law. The question I am concerned with, however, is whether their liability to punishment depended on this question about their state of mind.

Whatever the facts may have been in that case, this general question remains, and is raised by more humdrum examples. Consider, for example, the overconfident law graduate who is firmly convinced that he or she has found a way, without being guilty of murder or even manslaughter, to do away with the now burdensome spouse, who worked at a dull job to pay the law school fees. This state of mind does not seem to constitute a defense.

What is relevant in all these cases is not what the agent knew about the legal normative consequences of his or her action, but rather what the agent could, through the exercise of due care, have reasonable grounds for believing about these consequences. This suggests that the underlying value in these cases is not the deontological licensing power of consent but rather the value of having a fair opportunity to avoid falling afoul of the law—analogous to the "negative" appeal to the value of control which I discussed above. Both the overconfident law graduate and the members of real and imaginary juntas have this opportunity.[16]

What I would like to do, then, is to follow Carlos Nino's strategy for filling the "gap" in a nonretributivist account of punishment, but to deemphasize his literal appeal to *consent*.[17] This strategy runs the risk of minimizing, in an implausible way, the difference between civil and criminal law. The moral idea of consent, as Nino invoked it, was not an idea of desert. Nonetheless, insofar as it was a matter of the actual state of mind of the agent, it retained a link with that aspect of the criminal to which the criminal law and punishment are appropriately addressed: a state of mind that separates the criminal from the law-abiding citizen. In moving from consent to fair opportunity to avoid a sanction, we move away from the agent's state of mind to a mere benefit that the criminal has enjoyed, by virtue of which he cannot object to being punished. The result may seem a passionless and rather apologetic account of the mental element in criminal law, the sort of thing that is taken in some quarters to give "liberals" like me a bad name.

Newspaper editorialists and talk-show hosts would say that this view of punishment is so concerned with the rights of criminals that it pays no attention to the claims of victims. I can give this objection a more theoretical form by repeating that, as I said earlier, one thing citizens may reasonably demand of a system of law is that it affirm their rights and, in particular, their sense of having been wronged. To this I would add that a system that affirms a victim's sense of being wronged must condemn the agent who inflicted the wrong, and the mental element that makes this appropriate must go beyond merely having had the opportunity to avoid this sanction.

Here it is important to bear in mind the diverse elements that must go together to make punishment justified in Nino's view or mine, and to recognize the different contributions that these elements make to that justification.

The idea that justifiable punishment must be for something that is properly condemned figures in a theory of punishment in at least two ways. First, a defensible criminal law must defend something that the victim is entitled to have defended *and that the perpetrator cannot object to being excluded from.* (Otherwise that law would be an unacceptable deprivation of liberty.) Second, the fact that actions of a certain type are in this sense unjustifiable intrusions against their victims is a necessary condition for making these actions the object of a law with condemnatory force. A "mental element," in the form of specific intent or reckless disregard for the likely consequences of one's actions is important here: harms do not constitute unjustifiable intrusions if they were unavoidable.

The fact that an action is an unjustifiable intrusion (in the sense just described) is a necessary condition for condemning it, and usually also a sufficient condition for doing so. But it is not (on a nonretributive view) a sufficient condition for depriving the agent of liberty or inflicting other forms of harsh treatment on him. For such harsh treatment, some further justification is required beyond the desirability of expressing our judgments. This is where we must appeal to the utility of deterrence as a way of providing a kind of protection that we need and are entitled to, and to the fact that everyone will have a fair opportunity to avoid liability to the penalties involved.

This account enables us to put what I have been calling "affirmation" in its proper place. I said above that this notion has seemed puzzling because the expression of condemnation seems to be importantly connected with justifiable punishment, yet does not seem weighty enough to provide that justification. The central function of criminal law is to protect rights whose violation makes condemnation appropriate. So punishment will not be justifiable except where condemnation, and hence the affirmation of victims' rights, is appropriate, and just punishment will constitute such affirmation. In addition, as I pointed out in the case of Argentina, authoritative condemnation of certain acts as criminal can play an important role in building respect for the rule of law, and hence in a strategy of deterrence broadly understood.

The "mental element" in the definition of a crime plays two roles in the account I have just given. It occurs once as part of what makes an action an unjustifiable intrusion, which is justifiably condemned. It occurs again, in the form of "fair opportunity to avoid," as part of the account of why it is permissible not only to condemn certain actions but also to attach severe penalties to them as a mechanism of deterrence.

The mistake (as I see it) of retributive theories is that they lump together these two roles for the "mental element" in criminal punishment: its role as a condition for the appropriateness of condemnation and its role as a condition for the permissibility of inflicting loss. The weakness of nonretributive theories is that they may seem unsatisfactory because they separate these elements too widely and concentrate too much on the second (the permissibility of inflicting loss on the criminal) because the question it raises is seen as theoretically more challenging.

What philosophers do, of course, is to work hard at identifying the differences between theories of this kind and then try to decide which of them offers the most satisfactory account of "our" settled convictions. Reaching agreement about such matters is not easy, even when the "we" in question is just the group of people around a seminar table, or even when it is the single person in front of the computer screen.

The real-world political problems to which this inquiry is addressed involve building at least a partial consensus among a large and varied group of people on such issues as what the rule of law is, why it is to be valued, and what the pre-conditions are for just punishment. Some of us may think, after years of philo-sophical reflection, that we have answers to these questions. It would be hope-less to think that others will take our word for these conclusions, or even that everyone will agree with them. What we can do, however, is to try to call the al-ternatives we have distinguished to the attention of our fellow citizens, so that they can decide, for example, whether their view of punishment is actually ret-ributivist or just seemed to be so because they had not noticed what the alter-natives were.

Even imagining this role for philosophy in public discourse may seem opti-mistic, particularly given the abysmal level of recent debates in this country. But this is the hopeful model that Carlos Nino's idea of deliberative democracy seems to suggest. More remarkably, it is the model he put into practice in his life, in ways which made him an inspiration to us all.

NOTES

1. Nino, "The Duty to Punish Past Abuses of Human Rights Put Into Context" 100 *Yale Law Journal* 2619–40 at 2620, replying to Diane Orentlicher, "Settling Accounts: The Duty to Prosecute Human Rights Violations of a Prior Regime," 100 *Yale Law Journal* 2537–2615.
2. This rejection, on grounds close to those just mentioned, is spelled out in chapter 4 of Carlos Nino, *Radical Evil on Trial* (New Haven: Yale University Press, 1996).
3. H. L. A. Hart, *Punishment and Responsibility* (New York: Oxford University Press, 1968), 234–235.
4. Deterrence theorists may disagree as to whether the need for deterrence can be taken into account in adjusting the penalty in an individual case, some holding, perhaps, that this is required in any efficient system, while others see it as introducing an unacceptable form of arbitrary inequality.
5. It is recognized by Joel Feinberg in "The Expressive Function of Punishment," in his col-lection of essays, *Doing and Deserving* (Princeton: Princeton University Press, 1970).
6. Nino, *Radical Evil on Trial,* ch. 4.
7. The idea that one of the crucial functions of a system of criminal law is to give definite form to the sense of being wronged was emphasized by Nietzsche. See *The Genealogy of Morals,* second essay, sections 10–15.
8. Nino calls this more general view "preventionism." See *Radical Evil on Trial,* ch 4.
9. Nino describes these categories, which he says were first outlined by Alfonsín in a lecture

at the Argentine Federation of Lawyers' Colleges in August 1983, as follows: "(a) those who planned the repression and gave the accompanying orders; (b) those who acted beyond orders, moved by cruelty, perversity, or greed; (c) those who strictly complied with the orders." *Radical Evil on Trial,* 63.

10. As argued, with reference to the case of Chile, by Jorge Correa Sutil, in "Dealing with Past Human Rights Violations," 67 *Notre Dame Law Review* (1993), 1455–1494.

11. Carlos Nino, "A Consensual Theory of Punishment," 12 *Philosophy and Public Affairs* (1983), 295–296. See the essays in Hart's *Punishment and Responsibility,* especially "Prolegomenon to the Principles of Punishment" and "Legal Responsibility and Excuses."

12. Nino, "A Consensual Theory," 296.

13. Nino, "A Consensual Theory," 296.

14. Even here, it may be too strong a requirement, but I will not go into the details. As I have said, it does seem that the party to a contract must at least intend and believe that he or she is performing an act with normative legal consequences.

15. Nino, "A Consensual Theory," 299.

16. One way to make it particularly clear that violations of human rights incur legal liability would be to eliminate constitutional provisions licensing suspension of basic liberties by declaration of a "state of siege." This suggestion may be thought unrealistic, but such provisions (in addition to offering an air of legality to acts that do not merit it) invite a kind of cynicism by suggesting that even the law itself recognizes that civil liberties are something that can be enjoyed only in "good times."

17. I have presented a view of this kind in lecture 3 of "The Significance of Choice," *Tanner Lectures in Human Values,* vol. 8 (Salt Lake City: University of Utah Press, 1988), 151–216.

Chapter 17 From Dictatorship to Democracy: The Role of Transitional Justice

Ruti Teitel

Though Carlos Nino and I were both Argentine-born jurists and academics in the area of human rights, and we could have met in many ways, our paths crossed for the first time in Prague in 1991 at a conference where both of us had been invited to speak about the relevance of prior experiences in political transitions for the former communist bloc, and in particular regarding the question of how successor societies should respond to the crimes of the prior totalitarian regimes. To what extent were successor states obligated to punish the perpetrators of past abuses?

For a decade now it seems we have been struggling with the so-called successor "punishment-pardon" dilemma. Having had the anomalous experience of designing Argentina's punishment policy, and then having also to preside over the policy's undoing, Nino found himself locked in a sad debate against human rights advocates. In his writing about Argentina's trials, Nino always maintained that the notion that successor governments were obligated to punish abuses of prior regimes could be justified only under a retributivist theory of punishment. Yet among advocates of successor punishment, chiefly from within the international human rights community, the retributivist argument for punishment was generally dismissed as backward-looking, and even regressive. Advocates of successor criminal justice instead justified such policy in terms of forward-looking purposes, such as deterrence and the restoration of the rule of law.

There the debate remained. To the extent that forward-looking justifications were invoked for punishment, these were generally framed as a normative claim about the connection between punishment and the prospects for democracy. As time passed, and the interceding events of a wave of political transitions, it became clear that despite its interest as a theoretical matter, the terms of the punishment-pardon debate were more and more divorced from the actual experiences of successor societies. The pace of world events, as we would see, affected the terms of the debate over justice in transitions. Whereas the initial normative claims posited a positive relation between successor punishment and successful transitions to democracy, over time this claim appeared to give way, almost imperceptibly, to another claim: that successor regimes were obligated to investigate and to repair wrongs perpetrated under prior regimes. What is the relation between these two claims about the justification and even ostensible obligations of successor regimes to justice as conditions to democracy? I want to explore the question through a comparative look at the practices of societies in transitions from military rule in the Americas, with those now moving out of communist rule. What, if anything, might these developments tell us about the question of whether obligations are being assumed by successor regimes regarding the abuses of prior regimes?

FROM "PUNISHMENT OR PARDON" TO "TRUTH OR JUSTICE"
The Problem of State Impunity

At a certain point in the Latin American transitions, particularly those of the Southern Cone, it became evident that the question of whether punishment was necessary to democratic transition seemed strangely inapposite. Overwhelmingly as an empirical matter, the reverse relation seemed to be true: the precursors to democratic rule all over the region were agreements to amnesty. Most troubling was the level of societal support for such amnesties. In Uruguay, for example, the question of amnesty was approved in a popular referendum. Nevertheless, what also emerged was the apparently conflicting fact that despite the prevalence and societal acceptance of amnesty, the question of successor justice did not go away.

What seemed to be at stake in the deliberations was an agonizing choice between justice and utter impunity. Whereas repressive regimes are often characterized by state crime and its cover-up, the military repression of 1970s Latin America took state impunity to a new level. What emerged in the transitions were revelations of the depths of a state criminality whose very hallmark was impunity.

What does it mean if the victim's body disappears? Perhaps the crime never happened? In the 1970s Latin military repression revealed a new coercive state power—the power to make the body "disappear," the power to render citizens the disappeared or *desaparecidos* and thus a new form of impunity. In Argentina alone, more than ten thousand persons were abducted, detained, tortured, and disappeared. Every step of the military's process was characterized by cover-up and denial: of the kidnapping, detention, and torture; of the perpetrators, the methods, and the detention centers; culminating in the grossest denial—of the murders. By the disappearances all was denied. The question was whether all would continue to be denied if punishment were not brought to bear against military perpetrators. Failure to punish seemed to imply that victims and their survivors would be deprived of any possibility of a criminal investigation of their cases, and deprived of rights protected under the criminal law of the countries in the region as well as under international law. Would the failure to punish imply not even knowing the wrongs committed under the prior regime?

The framing of the transitional dilemma as a matter of "punishment or pardon" does not account for the fact that failure to exercise punishment did not put an end to the successor justice debates. Accordingly, I want here to move beyond the antinomies of the punishment-pardon debate to recognize alternative manifestations of successor justice. I want to consider three here: a "limited" form of criminal justice, historical justice, and finally poetic justice. I propose that there are affinities in these manifestations, informing the question of the nature of the successor regime's obligations undertaken respecting the prior repressive legacies.

THE "LIMITED" CRIMINAL SANCTION

I contend that to the extent that there is a turn to criminal justice in transitions, the dominant practice is prosecution followed by little or no punishment. The record of criminal justice in transitional periods confirms this pattern, which often culminates in pardons. I term this practice the "limited criminal sanction."

In Argentina, though there were trials of the military junta and others in the 1980s, soon after the trials began the limits on the trials, known as the "due obedience law" and the "final stop law," were promulgated. Ultimately, President Carlos Menem's pardons led to the release of every individual previously convicted of atrocities, including high-ranking junta leaders and the worst torturers. Argentina exemplifies trials without punishment.

In Chile, despite an amnesty law exempting from prosecution crimes committed through 1978, military officers were nevertheless called into court to cooperate in criminal investigations of torture and disappearances relating to prior military rule. These investigations were conducted pursuant to the "Aylwin doctrine," named after Chile's president who conceded that, under the prevailing amnesty law, the military were largely exempt from punishment. But Aylwin has nevertheless maintained that the amnestying of criminal liability should not imply exemption from the criminal investigation. In this abbreviated form of criminal process there is a judicial investigation of state wrongdoing, but no apportioning of individual culpability and sanction. Unlike Argentina, where punishment was limited after trial, under the investigations held pursuant to the Aylwin doctrine criminal penalties were dropped in advance, and in a sense on the condition of military confession to wrongdoing. The Chilean practice could be considered to be a conditional amnesty, amnesty given in exchange for the alleged perpetrators' participation in a judicial proceeding to clarify the relevant wrongs.

The limited criminal sanction is by no means particular to the Latin transitions. Review of the record of post–World War II successor trials, as well as more recent postcommunist cases, reveals a similar pattern: trials, sometimes followed by convictions, but often followed by little or no punishment. In contemporary transitions, a variant on the Chilean approach is emerging as a compromise solution to the problem of accountability after regime change. Thus, in postapartheid South Africa, despite an amnesty agreed to in the transitional agreements, amnesty from criminal liability will be allowed while judicial investigation of past wrongdoing may occur.

Depending on how limited the process (in some instances it is more abbreviated than others), the criminal investigations characterizing transitional justice may culminate in a verdict on individual perpetrators' culpability. Yet even where there are such verdicts, these are commonly followed by minimal sanctions. The notion of a verdict on a crime, separate from the verdict on an accused's culpability, is a feature existing in some versions of continental criminal law. But the limited sanction goes much further. The practice comprehends a novel use of the criminal sanction, one which does not result in the inflicting of punishment, nor necessarily the targeting of a particular defendant.

How should we understand the development of the "limited sanction?" What do successor trials and investigations, without ensuing penalties, signify? Despite the aftermath of Argentina's trials, why is there a generally held perception that in Buenos Aires federal court, justice was done? To understand the significance of this development of justice in transition requires us to deconstruct the limited criminal sanction. In the ordinary understanding of the criminal sanction the prosecution and penalties are considered to be a unitary practice we term punishment. This is seen in the language used to describe the practice, and in the absence of differentiation in the justification of the elements of prosecution and the penalties subsumed under the rubric of punishment. By contrast, in the transitional form of the criminal sanction, the prosecution and punishment components have become detached from each other. Successor practices suggest that to the extent that there is exercise of criminal justice, it is comprised largely of prosecution, often limited to a formal proceeding that consists chiefly of an investigation.

What purposes of criminal justice are served by the limited sanction? The limited sanction appears to have emerged in response to the distinct problem of massive crimes that are state-sponsored and covered up by a prior regime. This use of the criminal process implies a formal criminal investigation, enabling the clarification of past wrongdoing by a presumably neutral judiciary at the highest standard of knowledge—the most authoritative form of truth in the legal system. There is a turn to a limited criminal process to establish facts about past wrongdoing. Even ordinary criminal process establishes the truth of an event in controversy. Trials enable numerous historical representations, the re-creation of the event in the trial, as well as more enduring representations in the record and judgment. Thus, in Argentina's trial of its junta, the terrible events of the military period were aired openly.

Whereas the exercise of punishment is ordinarily justified in terms of traditional penal purposes relating to the guilty individuals such as retribution, deterrence, or rehabilitation, insofar as it elides the assigning of individual responsibility and the inflicting of individual punishment, the limited criminal sanction advances other purposes. This partial form of the criminal sanction enables clarifying the past and formally recognizing prior wrongdoing. The sanction thus advances epistemic and denunciatory purposes of the criminal law. Epistemic purposes relate to knowledge about the truth and hark back to an early meaning of "prosecution," signifying to know precisely. In the case of successor justice, the criminal investigation has a public historical dimension. These processes enable the country to recover its past.

Through a proceeding that formally recognizes past wrongdoing, the limited criminal sanction also advances the expressive denunciatory purposes associated with the full criminal sanction. Formal recognition that criminal wrongs occurred, even where liability remains unapportioned, expresses condemnation of the prior regime. Though liability remains unindividuated and punishment is not inflicted, merely exposing past regime wrongdoing implies the stigma of the criminal sanction often leading to noncriminal censure, such as the exclusion of the implicated public officials from positions of political leadership, or other comparable authority in the successor regime. Accordingly, even the limited sanction can advance political purposes such as the delegitimizing of the predecessor regime. In advancing epistemic and expressive purposes of the criminal law, the limited sanction appears to accomplish some of the forward-looking purposes associated with the full criminal sanction. These purposes can be considered to be "democracy-related." In the punishment-pardon debate we consider the purposes closely connected to forward-looking purposes such as the restoration of the rule of law. But the workings of justice in transition also suggest that the purposes advanced by the limited criminal sanction are closely intertwined with a retributivist view of punishment.

I propose that the developments of transitional justice should inform the content of our penal theory. These developments suggest that there are purposes relating to the retributivist idea which may well be satisfied by alternatives to punishment. I propose that the transitional manifestation of the criminal sanction illuminates the debate over the relation of criminal justice to democracy, and the related underlying debate about the proper justifications for punishment. Though retributivist justification is often eschewed for punishment's forward-looking democracy-related purposes, the limited sanction exposes a new way to think about the retributivist idea of punishment: if prior attempts to distinguish the varying senses of the retributivist idea—resort to "negative" and "positive," strong and weak retributivism—the nature of the limited sanction invites us to think about retributivist justification as comprehending a punishment process. In this regard we could distinguish a spectrum or range of broad and narrow senses associated with the retributivist view of punishment. The very claim to sanctions is couched in the language of rights and justice associated with the retributivist ideas of punishment. Few of these proceedings would occur if not for the demand from victims for redress of rights. The limited criminal sanction advances purposes retributive in nature in that they relate to the righting of prior injustice. Formal recognition that their rights were violated appears to vindicate victims. The workings of the limited sanction suggest that some of the purposes considered to be bound up in punishment in extraordinary periods are advanced by partial forms of the criminal process.

Returning to the question with which I began, what light might the criminal sanction shed on the punishment-pardon debate? The limited criminal sanction, I suggest, is one way successor societies have resolved the punishment-pardon dilemma characterizing periods of political transition. To what extent do the successor societies assume an obligation to punish prior regimes? If the eighteenth-century revolutions out of monarchy culminated in trials, and regicide, the practices associated with contemporary transitions are no doubt less radical for all sorts of reasons, such as political constraints, but nevertheless reflect a turn to alternative forms of justice. I now turn to a related manifestation, a form of historical accountability.

HISTORICAL JUSTICE
Impunity and the Advent of the Official
Truth-Tellings

The terrible problem confronted by societies in transition out of dictatorship was how to respond to the massive crimes of modern repressive rule. How to even establish the number of disappeared and dead enabled by the modern security apparatus? Military rule in Latin America and elsewhere, such as Africa, implied violence on a grand scale. Beyond the scope of the crimes were other elements further complicating the proof puzzle: how to establish what had happened during repressive rule when many of the victims had disappeared, when there were no eyewitnesses, and when for years the government covered up and the military could not be made to testify? The scope and nature of the wrongdoing defied ordinary criminal justice. Even where there were no criminal justice attempts, survivors and representatives of the disappeared nevertheless demanded that the successor regime tell the "truth" of what had happened. This demand led to the creation of the "truth commissions." The new mechanism created to cope with the crimes of the modern repressive state is the commission of inquiry.

Argentina's National Commission on the Disappeared (CONADEP) was mandated to establish what happened to the disappeared and to the country during the repression, leaving open the question of what remedies might follow.

After nine months CONADEP produced its voluminous report, identifying the disappeared and presumed dead, and documenting the systematic nature of junta repression. Though the CONADEP report did not name individual offenders, the report did apportion responsibility to distinct branches of the military junta, a determination that would become the basis of proof in the subsequent trials.

With its truth commission, Argentina spawned a new form of justice in political transitions: official truth-tellings. This new form of accountability responded to the pervasive dilemmas of amnesty in the region. When amnesty policies became pervasive in the transitions in the Americas and elsewhere, the ensuing dilemma was whether granting amnesty for criminal liability also meant that the underlying wrongs would be forgotten. The usefulness of truth commissions as solutions to the amnesty dilemma quickly spread to other countries. Wherever states were making delicate transitions out of brutal military rule, and where, due to political constraints, criminal justice was not a possibility, they turned to truth commissions. When political change occurred in Argentina's neighbor Chile, and bringing the military to trial was not possible because of Pinochet's ongoing hold in the country, the successor regime created the National Commission on Truth and Reconciliation. When the bloody civil war ended in El Salvador, the final peace accords stipulated the creation of an international truth commission to investigate past abuses. The truce agreed to in Guatemala was similarly conditioned on the "truth." Truth commissions have been established throughout Africa, in Uganda, in Chad, and most recently in post-apartheid South Africa.

Even in countries lacking the political impetus for an official investigation, nongovernmental organizations such as churches and human rights organizations took up the cause of documenting the past repression. Though Brazil and Uruguay's "truth-tellings" are private, the reports emulate the Argentine precedent, conveying the sense in which even private documentation can be perceived as delivering an "official" truth. Thus in Brazil, where military rule ended with no real political transition and governmental investigation was out of the question, the "truth" about the prior regime was left to two courageous members of the clergy. The church report drawn entirely from the government's own files constitutes a confession to state wrongdoing extracted by Brazil's leading clergy. To this day these private reports are the only records in the respective countries of the military repression of the 1970s.

The popularity of governmental and independent "truth-tellings" in countries forgoing criminal justice points to the development of a new paradigm of historical justice. How do truth-tellings enable a sense of justice?

THE HERMENEUTICS OF THE OFFICIAL TRUTH

The phenomenon of truth-tellings in periods of political transitions goes beyond the question of how states create collective memory. How does clarifying what happened under the prior regime enable a sense of transitional justice? And, relatedly, how does the truth become "official?"

What makes the truth "official" is defined to a large extent by principles generated within the legal system. How to establish authoritatively what happened during a much contested period of state history involving massive state crimes? Neither an official state trial nor private investigation, the truth commission stands at the juncture of our ordinary understandings of criminal and historical justice. The nature of the truth commissions reveal their relationship to the criminal justice system. The truth commission is quasi-governmental, with powers delegated from the executive branch, ordinarily the site of the prosecutorial power. Some of the commissions have broader investigative powers than others, such as being able to call the military to testify and having access to governmental archives. None of the commissions have full criminal subpoena powers, and thus they are clearly a compromise for the fact-finding associated with criminal justice.

THE AUTHORITY IN THE VICTIMS

The primary source of the official truth about the prior repression are its victims. Those who suffered at the hands of the state are its most credible witnesses. Survivors and other witnesses, many of whom have never before spoken openly, testify about their ordeal in "open-door" hearings convened by the commission throughout the country and abroad. Survivor stories are matched, exposing patterns of systematic rights abuses. Together with other documentation, these stories make up the "official truth."

The truth investigations are characterized by their open and participatory nature. Even the unofficial reports are like the official ones, largely based on victims' testimony. The right to a hearing, an ordinary part of governmental procedures, reinforces individual dignity rights. If the predecessor regime was known for its cover-up, the successor regime is known for its open door. If before the state failed to protect its citizens from violations of their security, under the successor government the practice of the open hearing undoes a small part of abuses perpetrated under the prior regime. The new democratic ritual is heightened when the truth hearings are held at the very state buildings that were sites of the prior persecution.

THE AUTHORITY OF THE OFFICIAL REPORT

The truth reports constitute a new paradigm of successor response to massive state persecution. In the commission reports, the testimony of victims and other witnesses is deftly reconstructed into a unified story of state repression that becomes the official truth. By what standard is the official truth known? The work of the commission of inquiry is to establish precisely what happened. The truth commission practices reflect adherence to a principle of documentation and to a standard of precise knowledge. The official truth of state atrocities is established by meticulous documentation. To know precisely is the way to close the gap upon past events, which by their very horror, and state sponsorship, would otherwise be disbelieved and forgotten. Thus, the record created in the truth reports are not general accounts but detailed documentary reports. The reports are a sea of details: the disappearances are reported by the street where the abduction took place, by the name of the detention center, the nickname of the torturers, the names of the other inmates, the witnesses who testified. Every detail is recounted in bare fashion, without literary license. In plain, matter-of-fact language, the unbelievable is made believable. The greater the detail, the stronger the counterweight to the prior regime's silence. The more precise the documentation, the less left to interpretation and even to denial. The paradigm of the official representation of statewide atrocity is the literal account.

From Official Truth to Historical Justice

How do truth-tellings enable historical justice? The goal of the official historical inquiry is to establish what happened under the prior repressive rule. Accounting for "what happened" during the prior repressive rule means going beyond amassing the facts. As in successor trials, what is at stake is a contested national history. Thus, the truth reports are constructed so as to enable historical accountability.

In transitions out of military rule, the truth that is most contested concerns the characterization of the prior regime's violence. According to the standard military account, the repression is justified as part of the "war against subversion." Reporting what happened under the prior dictatorship is conveyed in terms of known categories of violence: of "random violence," "war," "crimes against humanity." If the military characterize the violence perpetrated as "war," and the disappeared as the "guerrilla," the truth reports reply to these representations. The reports counter with an account that the government brutality was not a war against subversion; that those killed were not political terrorists but ordinary citizens; and that they were not killed for reasons of national security, but arbitrarily. Knowing who the victims are turns out to be inextricably related to representation of the nature of the prior regime's actions. Thus the truth reports are devoted in great part to identifying victims. When the Argentine truth commission soberly reports that one-fifth of the disappeared were students, this categorization refutes the military's claims that the disappeared were "combatants," and shows instead that they were unarmed civilians. When the Chilean report categorizes its disappearances according to state motive, it demonstrates that the state violence could not be considered motivated by reason of national security, but instead conclusively refutes the claim of the "war against terrorism." Just as a trial concludes with a determination of the veracity of one version of a contested event, so too the truth-tellings also conclude with such a determination. Refuting the predecessors' account of the repression provides historical accountability and hence a form of justice.

It is in presentment, the final stage of the truth-telling process, that historical and political accountability converge. After the reports are completed, they are presented by the truth commissioners to the governmental actor delegating the commission its powers, usually the country's president. Following this level of presentment by the truth commission is another level of presentment, that of the president to the country. This ritual of political accountability is often accompanied by a governmental apology. Thus, in the Chilean truth report's presentment, in an address held in a large public arena, President Aylwin acknowledged that the disappeared had been executed by agents of the state and pleaded for a societal apology.

TRUTH AS JUSTICE

Like the "limited criminal sanction," the "truth-tellings" are successor responses that also appear to advance purposes ordinarily associated with criminal justice. Affinities in the limited sanction and in the official truth-tellings regime converge upon the pursuit of some form of historical accountability. As with the representations enabled by criminal justice, the truth-tellings and the limited sanction both advance counteraccounts to prevailing regime accounts about contested events. Like the limited criminal sanction, the truth-tellings advance epistemic and denunciatory purposes ordinarily associated with the criminal sanction. Though historical accountability often remains collective in nature, this form of accountability nevertheless appears to advance purposes bound up in the retributive basis for punishment, previously discussed. Truth-tellings offer a way to recognize past wrongs, giving victims their "historical due." Such historical justice also enables delineating a line between the old regime and the new. The wrongdoing of the prior regime is exposed by the successor regime, and subjected to the fact-finding processes characterizing established democracies.

HISTORICAL JUSTICE IN THE TOTALITARIAN
LEGACY
The Challenge of "Living in Truth"

"To live in truth" was the opposition's challenge to the communist state apparatus. Yet after the fall of communism, whatever would it mean to "live in truth"? How to move from the closed society to an open one? In Latin America and Africa, where military persecution occurred largely outside any regard for state history, the pervasive response has been to establish the repressive period's official historical account. Unlike the repression of military rule, where people disappeared without a trace, under the Soviet system there was no lack of state "documentation." To the contrary, other than the Berlin Wall, there was no greater symbol of the communist repression than the miles of East German state police (Stasi) files. What distinguished totalitarian rule was precisely the totality of state power, and the attempt to control history and culture.

In the totalitarian legacy of the political uses of state history, the claim that official truth-tellings are necessary to successful transitions seems wrong. Whatever would an "official truth" mean without raising the old regime problem of the political uses of state history? Thus, in the transitions out of communism, successor regimes have generally eschewed creating official narratives about the prior dictatorship. After decades of the closed society, the response is to open the ancien regime archives. Whereas historical justice in the transitions out of military and communist rule share a common interest in the disclosure of suppressed evidence of prior state wrongdoing, beyond that there are differences. In the transitions out of military rule, historical justice has implied construction of state history, witness by witness, fact by fact. In the transitions out of communism, by contrast, historical justice has implied instead taking apart the existing state history, file by file. The meaning of historical justice appears contingent on the nature of the predecessors' persecution and the state's past uses and abuses of history.

In the aftermath of totalitarian rule, successor regimes in Eastern and Central Europe have generally eschewed truth-tellings. Despite little interest in constructing an official story about the prolonged period of communist rule, nevertheless the past state histories have been opened up to attempt to shed light on mysterious holes in history, the region's defining political moments, where the line between freedom and repression, and between resistance and collaboration were drawn. With the newfound access to Soviet KGB and communist party archives, the attempt has been to reconstruct critical turning points in the establishing of repressive communist rule: for Hungary, 1956; for the former Czechoslovakia, 1968; and for Poland, 1981. The pivotal question of historical justice after the collapse of communism is one of political responsibility. Whose dictatorship? We or they? The question has legal, political, and historical ramifications, informing whether the prior rule is fairly understood as a foreign occupation or as domestic repression.

In the Czech Republic there were two defining moments: 1968 and the crushing of the Prague spring is one turning point; and November 1989, the velvet revolution's beginning, is the other. With the end of Soviet control in the region, and newfound access to state files from all of the countries involved in the August 1968 invasion, the Czechoslovakian Government Commission for the Investigation of Events in 1967–70 was mandated to "uncover" the "full historical truth of the invasion." The relevant question is the extent to which the responsibility for the 1968 suppression of the Prague Spring was Czech or Soviet. The same question animates the special parliamentary November 17 Commission investigation into the attempted suppression of the former Czechoslovakia's 1989 velvet revolution. Like the responsibility for the repression of the 1968 Prague Spring, the parliamentary inquiry revealed that the violence at the November 1989 demonstrations was the joint responsibility of Czechs and Soviets.

In Warsaw, the promise of political change was raised and put out on December 13, 1981, the day Poland's General Jaruzelski ordered martial law, crushing the opposition Solidarity movement. This historical moment is the subject of investigation of a specially convened parliamentary committee, the Sejm Constitutional Accountability Commission. Again, the critical question driving the historical investigation is, who was responsible for the repressive period strangely known as "the internal invasion of Poland"? We or they? Was the country's repression attributable to national or foreign sources? And, if domestic, was the nineteen-month crackdown on Solidarity justifiable to avoid a Soviet invasion? Whereas Poland has in large part eschewed the prosecutions and purgings of its neighbors, its parliamentary investigation into the events of 1981 is a rare look back. The predecessor Jaruzelski regime is being held historically accountable.

October 31, 1956, was the historical turning point in Hungary, the date of the popular uprising against Soviet dictatorship and its violent suppression. Again, the question driving the governmental 1956 investigation is where ultimate responsibility lies for the 1956 suppression: we or they? Was it outside the country in the Soviets, or with the predecessor Hungarian regime? The promise of an independent account of what happened at the uprising is fanned by newfound access to Soviet files. But as the historians in the region are finding, the communist archives do not fully clarify the question of historical accountability. There is enough to suggest collusion between the Soviets and the domestic communist party apparatus in the 1956 suppression. Though the historical inquiry begins with exploration of the "they," of the invasion externalized, it ends in the "we," with the profound question of national responsibility.

A more subtle historical question than that of physical invasion is the focus of research in Germany. The question now before a parliamentary commission concerns political responsibility for the dictatorship in East Germany. The Eppelman Commission is charged with reviewing *Ostpolitik*, and the question of the extent to which West Germany's accommodationist policies were responsible for supporting the communist dictatorship.

Exploration of the successor efforts after communism illuminate the contingencies of historical justice. As a general matter, the responses to totalitarian rule have not been the creation of massive historical investigations and metanarratives characterizing the transitions out of military rule. If communist rule implied the attempt to assert hegemonic control over history, the postcommunist successor response is localized knowledge. Localized knowledge is antitotalizing. In the posttotalitarian period the response has been to establish precisely what happened at particular critical junctures in the dictatorship. As with the postmilitary historical inquiries, the postcommunist inquiries into these historical moments contest the predecessor accounts of these controversial moments in the nation's history.

Though the postcommunist historical inquiries all commence with the question of national responsibility, as the investigations proceed the lines of responsibility lead closer and closer to home, and the question of national responsibility gives way to a question about individual responsibility in the prior regime. This is reflected in the turn to criminal justice. Thus, for example, in the Czech Republic, immediately after the events of the velvet revolution, in the first wave of prosecutions, former communist party leaders were investigated on treason charges for collaboration in the suppression of the Prague Spring. Similar consequences followed the investigations of the 1989 events. Shortly after it was created, the November 17 Commission mandate was expanded to include investigation for collaboration of the past records of parliamentary deputies and other public officials. These parliamentary investigations would lead to widespread administrative purgings from political office. Similarly, to the extent that there has been successor criminal justice in Hungary, it concerns treason charges for collaboration with the Soviets in the bloody suppression of the 1956 uprising. Treason prosecutions were blocked from going forward when Hungary's Constitutional Court held that the legislation suffered fatally from retroactivity in its definition of treason. Constitutional review of the 1956 treason law illuminates the rule-of-law implications of using treason charges to prosecute what was encouraged under the prior regime. Under a subsequent law proscribing "war crimes," the prosecutions of the 1956 collaborators are under way today. As with the Czech 1968 trials and Hungary's 1956 trials, in Poland the former regime's 1981 imposition of martial law could be shown to be a sign of all too willing Polish collaboration, and could become the basis of criminal charges against the former leadership for treason.

To the extent that there have been trials in the former communist bloc, most have been bound up in pivotal historical moments where freedom hung in the balance. Those held responsible are those who happened to be in the communist leadership at those fateful historical moments. The postcommunist transitions highlight the relation between historical and criminal justice. The truth about what happened to the country is conflated with the "truth" of its citizens, that is, with the steadfastness of their allegiance to the country. As the historical investigations culminate in trials they expose the interplay of truth and treason in the crucible of postcommunist political transitions.

POETIC JUSTICE

Both the postmilitary and postcommunist practices reflect transitional response of some form of historical accounting for the prior repressive rule. What is the significance of these accountings? I want to return to the question posed at the

beginning of this chapter about the nature of the relationship of successor justice to democracy. I want to reconsider the normative thesis positing a relation
between successor justice and the prospects for democracy—the democracy justification for successor justice. I contend that the democracy justification is best
borne out in the historical accountings common to the transitions. I suggest that
these evince a poetic relation between the knowledge of the country's repressive
past and its future. Through the historical accountings, what is being pro-
pounded is a sense of poetic justice.

Consider the successor accounts about the predecessor repression. I argue
that these take a distinct form. The form of the narrative, I contend, follows the
line of the normative thesis—positing that there is a positive relation between
knowledge of the past repression and the potential for democratic transformation. Thus, both official and unofficial reports of the preceding dictatorships, as
well as fictionalized accounts, generally follow the following narrative. The successor histories begin in a tragic mode. As in the classical understanding described by Aristotle, the stories incorporate elements of tragedy (such as a re-
versal of fortune) and suffering (such as murders, torture) and a discovery. But
at a certain point the narratives switch over to a nontragic optimistic resolution.
In classical literary categories, this would constitute a turn to the comic phase.
In the successor narratives, the country's past suffering is somehow transformed
into something good for the country—the transition to democracy.

Transitional Narratives: From Tragedy
to Hope, from Truth to Reconciliation

Consider the stories being told in the truth reports coming out of Latin America. What is the form of these transitional narratives? Whereas in large part the
successor narratives reflect elements of the tragic form, in their final part the successor accounts end in a nontragic mode. Despite the most terrible atrocities,
the stories about the past nevertheless end in societal reconciliation. Such societal reconstitution is characteristic of comic structure. When the country's story
is told this way, the past suffering becomes redemptive. The "lessons" of a tragic
history are said to enable the transition to democracy.

This story line is very clearly seen in the national histories reported by the
truth commissions. To begin with are the reports' names. Entitled "Never
Again," the reports' very titles promise that discovery and self-knowledge will
deter future suffering. Even the private Latin reports, such as Brazil's "Nunca
Mais" and Uruguay's "Nunca Mas," follow the title of the Argentine precedent.
The promise of deterrence, ordinarily the province of criminal justice, is thought

to result from the truth-tellings. Beyond their names, in the first such report of the Argentine National Commission on the Disappeared, the account of the country's repression begins with a prologue declaring that the military dictatorship "brought about the greatest and most savage tragedy" in the country's history.[1] Nevertheless, the preface asserts that "[g]reat catastrophes are always instructive." In what way are great catastrophes instructive? What are the "lessons of history"? "The tragedy which began with the military dictatorship in March 1976, the most terrible our nation has ever suffered, will undoubtedly serve to help us understand that it is only democracy which can save a people from horror on this scale." According to the account, the nation's knowledge of suffering plays an important role in the political transition.

The narratives in the other Latin truth reports follow a similar story line. Discovery and confrontation with the past suffering is described as a necessary stage in the transition to democracy. The report of the Chilean National Commission on Truth and Reconciliation asserts that the historical accounting is necessary to the country's reconciliation.[2] Disclosure and knowledge of suffering are said to have been instrumental in bringing the country together. According to the decree establishing the commission, "the truth had to be brought to light, for only on such a foundation . . . would it be possible to . . . create the necessary conditions for achieving true national reconciliation." According to Chile's "Never Again" report, the truth is the necessary precondition for democracy. This is also the organizing thesis of the Report of the Commission on the Truth for El Salvador.[3] The story line is manifest even in the report's optimistic title: "From Madness to Hope" tells a story of violent civil war that is followed by "truth and reconciliation." According to the report's introduction, the truth's "creative consequences" include "settling political and social differences by means of agreement instead of violent action." "Peace [is] to be built on transparency of a knowledge." The report describes the truth as an illuminating bright light: "always in the search for lessons that would contribute to reconciliation and to abolishing such patterns of behavior in the new society."

The historical accountings in and of themselves are said to constitute a measure of justice. The preface to the Uruguayan report, for example, claims that the writing itself constitutes a triumph against repression. The preface refers to the prevailing notion that the lack of "critical understanding created a risk of having the disaster repeated . . . to rescue that history is to learn a lesson." The normative claim is expressed through the successor narratives. "We should have the courage not to hide that experience in our collective subconscious but to recollect it. So that we do not fall again into the trap." Successor accounts of past tyranny have given rise to a distinct form of national narrative—narratives that propound a sense of poetic justice.

In transitional history-making, the story must come out right. Yet it is clear that the stories being told in the transitions imply a taking of poetic license. Did the discovery of the truth bring on the restoration of democratic government, or was it the political change that enabled the truth-telling? The claim that the truth-tellings enabled transitions to democracy seems wrong almost everywhere. The transitions out of dictatorship in Brazil, Uruguay, and El Salvador did not await the truth. Indeed, transitions to freer political systems, and free elections, generally precede the truth as well as other successor justice. Political change often occurs in what is arguably a state of deception about the past. It is only much later in the transition that the "truth" becomes known. Nevertheless, in the stories told in the reports, the switch from the tragic past to the hopeful future occurs through the truth-tellings. An awful destiny is averted by a marvelous switch, enabling the societal reconciliation as in comic drama, by the introduction of a device, of witnesses or people with special knowledge, that is, some form of justice.

Transitional Justice: Romantic
and Ironic Permutations

In the contemporary postcommunist transitions, the creation of parliamentary commissions has been directed to the writing of national histories establishing the story of the popular resistance to Soviet invasions. Yet strangely, the historical commissions documenting the resistance have turned instead to documenting collaboration. Throughout Eastern Europe, the stories told about the past begin with the representation of the enemy as the foreigner and then proceed to the progressively more and more troubling discovery of pervasive collaboration throughout the society. In the narratives unfolding in the former Soviet bloc, the most pronounced element is the tragic discovery.

In the former Soviet bloc the historical investigations too have revealed profound suffering and attempts to isolate perpetrators from the society. These are tragic stories. Yet again, as in the stories of the Latin transitions, there is a competing story line by which the tragic is converted into a happy ending, into prospects for a democratic future. Again, this switch occurs through some form of justice. Whereas in Latin America, it has been through truth-tellings, in the former Soviet bloc the transition to a new society occurs through trials and purges.

Whereas the stories of transformation in the Americas are romanticized, in the former Soviet bloc the tone is ironic. The efforts to attain justice are described as they are in reality, where the difficulty of bringing those most responsible to trial has resulted in attempts that often seem besides the point. A note of irony threatens to undermine the entire endeavor. What rationalizes the postcommunist prosecutions and the purges is the degree to which there is a perception of responsibility for the regime's repression. But the ironic tone heard in so many of the accounts from the region emphasizes the seemingly arbitrary nature of successor justice. Those prosecuted or purged in many cases are simply those who happen to have been in a particular place at a particular moment in time. Insofar as the ironic tone suggests that those individuals isolated from the society are no more guilty than the rest of its members, this tone threatens the successor justice project in the region. In haunting fashion the arbitrariness of the latter-day exclusions of individuals from the postcommunist society evokes the arbitrariness, the Kafkaesque nature, of the prior repression.

Whether in the romanticized Latin versions or the ironic East European versions, it is in the narratives constructed in contemporary transitions that we most clearly see support for the normative claim about the positive relation between justice and the prospects for democracy. In these stories, it is transitional justice that is the device by which the state moves from catastrophe to democracy. The democracy thesis we have long debated is best borne out in the stories we are telling today.

NOTES

1. *Nunca Más: The Report of the Argentine National Commission of the Disappeared,* trans. (New York: Farrar, Straus and Giroux, 1986).
2. *Report of the Chilean National Commission on Truth and Reconciliation,* trans. Phillip E. Berryman (South Bend, Ind.: University of Notre Dame Press, 1993).
3. *From Madness to Hope: The Twelve-Year War in El Salvador,* Report of the Commission on the Truth for El Salvador, U.N. Security Council S/25500 (April 1, 1993).

Chapter 18 Dictatorship and Punishment: A Reply to Scanlon and Teitel

Ernesto Garzón Valdés

In what follows I offer a few comments on T. M. Scanlon's and Ruti Teitel's reflections on what Carlos Nino has called "radical evil" and its punishment. Specifically, I will consider the two aspects of the problem analyzed by Scanlon, that is, the problem of "building a legal order that preserves the rule of law and provides remedies for victims of past human rights abuses." My comments on Teitel's chapter will concentrate on the question of transition. A few references to the Argentine case will serve to clarify my own position on this problem. My remarks will be made from the moral point of view, paying special attention to the justification of a legal *system of punishment*.

The system of punishment obviously plays an instrumental role in the preservation of the rule of law. People do not always act as they ought to, even if they recognize their obligations and express their consent to the rules of the social game. Therefore, as long as people are as they are, and as long as admonition is not enough to ensure the effective functioning of an order of peaceful coexistence, any legal system needs what Hart has called "primary norms" of obligation, that is, norms the violation of which is threatened with punishment.[1] In that sense, the justification of punishment is intimately related to the justification of the imposition of a heteronomous political order, and that means the justification of the state which, in its minimal version, implies at the very least the prohibition of the exercise of self-justice.

The problem of punishment, therefore, is a double one: on the one hand, we need to justify the infliction of a harm on those who violate primary norms; and on the other, we must justify the prohibition of self-justice. Both aspects are important, and Scanlon explicitly refers to them in his essay.

From a liberal point of view, which many share, the justification of a sanctioning state can only proceed within a framework that requires, above all, respect for the autonomy and for the dignity, or self-respect, of individuals. Nino incessantly emphasized these two values, which must be taken into account as they relate to the offender as well as to the victim. It is precisely this question of how to reach a fair equilibrium between these two perspectives that gives rise to the discussion about punishment.

At the beginning of his chapter, Scanlon announces that in this context he will distinguish four moral ideas: retribution, deterrence, affirmation, and fairness. With respect to this list, I doubt that its elements are all on the same level. In fact, it seems to me that the value of fairness belongs to a different level, because it can be used as a criterion for judging the other three but not vice versa.

Let us look at the list from the standpoint of the offender. Like the great majority of liberal criminal lawyers, Nino and Scanlon agree that there do not seem to exist good justificatory arguments for the retributivist theory. Scanlon, however, seems to hold a less radical position than Nino when he says, "part of my message . . . is that something *like* retributivism is not so easy to avoid." The question, of course, is what that "something" could be. Apparently, it may not be too similar to retribution, because Scanlon also says that "it is not appropriate for [citizens] to demand retribution." According to Nino and Scanlon, that "something" also must not require the punishment of all those who are guilty, since that would mean a relapse into a totally retributivist theory. Scanlon thus seems to accept the permissibility of "selective punishment." The "something" we are looking for would not lead us to a pure deterrence theory, either, because, as Scanlon says, such a theory, for its "future orientation," "seem[s] deficient from the perspective of another moral idea, which I [Scanlon] will call *affirmation* of the victims' sense of having been wronged." Finally, then, that "something" could consist in a theory that gives greater weight to the aspect of affirmation, that is, one that emphasizes the attitude of resentment, of indignation.

This last point obviously is related to the symbolic meaning, or to what Feinberg has called the "expressive function," of punishment. A crime produces public indignation, on the one hand, and an insult to the victims, on the other.[2] Punishment, in that sense, expresses—in Feinberg's words—"a kind of vindictive resentment."[3]

But we must also remember that the expressive or affirmative character of punishment, its symbolic meaning, is only secondary, because it is "merely a consequence of the fact that it is thought to have retributive or instrumental objectives."[3] This observation may seem unimportant at first, but it becomes relevant when we try to follow Nino and Scanlon in their attempts to bridge the gap between retributivist and deterrence theories.

To take the affirmative aspect seriously means to acknowledge it in all cases. This seems to exclude the possibility of "selective punishment." In fact, even defenders of the idea of deterrence like Viktor Vanberg do not hold that punishment should be applied selectively. Rather, Vanberg stresses that we must distinguish the theory of deterrence from utilitarian approaches that suggest the convenience of a selective infliction of punishment, and sometimes even the infliction of "punishment" on innocent people. Such a version of "deterrence" would actually undermine a deterring effect, since those who have a taste for risk could speculate on their good luck that they will be among those not punished; and the inclusion of innocent people among the punished would transform the system of punishment into a system of terror and thus contradict the rule of law.[5]

While it is true that deterrence justifies the system of punishment by referring to its effects in the future, this does not mean that the infliction of a penalty is not justified in each particular case by referring to the past, that is, to a crime that has been committed. Thus, neither with respect to the legislator nor with respect to the judge can the permissibility of selective punishment be inferred. In any case, deterrence theory does not deny the affirmative value of punishment; on the contrary, if a penalty expresses disapproval and resentment, it produces an additional motive for not committing a crime. It is, in Bentham's words, a "restraining motive" counteracting an "impelling motive" for committing a crime.[6]

This approach takes into account what Scanlon correctly points out when he says: "People whose sense of being wronged is not recognized and affirmed by the law have less respect for and less investment in it." Indeed, when people feel that their condition as a victim is not taken seriously, this can have two consequences, both of which are morally unacceptable.

First, the victim is doubly harmed: because after having suffered the transgression of the offender, he or she now suffers the psychological harm of feeling unprotected against the former and other potential future offenders. Second, the victim may thus feel impelled to take justice into his or her own hands. The first consequence violates the value of fairness the importance of which Scanlon rightly emphasizes.[7] From a liberal point of view, such a violation is unacceptable. And with the second consequence, the legal system becomes unsafe—an outcome that is a large step in the direction of a Hobbesian prepolitical situation. With respect to the necessity of affirmation Scanlon correctly observes that: "It does not seem likely that a system of law that fails, in general, to respond to such demands is likely to survive." But this is precisely why I find it hard to accept the second part of Scanlon's thesis, according to which "a defensible legal order must, in general, define and defend citizens' rights, but this does not require that every offender be punished."

Even when prudential reasons suggest in a particular case that no penalty should be imposed, this can provoke the (under the rule of law) undesired effect of vigilante justice, as the following anecdote illustrates: "A French king once had to deal with a delicate legal case: one of the most influential dukes of his kingdom had raped and killed the daughter of a wealthy peasant of a certain social standing. To sentence the duke as he deserved would not have been politically wise, but neither could his crime go totally unpunished. In public hearing, the king sentenced the noble murderer: 'Go freely, I pardon your crime . . . as I will also pardon the man who might kill you.' Poor duke! He did not last long."[8]

The fact that those who committed, or were responsible for, the crimes of state terrorism in Argentina have (so far) not shared the duke's fate tells us a lot about their victims' respect for the rule of law. But it is neither prudent nor fair to test the limits of that respect by way of a systematic denial of "affirmation."

The duke, in any case, knew very well that to rape and kill—even a peasant girl—was a crime, and that therefore he legally (and morally) deserved to be punished. It is this prior knowledge that Scanlon underscores when in principle he accepts the idea of consent, which is an expression of respect for individual autonomy, as fundamental for the justification of a punishment. Scanlon, in fact, proposes the idea of a "fair opportunity to avoid a sanction" as a weaker version of Nino's consensual theory.

However, it should be remembered that the notion of consent, or fair opportunity, is also taken into account by deterrence theory. As Vanberg observes: "With respect to . . . the need for a 'system of rules of the game' as well as the necessity of their effective implementation, the assumption of an interest in these aspects common to all the participants cannot be dismissed as mere fiction. This is, then, the most appropriate way to interpret the 'implicit assumption of consent' of general deterrence theory."[9]

Finally, I end my comments on Scanlon with a short remark on what could be called Scanlon's hopes. There are at least two. Scanlon's first hope is that "One can hope that occasions like the dramatic trial of the members of the juntas in the Federal Court of Buenos Aires will lead to greater public commitment to the rule of law. Surely they are one of our best hopes." Unfortunately, this hope was not realized. Many protagonists of the *Proceso*[10] and their accomplices kept their positions in the armed forces, the judiciary, the foreign service, and the universities. Leaders of the so-called *carapintada* movements, which destabilized democracy during Alfonsín's presidency, have become active political leaders accepted as equals by the traditional parties.[11] In addition, corruption in the Argentine public administration and judiciary system, so aptly analyzed by Nino in an excellent book,[12] has reached a level that can only be compared with the golden age of the Italian mafia.

All this may have happened because another aspect of the system of punishment was not taken into account—an aspect emphasized by the so-called theory of positive general deterrence—namely, that it is important to convince people not only that sometimes it does not pay to commit some crime or other, but that it does not pay to be a criminal. When people see that criminals go unpunished, this does anything but strengthen the population's internal point of view toward, or "dispositional subjection" to, the norms of the system.[13]

Scanlon's second hope refers to the possibility of "call[ing] the alternatives we have distinguished to the attention of our fellow citizens, so that they can decide, for example, whether their view of punishment is retributivist or just seemed to be so because they had not noticed what the alternatives were." Here again, I am somewhat skeptical about the practical implications of this rise in our fellow citizens' consciousness: The *victims*—like the Madres de la Plaza de Mayo whose claim, it should be remembered, was not retribution but rather "Punishment of the offenders!" according to the criminal code, that is, the application of the rule of law—will rightly continue to insist on the affirmative-vindictive aspect of penalties and request that offenders be punished. And potential *offenders,* if they are rational, will continue to calculate expected utilities and act accordingly. For both groups, theoretical distinctions will hardly make a difference.

With respect to Ruti Teitel's chapter, I shall comment briefly on the Latin American and especially the Argentine case. In this context, we should distinguish two basic types of transitions: *negotiated transitions,* and *transitions by defeat* of the dictatorial regimes. In the first case, the possibilities for punishment are fixed in advance, which basically means that there are none (the most recent example of this is perhaps Haiti). In the second case, on the contrary, the transitional or first democratic administration has a wide range of possibilities: they have what Bruce Ackerman calls a "window of opportunity." The Chilean case is paradigmatic for the first type: Pinochet negotiated the path to democracy with the opposition and continued to be a factor of power and control. The Argentine case is of the second type: the defeat in the Falklands-Malvinas was decisive in ending the dictatorship. An Argentine military victory certainly would have delayed the transition to democracy, which would then probably have been a negotiated one.

Some 160 years before Ackerman, Mariano José de Larra, a fervent Spanish liberal, observed that in Spain, "Liberals may be satisfied with having gone halfway, when there were occasions for going all the way." Ackerman's "window of opportunity" is Larra's "occasion," and what many Argentines regret is that the occasion of military defeat has not fully been taken advantage of.

If on that "occasion" the criteria established by Alfonsín and mentioned by Scanlon had been applied, almost all members of the armed forces would have had to be punished. What's more, Alfonsín's classification does not add much to the provisions of the Argentine Criminal Code and Code of Military Justice: In fact, article 514 of the Code of Military Justice literally repeats the first part of article 47 of the German Code of Military Justice of 1872, which read: "If the execution of an order, carried out in due obedience, violates a disposition of the Criminal Code, the only one responsible is the superior who gave the order." The second part of the German Code—"But the subordinate who obeys that order may be punished as an accomplice if . . . he knew that the order implied an act the execution of which is a crime or a civil or military offence"—is omitted in article 514. But still, as Nino,[14] as well as Supreme Court Justice Jorge A. Bacqué in his dissenting vote in the so-called Law of Due Obedience[15] case, and other well-known legal scholars in Argentina have pointed out, article 514 neither establishes a duty to blind obedience, nor does it promise immunity from the consequences of such obedience.

The last military government's law of self-amnesty (Law 22.924), which was later declared unconstitutional (Law 23.040), openly admitted that crimes had been committed, since in its article 1 it extended "the benefits conferred by this law . . . to all criminal acts carried out on occasion or with the objective of action designed to prevent or impede the aforesaid terrorist or subversive activities, regardless of their nature or the legal good they may have violated."

Before the 1976 military coup, the Argentine Criminal Code already sanctioned with a term of three to ten years the crime of "rebellion" that consists in "rising in arms to change the Constitution, depose any of the public powers of the national government [or] impede the free exercise of its constitutional competencies," and article 652 of the Code of Military Justice stipulated that "while the rebellion lasts, all soldiers who participate in it are stripped of the authority and the prerogatives of their rank."

After the coup the military leadership never bothered to derogate a single one of these provisions, so at all times during its reign it lacked any legal competence to give orders that anyone felt obligated to obey. And, what is even more relevant, this also means that in the case of Argentina, the objection against the punishment of those actively involved in implementation of state terrorism, which argues that this would amount to a retroactive application of criminal laws, does not apply.

The Argentine experience shows that the victims of state terrorism do not perceive that their rights have been sufficiently affirmed. For them, the so-called Law of Due Obedience was the first step on a road that inevitably had to end in Decrees 1.002–1.005 of October 7, 1989, and 2.741–2.746 of December 29, 1990, signed by President Menem and pardoning all those who took part in the military rebellions during the Alfonsín administration, as well as the protagonists of the so-called dirty war. For many, these measures were only a logical consequence of Alfonsín's military policy. The illustrative expression of "due pardon" was coined for them.[16]

Teitel is right in insisting on the importance of bringing out the truth of what happened and thus correcting the former "official history." The installation of investigation committees is indeed a necessary step toward the punishment of the guilty in the case of a transition by defeat, and perhaps the only possible step in a negotiated transition. But if the true facts are known, and if those facts constitute the necessary and sufficient base for the infliction of a penalty according to the legal precepts that were in force at the time the acts were committed, and if then punishment is not applied, the only excuse for it could be that it would endanger a higher good—as, for example, the success of the transition to democracy. This, allegedly, was the situation Alfonsín believed himself to be facing. In the case of Menem, he took the trouble to give a justificatory explanation: "I can't stand to see even a little bird locked up in a cage." And the commander-in-chief of the navy, Counteradmiral Ferrer, publicly welcomed Menem's pardon "deeply moved and with tender feelings."

However, I am not so sure that knowing the truth is sufficient to avoid future catastrophes, as Teitel's remarks on reports such as *Nunca Más* seem to imply. Knowledge must be accompanied by a strong attitude of vigilance in the citizens, by the daily experience of what Carlos Nino has called "deliberative democracy"[17] and what in Germany is know as "vigorous democracy." To refuse to become an accomplice of a regime that violates the autonomy and dignity of people is surely one of the most fundamental aspects of a *citoyen*'s responsibility.

One of the most tragic consequences of dictatorship is that it turns a great part of the frightened population into accomplices, and that it reduces the solidarity with the direct victims of state violence to a minimum. Once democracy is reestablished, it is therefore only natural that the accomplice majority eagerly stresses the need for reconciliation and recommends to the victims an attitude of benevolent pardon for the harms done to them.

But this appeal for "reconciliation," explicitly mentioned by Teitel with respect to the Chilean case, and which in many Latin American countries has been heard in the first years of reestablishing democracy, is something that, just as naturally, the victims of state terrorism and governmental arbitrariness find hard to understand. A very similar situation can currently be observed, for example in the former East Germany. For the victims of the GDR system, it is difficult to understand why they should seek reconciliation with the old communist nomenclatura, which in many cases still holds politically influential positions. Here we have another case of the feeling of double harm I mentioned at the beginning.

As for another point made by Teitel, I am not in a position to pass judgment on "classical literary categories" and the passage from tragedy to comedy. But I find it hard to understand how "In the transitional narratives, the country's past suffering is somehow transformed into something good for the country, enabling the turn to democracy." This seems to imply that some amount of tragedy in the history of a people is a good thing because, in hindsight, it strengthens democracy. But that would be just like saying that it is good to suffer a few illnesses—the worse they are, the better one appreciates health. Ruti Teitel concludes her essay with a reference to "poetic justice." I too would like to conclude my comments with a reference to two poets: one from Argentina, the other from Spain. The Argentine Jorge Luis Borges used to say that to really forgive is to forget. It is no coincidence that neo-Nazis in Germany have been talking of the *Auschwitzlüge*—literally, "the lie about Auschwitz"—in their attempt to wipe from history, or at least from the *memory* of the German people, the atrocities of the Holocaust. Therefore, I completely agree with Teitel when she accords such great importance to the fact of "living in truth."

The Spanish poet Juan Ramón Jiménez once said, "There is no irreconcilable hatred; there are only invincible revulsions."[16] For me and for many Argentines, one of these "invincible revulsions" is the one produced by having to see those who attempted to destroy Argentine democracy in positions of public responsibility, as if nothing had happened. Knowledge of the facts, of the truth of what happened, is precisely what nurtures and justifies this revulsion. And in my view, it is good that this is so.

NOTES

1. See H. L. A. Hart, *The Concept of Law* (Oxford: Clarendon Press, 1961).
2. In Feinberg's words: "[P]unishment is a conventional device for the expression of attitudes of resentment and indignation, and of judgments of disapproval and reprobation, on the part either of the punishing authority himself or of those in whose name the punishment is inflicted." See J. Feinberg, "The Expressive Function of Punishment," in *Doing and Deserving* (Princeton: Princeton University Press, 1970), 95–118.
3. Feinberg, "The Expressive Function of Punishment," 100.
4. Michael Baurmann, "Vorüberlegungen zu einer empirischen Theorie der positiven Generalprävention," *Goldtammer's Archiv für Strafrecht*, 8 (Aug. 1994), 384.
5. Viktor Vanberg, *Verbrechen, Strafe und Abschreckung* (Tübingen: Mohr, 1982), 9ff.; see also the essay by Jaime Malamud Goti in this volume.
6. Jeremy Bentham, *An Introduction to the Principles of Morals and Legislation,* ed. J. H. Burns and H. L. A. Hart (London and New York: Methuen, 1970), 166.
7. E.g., when he says that: "In principle, it might provide a reason for insisting on punishment in a particular case insofar as refraining from punishment was seen as unfair or arbitrary, in view of the fact that others were punished for similar crimes."
8. Fernando Savater, "Para reinsertar la reinserción," *El País* (Madrid), Sept. 11, 1994, 11.
9. Vanberg, *Verbrechen, Strafe und Abschreckung*, 13.
10. I.e., the Process of National Reorganization, as the military dictatorship had euphemistically baptized its own regime.
11. *Carapintada*, literally "those with painted faces," refers to rebellious Argentine soldiers who hid their faces behind camouflage during their actions.
12. Carlos S. Nino, *Un país al margen de la ley: Estudio de la anomia como componente del subdesarrollo argentino* (Buenos Aires: Emecé, 1992).
13. Baurmann, "Vorüberlegungen," 375.
14. Carlos S. Nino, "The Human Rights Policy of the Argentine Constitutional Government: A Reply," *Yale Journal of International Law* 12:1 (1985), 217 ff., 227 f.
15. Law 23.521 of June 22, 1987.

16. By Carlos Gabetta; see *El País* (Madrid), Oct. 31, 1989.
17. Carlos S. Nino, *The Constitution of Deliberative Democracy* (New Haven: Yale University Press, 1996).
18. "No existen odios irreconciliables, sólo repugnancias invencibles." Savater, "Para reinsertar la reinserción."

Chapter 19 Human Rights and Democracy in Practice: The Challenge of Accountability

John Shattuck

This is a time of great global transitions, and those transitions affect the nature and thrust of human rights advocacy in U.S. foreign policy. During the Cold War, especially in its last decade, threats to human rights and democracy were seen as deriving from two primary sources: the threats posed by communist totalitarianism were clearly perceived both by the U.S. government and the human rights community; and the human rights community for its part did not limit its critique to totalitarian states, but also crusaded against human rights abuses by authoritarian regimes, even those considered friendly to the United States and its allies. In both cases, the threat to human rights was seen as deriving from centralized authorities. The U.S. government saw the human rights challenge through the prism of the Cold War; while this was understandable, it often led Washington to define democracy-building as requiring the creation of strong central governments, to rely on counterinsurgency to defend them, and often to ally itself with authoritarian regimes, which justified their repressive tactics as necessary to meet the communist threat.

The human rights community, for its part, developed the forms of advocacy with which we are familiar—monitoring, reporting, publicizing cases, advocacy on behalf of individual victims of human rights abuse and advocacy for the imposition of bilateral and multilateral sanctions against abusive governments—in the process displaying much imagination, doggedness, and personal courage.

Today, in the post–Cold War world, things have changed. Although the familiar paradigm of human rights abuse by strong central governments is still very real, we are faced with unfamiliar and daunting challenges as well, which may be usefully thought of as internally driven human rights abuses, that is, abuses arising from social groups, from weakening and disintegrating governments and states, from ethnic and other intergroup conflicts, all exacerbated by economic, environmental, and demographic pressures.

At the same time, the human rights movement has gathered steam the world over. As we saw most dramatically at the 1993 UN World Conference on Human Rights in Vienna, the human rights movement is one of the most powerful, and growing, political phenomena in the world today. This growth has not happened in a vacuum—it is the result of tireless efforts by brave men and women, and is a function of the broader growth of nongovernmental organizations worldwide. Around the world we are seeing increasingly assertive indigenous grass-roots forces pressing for democracy and human rights both in the familiar sense and in the broader sense of government transparency and accountability.

This phenomenon results from the confluence of a number of factors: the failures of strong central governments to shepherd satisfactory economic and political development; the burgeoning environmental movement, which is about rendering governments and corporations accountable for the use they make of resources and for the effects of development on communities; the global movement to empower women; the communications revolution, which has fostered ties among otherwise isolated groups of activists in both the developing and developed world; and the spread of free-market economics, which creates dynamic middle classes who seek to realize the political and social dimensions of their new economic mobility and freedom.

All this is taking place in the context of a multipolar world, in which states are drawn into cross-cutting and sometimes contradictory relations with one another on a range of issues—economics, environment, security, population, migration—while encountering forces of integration at some levels and disintegration at others.

In this sort of world, traditional bilateral enforcement measures—in the form of sanctions, linkages, and conditionalities—are of uncertain use, particularly in light of other policy objectives, such as promoting global community through ties of trade and commerce and helping to stabilize imperfect democracies which nonetheless enjoy significant regional influence. In a multipolar world the United States has far less leverage when it acts on its own, and may even reap counterproductive results if other countries choose not to support U.S.-imposed sanctions against human rights abusers. Although traditional "sticks" still have their time and place—particularly in a multilateral setting—they are never universally applicable, but always have to be tailored to the specific situation of the countries involved. This is all the more true today when the challenge facing us is how to help countries in the midst of wrenching political, social, and economic transitions achieve effective institutions that will foster human rights and sustainable democracy.

All the while, we are seeing a mounting coincidence between U.S. strategic interests and human rights and democracy. The relationship between those two terms, both conceptually and practically, is not without its difficulties. As Tom Carothers has pointed out in the *Washington Quarterly,* the human rights and democracy communities have over the years come to rather different perspectives on a number of issues, including the relative emphases to be placed on law versus politics, on strengthening government institutions, and on how to allocate U.S. funds abroad.[1]

The way to reconcile this conceptual conflict is to recast human rights and democracy issues in terms of accountability. Accountability, as we are coming to see it, moves simultaneously in two directions: vertically, as ruling elites are to be held accountable to the people whose lives they rule, and horizontally, toward the broader international community. And indeed, the passing of the Cold War makes it more urgent and more possible than before to construct an international system of accountability and justice based on law and respect for human rights in the processes of government and politics.

Accountability becomes even more compelling in light of the horrific interethnic conflicts we are witnessing today. The genocides in Rwanda and the former Yugoslavia did not arise spontaneously out of the ether. They were fomented by individuals who sought to gain political ends through hideous means. Unless these leaders are held accountable, reconciliation and reconstruction will not be possible. In Rwanda and the Balkans, but not only there—indeed everywhere we see massive, genocidal human rights violations—the international community must investigate and assign responsibility by establishing international criminal tribunals. Why do we need such tribunals? Why is accountability so central to reconciliation?

First, unless the leaders of violence are made responsible for their acts, the cycle of retribution will continue and claim more lives. Fixing responsibility on those who have directed acts of mass violence can transform revenge into justice, affirm the rule of law, and break the cycle of violence.

Second, justice is necessary in order to lift the terrible burden of collective guilt that settles on any society whose leaders have directed such terrible violence. If countries like Rwanda and the states of the former Yugoslavia are to rebuild themselves, that burden must be lifted. Moreover, assigning responsibility enables the international community to differentiate between victims and aggressors, and helps expunge the cynical illusion that conflicts with an ethnic dimension are hopelessly complex and therefore insoluble.

The new international war crimes tribunals for the former Yugoslavia and Rwanda are not a cure-all but rather an example of the sort of human rights accountability institution that we are now able to create in the post–Cold War world. War crimes tribunals, by definition, arise after the fact. Yet beyond dealing with present crises we must work to prevent future crises and conflicts. Meaningful accountability in tribunals will, with time, have a deterrent effect. But we must be creative in other ways as well.

The ambiguities in the nexus between democracy promotion and human rights protection are also at play in the context of accountability. From the perspective of democracy promotion, the overriding goal of political reconciliation among contending groups necessitates a lessening of personal accountability in order to create viable democratic institutions in divided countries, and to give elites of the *ancien régime* a stake in the viability of those institutions. From a human rights perspective, by contrast, marking the individual criminal responsibility of those responsible for human rights abuses is of overriding importance, not merely for reasons of principled humanitarianism, but to ensure that violations do not recur.

There are strong arguments to be made on both sides of this debate. It can and must be resolved by a commitment on the part of both the democracy and human rights communities to learn from each other and to develop a range of appropriate institutions of accountability that can be tailored to different countries.

The term *accountability* must be turned from an idea into a reality by developing a spectrum of institutional responses to human rights abuse, supple enough to respond to a range of issues, and concrete enough to actually bring about change in troubled societies, and not just burden the workload of the International Court of Justice or add new volumes to the statute books.

The challenge is not one of advocacy as such but of institution-building. It is essential to construct viable domestic institutions of accountability and justice, undergirded by an international framework of human rights protection and democratic governance, whose overarching aim is not only to realize the inalienable rights which we believe to be the birthright of every person, but also to defuse and ameliorate political and social tensions, to create safety valves for societies undergoing difficult economic and social transitions, to cultivate local means of conflict resolution, and, over the long haul, to foster a more peaceful and just world.

The human rights policy of the Clinton Administration is working toward these ends, sometimes with forethought, sometimes reactively, in the mix of concept and improvisation that characterizes hands-on policymaking:

war crimes tribunals in the former Yugoslavia and in Rwanda;
truth commissions, like the one in El Salvador, which will publicly identify the perpetrators of past human rights abuses;
national human rights commissions of the sort we have encouraged for Mexico and India, which can take an active role in countries with democratic institutions, whose human rights practices often fall short;
strengthening the United Nations human rights system through the creation of the new position of High Commissioner for Human Rights, and generally working to coordinate UN human rights institutions, such as special rapporteurs, commissions, and observer teams;
working with regional bodies like the Organization of American States, as we have in supporting Haiti's human rights monitors;
launching the U.S. government's Interagency Working Group on Democracy and Human Rights, and giving a greater role to the State Department's human rights bureau in the allocation of foreign assistance monies;
developing rule of law and administration of justice assistance programs in a wide range of countries. These programs have already met with substantial success in Central and Eastern Europe and their successes can be replicated elsewhere.

The common denominator of all these activities is that they support the building of institutions and structures that can foster human rights at the national and international level over the long haul.

This is not a substitute for traditional human rights advocacy, but an augmentation of it. Our objective is to address the new challenges of a chaotic post–Cold War world in which forces of disintegration threaten to overwhelm the possibilities of international order. That is why we must develop new institutions for conflict prevention and accountability, and new strategies for sustainable economic and political development.

NOTE

1. Thomas Carothers, "Democracy and Human Rights: Policy Allies or Rivals?" *Washington Quarterly*, 17, no. 3 (summer 1994).

Contributors

Alberto Calsamiglia is professor of legal philosophy at the Universitat Pompeu Fabra in Barcelona.

Ronald Dworkin is professor of jurisprudence at Oxford and professor of law at New York University School of Law.

Martin D. Farrell is professor at the Centro de Estudios Institucionales and Universidad de Bueno Aires.

Owen Fiss is Sterling Professor of Law at Yale Law School.

Amy Gutmann is Laurance S. Rockefeller University Professor of Politics at Princeton University.

Stephen Holmes is professor of law at New York University School of Law.

Paul W. Kahn is Nicholas deB. Katzenbach Professor of Law at Yale Law School.

Harold Hongju Koh is Gerard C. and Bernice Latrobe Smith Professor of International Law at Yale Law School.

Jaime Malamud Goti is professor of law at the University of Buenos Aires and professor at the Center of Advanced Studies at the University of Buenos Aires.

Thomas Nagel is professor of philosophy and law at New York University School of Law.

Carlos F. Rosenkrantz is professor at the Centro de Estudios Institucionales and Universidad de Bueno Aires.

T. M. Scanlon is Alford Professor of Natural Religion, Moral Philosophy, and Civil Polity at Harvard University.

Elaine Scarry is professor of English at Harvard University.

Ian Shapiro is professor of political science at Yale University.

John Shattuck is Assistant Secretary of State of the Bureau of Democracy, Human Rights, and Labor.

Ronald C. Slye is professor of law at Seattle University School of Law and former associate director of the Orville H. Schell, Jr. Center for International Human Rights.

Irwin P. Stotzky is Professor of Law at the University of Miami School of Law.

Ruti Teitel is Associate Professor of Law at New York Law School.

Ernesto Garzón Valdés is Professor of Political Science at the University of Mainz in Germany.

Jeremy Waldron is the Maurice and Hilda Friedman Professor of Law at Columbia University.

Bernard Williams is Monroe Deutsch Professor of Philosophy at the University of California, Berkeley, and White's Professor of Moral Philosophy at Oxford (Emeritus).

Index